The
Seymours of
Wolf Hall
A Tudor Family Story

The Seymours of Wolf Hall

A Tudor Family Story

DAVID LOADES

AMBERLEY

First published 2015

Amberley Publishing
The Hill, Stroud
Gloucestershire, GL5 4EP

www.amberley-books.com

Copyright © David Loades, 2015

The right of David Loades to be identified as
the Author of this work has been asserted in
accordance with the Copyrights, Designs and
Patents Act 1988.

ISBN 978 1 4456 4788 3 (paperback)
ISBN 978 1 4456 3495 1 (hardback)
ISBN 978 1 4456 3516 3 (ebook)

British Library Cataloguing in Publication Data.
A catalogue record for this book is available
from the British Library.

Typesetting and Origination by Amberley Publishing
Printed and bound by
CPI Group (UK) Ltd, Croydon, CR0 4YY

CONTENTS

PREFACE

The Seymour family was one of the most prominent at the Tudor court.

They traced their origins from the seventh century to the village of St Maur, to the south-east of Paris, and having accompanied William the Conqueror to England they became established in Hampshire and the Welsh Marches, and served the Crown there in an administrative and military capacity for many generations.

The first of the Tudor Seymours, Sir John, lived at Wolf Hall near Marlborough and served at court in a modest capacity. However, it is the second generation of the Tudor Seymours which truly merits study. The daughter, Jane, about whom I have already written, was Henry VIII's third queen, and played a problematic part in the downfall of her predecessor Anne Boleyn. However, her brothers, Edward and Thomas, will be the main subject of this book.

Edward had already established himself at court before his sister's rise to prominence, but he benefited considerably from her position, becoming Viscount Beauchamp in 1536 and Earl of Hertford in the following year. In the years following Jane's death he became the leader of that party at court which favoured reform in the Church, taking over that role from Thomas Cromwell, who fell from power in 1540.

Thomas was closely linked with Henry's last queen, Katherine

Parr, and through her with the young Elizabeth, who was in her care. He made his own way at court under the influence of his brother Edward, receiving a knighthood and several grants of monastic lands. So successful were the Earl of Hertford's tactics that when Henry died in January 1547 he was able to proclaim himself Lord Protector, although not named to that position in Henry's will. At the same time he became Duke of Somerset, and his brother Thomas became Lord Seymour of Sudeley and Lord High Admiral.

Both were uncles to the king, Edward VI, and for the next two and half years Somerset directed the policy of the state, particularly in relation to Scotland and the Protestant faith. Thomas became increasingly jealous of his elder brother, scheming to overthrow him and marry the princess Elizabeth, offences for which he was charged with treason and executed in March 1549.

Meanwhile Edward's style of government had offended the majority of the Regency Council, and he fell from power in October 1549. His successor John Dudley, Earl of Warwick (later Duke of Northumberland) did not take the title of Protector, but styled himself President of the Council. Edward was eventually executed for scheming to recover power in January 1552. His son and heir, also Edward Seymour, was restored in blood in January 1559, and created Earl of Hertford. Unfortunately Hertford later entered into a clandestine marriage with Catherine Grey, Jane Grey's sister, which Elizabeth never recognised. Catherine was Elizabeth's Protestant heir, so to marry without her permission and to have a child were offences. Both were sent to the Tower.

Hertford's grandson and heir was created Marquis of Hertford in June 1641 and Duke of Somerset in 1660. The dukedom then ran through three further incarnations, lapsing from the direct line eventually with Algernon Seymour, the seventh duke, in 1750. The power of the restored Seymours was, however, social rather than political, none of the later dukes serving in high office.

My thanks are due on this as on previous occasions to the History Faculty of the University of Oxford, which has given me a base in my retirement, and enabled me to attend its postgraduate seminars. I am grateful also to the staff of the Bodleian Library, who have responded to my enquiries with consistent patience and courtesy, to Jonathan Reeve of Amberley, who suggested that I should look at the Seymours, and above all to my wife Judith, who has supported me throughout the writing process. I have discussed this project with numerous colleagues, but any mistakes or infelicities remain my own responsibility.

David Loades

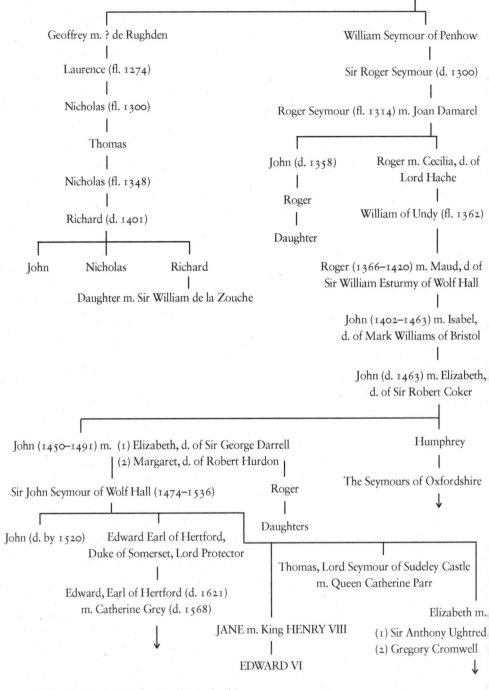

Richard de St. Maur (late 7th century) – Goscelin de St. Maur (fl. 1000) – Guillaume – Wido (fl. 1066) –

– William (fl. 1087) – Roger (fl. 1129) – Bartholomew (fl. 1170) – William – Milo (fl. 1215)

Geoffrey m. ? de Rughden

Laurence (fl. 1274)

Nicholas (fl. 1300)

Thomas

Nicholas (fl. 1348)

Richard (d. 1401)

John   Nicholas   Richard

Daughter m. Sir William de la Zouche

William Seymour of Penhow

Sir Roger Seymour (d. 1300)

Roger Seymour (fl. 1314) m. Joan Damarel

John (d. 1358)

Roger

Daughter

Roger m. Cecilia, d. of
Lord Hache

William of Undy (fl. 1362)

Roger (1366–1420) m. Maud, d of
Sir William Esturmy of Wolf Hall

John (1402–1463) m. Isabel,
d. of Mark Williams of Bristol

John (d. 1463) m. Elizabeth,
d. of Sir Robert Coker

John (1450–1491) m. (1) Elizabeth, d. of Sir George Darrell
(2) Margaret, d. of Robert Hurdon

Sir John Seymour of Wolf Hall (1474–1536)

Roger

Humphrey

The Seymours of Oxfordshire

↓

John (d. by 1520)   Edward Earl of Hertford,
Duke of Somerset, Lord Protector

Edward, Earl of Hertford (d. 1621)
m. Catherine Grey (d. 1568)

↓

Daughters

Thomas, Lord Seymour of Sudeley Castle
m. Queen Catherine Parr

Elizabeth m.
(1) Sir Anthony Ughtred
(2) Gregory Cromwell

↓

JANE m. King HENRY VIII

EDWARD VI

1. The Seymour family genealogical table.

Introduction

THE IMPORTANCE OF THE SEYMOUR FAMILY

Just as Elizabeth was the third Boleyn Girl, so Edward VI was a Seymour. Not in his tastes, or in his intellectual ambition in which he closely resembled his father, but in the general amiability of his disposition to which there is plenty of contemporary testimony. In this respect he took after his mother, whose sweetness of character was famous. The Seymours were a courtly family, not in the same political sense as the Boleyns, who had led a court faction, but in their general presence. The court was the focus of Tudor politics, because it was the king's immediate context, and access to the king was the essential ingredient of political success. Henry and his children were more than mere chief executives, they were also the Lord's Anointed, and that implied a special relationship with God. From 1535 onward this meant the headship of the English Church, because legislation had made Henry Supreme Head, but it had been present before that, and during the reign of Henry VII had been reflected in an unwritten but powerful concordat with the papacy. Consequently anyone wishing to gain access to the king needed to have their godly credentials in good order, and this meant support for the king's dealings with the Church, whether pro-papal as in

1521 or anti-papal after 1535. Cardinal Wolsey's successful career has to be seen in this light. Another aspect of the king's persona was majestas or magnificence.[1] This was expressed not only in splendid entertainments, feastings and jousts, but in the sheer scale of his housekeeping, and in the number and status of his servants. The court was divided into two sections: the Household and the Chamber. The Household consisted of the service departments, which provided for the comfort and wellbeing of the whole establishment. There were twenty-four of these departments, ranging from the kitchen to the cart takers, each under the control of a sergeant, and at the end of Henry VIII's reign there were some 450 servants altogether.[2] They were supervised by an office variously known as the Counting House and Board of Greencloth, which controlled their budgets, and were under the general oversight of the Lord Steward assisted by the Controller and the Cofferer. Both the Lord Steward and the Controller were supposed to attend the Board of Greencloth on a regular basis, but by 1547 this duty was largely discharged by the Cofferer, who normally presided. The Lord Steward was a great officer of state and a member of the Privy Council. He also had, by virtue of his office, jurisdiction over all the members of the court, who would appear before him to answer for any crimes or misdemeanours committed within the verge, or boundary. The verge of the court was clearly defined for the major palaces, such as Westminster and Hampton Court, but was set up on an ad hoc basis when the court was on progress, which occasionally led to clashes of jurisdiction with the local authorities in the area around London. The household was bureaucratically organised, with promotion going by seniority, and when a member retired or died he was replaced by the sergeant of the relevant department, with the consent of the Lord Steward. The staff of the Household normally had little or no contact with the monarch, being of relatively humble status.

The other main division of the court was the Chamber, which was the monarch's normal location and where political business was conducted. Unlike the household, the Chamber staff were aristocratic, ranging from noblemen like the Earl of Oxford to the numerous gentlemen ushers and sewers, many of whom were part-time. The Chamber also had its departments, but they were less bureaucratic than in the Household, and both appointments and promotions were made by the Lord Chamberlain, with the king's consent. The Guard, the Gentlemen Pensioners, the Wardrobe of the Robes and the Wardrobe of the Beds were each supervised by a senior gentleman, and the captaincies of the Guard and of the Gentlemen Pensioners were positions of high confidence. It was in the Chamber that ambassadors were received, and presented their credentials, that petitions were submitted, and distinguished visitors entertained.[3] By the sixteenth century it was accommodated in a suite of rooms, including a Presence Chamber where the king conducted his business and a Great Chamber where the senior officers of the court 'kept their tables'. The senior courtiers no longer dined in the Great Hall, which by this time was kept only for the benefit of the household servants. The king did not eat in the Chamber either. By the end of Henry VII's reign he had further withdrawn into the Privy Chamber, where he dined only in the company of specially invited guests. The Privy Chamber was the inmost closet of the court, where the king could enjoy what little privacy was available in the public world which he normally inhabited. At first he was served in this retreat only by menial servants, but Henry VIII turned it into something different, adding his close companions to the staff who, from about 1516, were known as the Gentlemen of the Privy Chamber.[4] Because of their regular proximity to the king, these gentlemen came to exercise a large measure of control over access, and this worried the regular council, who considered it to be their right to control such access themselves, the companions not being councillors. However, these appointments were made by the king personally and could only be limited with his consent. This meant that extreme care had to be exercised in removing members of the Privy Chamber. It was accomplished on two occasions, in 1519 and 1526, by appealing to Henry's sensitivity on the subject of his honour. It was represented to him that the behaviour of certain of his companions was not conducive to that honour, and he was persuaded by Cardinal Wolsey to remove them.[5] They returned six months later, so the victory was only a temporary one, but it made its point. After Wolsey's fall the king expanded the staff of the Privy Chamber, from the six originally intended to about twenty by the end of his reign, but he exercised extreme caution over whom he appointed. The rise of the Privy Chamber was the most significant shift in the political focus of the court during Henry's reign, but it was also temporary because the Privy Chamber of the minor Edward VI who followed Henry was a different kind of set-up, and for the remainder of the century the female monarchs required female body servants, and, although influential, these ladies played no overt political role.[6]

The queen consort also had her own Privy Chamber, which was similarly debarred from active politics. Although Anne Boleyn, Henry's second consort, was certainly active politically, such activity did not extend to the members of her Privy Chamber, who were seen primarily as representatives of their husbands or kindred. Such ladies were mainly useful to the court for the part which they played in the entertainments, for example the assault on the Chateau Verte in 1522 in which leading roles were played by the two Boleyn sisters and Jane Parker, soon to be married to George Boleyn. They also played their part in sustaining the games of courtly love which kept the young men of the Chamber occupied, and in which the king himself indulged from time to time. The court as a whole was heavily male dominated, and this led to disciplinary problems as the unattached men made extensive use of the local prostitutes, who were regularly having to be evicted from the premises by the Lord Steward's officers.[7]

The king's magnificence also involved the taking of counsel. When he appeared on formal occasions he would be accompanied by the members of his council, ranked in order of importance by their proximity to the monarch. It was on one such occasion in 1533 that the Imperial ambassador, Eustace Chapuys, was alerted to the importance of one whom he knew only as Mr Secretary, standing among the magnates and close to the king's person. Thomas Cromwell was not a courtier, but he was a royal servant, and his position on this occasion told Chapuys that he was a man to be reckoned with – indeed that he was already Henry's right-hand man. Before he was Earl of Leicester, or a member of the Privy Council, Robert Dudley was accorded a similar precedence, although this was disguised by the fact that, as Master of the Horse, he had an *ex officio* right to be in attendance.

In the fifteenth century the court had been very much the preserve of the nobility, and this tendency had been strengthened by Edward IV's policy of relying heavily on nobles for the local government of the country. The marriages which he arranged for his wife's kindred also reinforced this trend. Richard III's brief reign had served only to replace one set of nobles with another, and it was left to Henry VII to break this mould. Although he was on good terms with many of his nobles, whom he counted among his friends, he was distrustful of the political ambitions of the nobility as a whole, and sought to break down their locally based affinities, or regular followings. This he did by retaining prominent gentry himself, through fees and positions at court. Many of them became sewers and gentlemen ushers of the Chamber, and this led to a considerable expansion of its size, and a consequent increase in its cost. Henry was not mean when he perceived a political advantage to himself, and his generous hospitality was famous.[8] The gentlemen concerned welcomed this development, because not only did it increase their prestige to be members of the court, but it also enlarged their opportunities for networking outside their home regions. A gentleman from Kent might have no other chance to meet his equivalent from Shropshire or Warwickshire, and if he had daughters to marry, such contacts were obviously useful. He might also wish to introduce his own sons at court, or find positions for his daughters among the queen's ladies. Henry VIII continued this policy, and both he and Catherine welcomed the opportunity to widen the circle of their retinues. Military service might also provide a means of access to the court, and both Sir Thomas Boleyn and Sir John Seymour first entered into the king's consciousness by that means.

1535 was a year which saw more rumours of the king's love affairs, and during which the Earl of Wiltshire and Viscount Rochford served on the commissions of oyer and terminer which tried both the Carthusian priors and Sir Thomas More. In May and June of that year Rochford undertook another fruitless mission to France in an attempt to arrange a marriage between Princess Elizabeth and Francis's third son, the Duke of Angoulême. Both Henry and Anne were relieved by Catherine's death, and Anne had another chance to deliver the much-needed prince. However, the situation was also fraught with danger. Now that there was no chance of his being forced to return to his first wife, the king would have a free choice if he should choose to abandon his queen, and she knew perfectly well that if she should produce a second daughter, he might decide to do just that. In the event, it was worse than that, because on 29 January she miscarried of a male foetus, and the king was devastated. By the middle of the following month he was paying serious attention to Jane Seymour, and the writing was on the wall.[9] Henry did not make up his mind at once, but by the end of March he had called upon Thomas Cromwell to investigate his wife's conduct, and the secretary was given his chance to end what had by then become a serious conflict of interests. By that time another disagreement had added to their estrangement. Anne was, by nature and background, pro-French, while the Secretary was in favour of rebuilding ties with the Emperor. Moreover, under pressure from Cromwell, small abbeys had been surrendering to the king over the last few months, and Henry had begun to redistribute their property among his servants. Anne believed that such property should be allocated for religious purposes, education and the augmentation of poor livings, and that ran directly counter to the Secretary's advice. That alone would not have been sufficient to motivate him, but taken in connection with the king's changing attitude, and with Anne's obstruction of his cherished imperial alliance, it was enough to convince him that the whole Boleyn faction must go.

Anne did not help herself in this dilemma. On 29 April she had a conversation with Sir Henry Norris which could easily be construed as treasonable, and she had flirted with several members of the court.[10] At some point between 30 April and 2 May the king became convinced that she was guilty of adultery, and the agent of this conviction was almost certainly Cromwell. On the 30th he had Mark Smeaton, a musician of the Chamber, arrested and interrogated. Under pressure, Smeaton confessed to having had sex with the queen, and this was sufficient for Cromwell's purposes. On the 2nd he confronted the king with this evidence, and Henry immediately ordered Anne's arrest. To the Secretary, however, this was not sufficient. Using his contacts in the Privy Chamber he built a case of a sort against George Boleyn for incest with his sister, and George was also arrested.[11] This case seems to have convinced very few at the time – even Chapuys was sceptical

– but it persuaded the king, and that was all that was necessary. Norris, Smeaton and two others were put on trial and convicted. On the 14th Lord Rochford was also convicted, and that left the queen with nowhere to go. On the 15th she was also found guilty, a process which many people found 'very strange', and on the 17th the Archbishop's court dutifully annulled the marriage which it had found good three years earlier. The papers for this case do not survive, but the decision appears to have been reached on the basis of Henry's confessed relations with her sister, Mary.[12] Mary herself had been banished from the court in the autumn of 1534 for her clandestine marriage to William Stafford, a union which had deeply offended the then queen, whose permission should have been sought. By this time she was living in obscurity and some financial hardship. However, obscurity proved a protection against the ruin which overcame the rest of her family. Anne and George were executed on 19 May, and the Earl of Wiltshire lost his position as Lord Privy Seal, an office in which he was replaced on 29 June by no less a person than Thomas Cromwell.

At this point Jane Seymour came on the scene, the daughter of Sir John Seymour of Wolf Hall, near Marlborough. Sir John had been present at the Battle of Blackheath against the Cornishmen in 1497, and had been knighted on the field. In about 1498 he had married Margery, the daughter of Sir Henry Wentworth, and was almost exactly of an age with Sir Thomas Boleyn.[13] He was a regular attender at court, but unlike Sir Thomas played no part in the jousts and other festivities. He was a Knight of the Body at the beginning of Henry VIII's reign, but that conferred no particular intimacy, and his career thereafter was largely confined to Wiltshire, where he served on numerous commissions for the rest of his life. He did, however, accompany the king to the Field of Cloth of Gold in 1520, and enjoyed a number of small military commands. It was probably on this occasion that he is alleged to have joked with Henry about his ability to father sons, a subject which would soon be too bitter for jest. His firstborn, John, was probably dead by then, but there had followed Edward, born about 1500, Henry and Thomas. Edward was already a courtier, having accompanied Mary to France as a page in 1514, an assignment which had, however, a short duration as he returned to England with the balance of her household as soon as the wedding was over. Jane was the youngest of this brood, having been born in about 1508 or 1509, no doubt to her mother's great relief. Very little is known about her upbringing. She was later literate in English, but seems to have had no knowledge of Latin, which indicates home tuition, probably by a chaplain of her father.[14] She seems to have remained at home until in 1529 Sir John secured for her a position in the household of Queen Catherine. How he managed to achieve that from the fringes of the court is not known, and it may indeed have been Edward, who was a courtier in good standing, who accomplished the feat. The queen must have been complacent because no one could be placed in her service without her consent and the king had no incentive to override her in such a matter. She was not looking for beauty or intellect among her attendants, but Jane, in spite of her twenty years, was still a virgin, and that would no doubt have been a commendation. She was pious and well seen in those domestic skills such as needlecraft, which would also have attracted the queen's favourable attention. She may indeed have been in the service of one of the ladies of the court before being brought to Catherine's attention. If so it would have been one of the patronage brokers, such as the Countess of Sussex, but there is no evidence to that effect. She obviously made a good impression, and when Catherine's chamber was downsized in the summer of 1533, Jane was transferred to the service of the new queen, Anne Boleyn.[15] It was from that position that she may have caught the king's eye in the summer of 1534. If so, it is unlikely to have gone beyond a game of courtly love, a skill which Jane would have had time to learn by then. Flirtation had not been one of the accomplishments which she had learned at Wolf Hall.

It was not until February 1536, in the aftermath of Anne's miscarriage, that Jane was first named as Henry's new 'love interest'. According to Chapuys, who was concerned with anything that would unsettle Anne, the king sent her a purse of sovereigns and a letter, which she returned unopened and with a coy message, which aroused Henry to new efforts.[16] How successful these may have been we do not know, but by the time of Anne's execution, Edward and his wife were aiding and abetting his sister's unique but vulnerable position. The king was by this time set on matrimony, and on the very day of Anne's death, the two were betrothed. This was supposed to be a secret, but like most secrets of the court it soon leaked out, causing outrage among the conventionally minded, who expected at least a show of mourning on Henry's part. The king ignored this reaction and the couple were married on 30 May, Jane being 'shown as queen' a few days later. She was by this time about twenty-seven years old, no great beauty, as her portraits confirm, but of a singularly sweet nature. She also came of a good breeding stock, having had four brothers, and that may have been crucial in the king's process of selection. Sir John Russell commented shortly afterwards that Henry was 'in heaven' thanks to the docility of his new wife, a situation which he pointedly contrasted with the 'cursed nature' of the other – by whom he plainly meant Queen Anne.[17] Within a few weeks there began a 'pregnancy watch' in which the members of the court commented repeatedly upon the state of the queen's health, although it was to be some eight or nine months before there was anything positive to report.

The Seymours were thus a courtly family, but in rather a different sense from the Boleyns. Unlike Sir Thomas Boleyn, Sir

John Seymour was not a courtier himself, nor the leader, however theoretically, of a court faction. His sons, Edward and Thomas, moreover had made considerable progress with their court careers before Jane came on the scene at all. Edward had been knighted by the Duke of Suffolk in the course of his campaign in 1523, and was a Gentleman of the Privy Chamber by 1533, while Thomas was a junior member of the Chamber Staff by the time of Anne Boleyn's coronation. Unlike George Boleyn, their careers owed nothing to the position of their sister in the king's bed. It cannot be proved, but it seems likely that George owed his diplomatic postings to Anne's influence, because his various missions to France were mostly designed to further her interests, and it was her alleged indiscretions which brought about his ruin and death. He owed his elevation as Viscount Rochford to the creation of his father as Earl of Wiltshire, an event which occurred well before Anne's marriage to the king, whereas Sir Edward Seymour only became Viscount Beauchamp on 5 June 1536, after Jane's marriage to Henry. He became Earl of Hertford in October 1537 in recognition of the fact that he was now uncle to the heir to the throne, just a few days before Jane's untimely death. As earl he became a close confidant of the king, but he never led a family-based faction in the sense that Sir Thomas Boleyn had, and his sister kept assiduously out of the political limelight, in a way which would have been alien to Anne's whole nature.[18] Nor did Edward's brother Thomas aspire to a political career, although as a member of the Privy Chamber he could not avoid politics altogether. Their other brother, Henry, who could possibly have made an impact at court, chose not to do so, remaining in the country and supporting their father in his work on the various commissions for Wiltshire. It is true that the Earl of Hertford was close to Thomas Cromwell, but he survived his fall without difficulty, and although he became a leader of the reforming group on the council in the 1540s, that owed little to his family connections and much to the trust which the king reposed in him. So although the Seymours were a courtly family, they never became a faction as long as Henry VIII was alive. Their dominance belongs to the following reign.

I

THE ORIGINS

The Seymours were an ancient family, according to one tradition tracing their origins back to the village of St Maur sur Loire in the seventh century. A Richard de St Maur is allegedly mentioned in a grant of Queen Fredegunde to the abbey of Villers in 679, and a Guy de St Maur, who may have been his son, performed fealty to the same abbey for his lands in 701.[1] Thereafter the family disappears from view for almost two hundred years save for a certain Ludo de St Maur, who was alive in 919 and was presumably a descendant. We are on slightly firmer ground with Goscelin de St Maur, who was styled 'Castri Sanctae Maurae dei gratia hereditario possessor et dominus' ('of the Castle of St Maur by the grace of God hereditary possessor and lord') in a charter of Foulque Martel, Count of Anjou, which is dated to about 1000.[2] Pope Gregory VII also wrote him a letter, a copy of which survives in the Vatican archives. Goscelin must have been a young man at the time, because he did not marry until 1009, when his bride was called Annebury, about whom nothing is known. By her he had four sons, the eldest of whom appears to have been a priest from whom no legitimate descendants were derived. It was through his second son, Guillaume, that the connection with England first arose. He must have been born around 1012, because he had married and had children of his own by the mid-century. His son, Wido, appears to have accompanied the Conqueror in 1066, although this cannot be firmly established because of the incompleteness of the surviving lists. However, a Wido de St Maur received an extensive barony soon after the Conquest which covered parts of Somerset, Wiltshire and Gloucestershire, a substantial reward which indicates significant service. He had died before the Domesday survey of 1086, because by then the barony was held by his son, known as William Fitz Wido, who was clearly legitimate in spite of his name.[3] It is from that survey that we learn that the barony was held by gift of William I. Nothing very much is known about Fitz Wido or his circumstances, but he clearly married and his son Roger was born at some point before 1100. He witnessed a charter by Richard of Cormeil to the priory of Monmouth in 1129, appearing as Roger de St Maur, not Fitz Wido, which was clearly not adopted as the family name. Roger may well have been given some responsibility in the Welsh Marches, although that cannot be proved from the surviving records, and may even have settled at Penhow, which the family certainly owned a few years later, although that cannot be proved either.

A Bartholomew de Sancto Mauro, who was almost certainly Roger's son, witnessed a charter to Keynsham abbey from William, Earl of Gloucester in about 1170, and his son, William, was one of the king's esquires in 1175. A Milo de St Maur appears among the barons who forced King John to sign Magna Carta in 1215, who is described as a descendant of Roger and was thus almost certainly William's son.[4] Nothing very much is known about the life or career of this Milo beyond this one appearance, although he does also appear on the fine roll of King John. He left two sons, Geoffrey and William, and it is from them that the two branches of the medieval St Maur (or Seymour) family descended. Geoffrey, who seems to have been the elder, settled at Kingston Seymour in Somerset, and from him sprang five generations, culminating in Richard who died in 1401 leaving three sons, John, Nicholas and Richard. Nothing is known about John and Nicholas, who may have died young, but Richard lived to marry and beget a daughter, Alice, who married Sir William Zouche at some time in the early fifteenth century. He had no son and Alice conveyed Kingston Seymour to her husband after his death. Meanwhile the younger son, William, based himself at Penhow, which he seems to have inherited. Milo may have married twice, which would explain the inheritance arrangements, and also the fact that the two families wanted nothing to do with each other. They seem to have denied any connection between them, and even chose quite different coats of arms, when that became relevant.[5] It was from this family that the courtly Seymours of the sixteenth century were descended. Geoffrey married a daughter of William de Rughdon and left a son, Laurence, who in 1274 was granted by Edward I a market which was to be held at his manor of Rode in Somerset, and an annual fair to be held in the same place on the morrow of St Margaret the Virgin, which was 21 July. He does not seem to have lived at Rode, however, continuing to be known as 'of Penhow'. Meanwhile Nicholas seems to have been high in favour with Henry III. In 1260 he received a gift of £10 from the king 'for a horse'. In 1263 he appears to have served the king overseas, and in the same year was given a present of wine via the port of Southampton. At the same time he received a letter from Henry relating to the affairs of Wales, which perhaps indicates where his main interests lay.[6] Other members of the family surface from time to time. A Henry de Saint Maur, whose relationship to Nicholas is obscure, acknowledged a debt of 200 marks to one Geoffrey Gracelin in 1267, and in 1269 was released from prison in Northampton, where he had been incarcerated for a crime of which he was not guilty. He appears to have died in 1276 and is described as the son of Geoffrey, which would have made him Lawrence's younger brother and the uncle of Nicholas.[7] Lawrence de Saint Maur appears in 1288 in a quittance for the service of Common Pleas in Somerset, and in 1289 an allowance was made to him for his service with the army in Wales. He died at some point before 1 August 1297, when the escheator beyond Trent was ordered not to interfere with the lands which his widow, Sybil, had inherited from him.

Nicholas was summoned to war against the Scots in 1298 and in 1300, and in 1313 was pardoned for an unspecified involvement in the death of Piers Gaveston. In the same year he was summoned to Parliament as a representative of Gloucestershire. By May 1314 he was married to Ellen the daughter and heir of Alan de Zouche, who died in that year leaving her certain lands, which the escheator was ordered to hand over to her in September, together with the advowsons of certain churches in Hertfordshire and in Devon.[8] Nicholas had died by 18 May 1317, leaving his son Thomas, aged nine, in the wardship of Hugh le Despenser. Thomas also appears to have died young, but not before he had married and begotten a son, another Nicholas, which must have occurred before 1330, because Nicholas served in the French wars in 1348. He had settled certain debts with Hugh le Despenser in 1325, which presumably occurred when he attained his majority, at which point he seems to have married. Nicholas was summoned to Parliament from 1352 to 1361 and served again in the French wars in 1360. He appears to have died in 1361, leaving a son, Richard, who inherited all his lands, and must therefore have been of full age, which means that he had been born not later than 1340. Meanwhile Ellen had remarried, and the escheator 'this side of Trent' was instructed to release her dower land to her on 3 February 1319.[9] Her second husband was a certain Alan de Charleton. John de Saint Maure, who is described as a knight and who acknowledged a debt of £20 to John de Potteshall of Crawley on 16 May 1329, appears to have been the elder son of Roger of the Penhow family by his wife Joan Damarel. If this is so, then his nephew William served as sheriff of Northamptonshire in 1327–8, when he was allowed £14 8s 2d for the wages which he had paid to the king's huntsman. Who the Edmund de Saint Mauro under arrest in Norwich Castle in March 1331, indicted of various felonies, may have been is not known, but he probably did not belong to either of the families whose fortunes we have been following. The same is true of the Nicholas de Saint Maur who served as escheator of Northamptonshire and Rutland in 1373, although he may have been a sibling of Richard, about whose family circumstances we know little.[10] Richard served in the French war in 1387 and was summoned to Parliament from 1381 until his death in 1401. He begot three sons, John, Nicholas and Richard, but only Richard seems to have survived him. This young man was old enough to have served in Ireland in 1399, and in France in 1402. He was summoned to Parliament from 1402 to 1407, and also married, but left only a daughter when he died in 1408. By that time she was married to Sir William de la Zouche of Totnes, and conveyed the whole of her inheritance to him in 1409.

William Seymour, the younger son of Milo, had dug himself into the Welsh Marches, where he was known as Sir William of Penhow. In about 1235 or 1236, with the connivance of William Marshall, Earl of Pembroke he wrested the manor of Undy from Morgan ap Howell in the course of a border campaign. Nevertheless he continued to reside at Penhow, where he rebuilt the castle, and laid out a splendid park for the benefit of his hunting. He also built a church in the vicinity, which he dedicated to St Maur, which was an eccentric thing to do in that part of the country. Clearly he felt that the family owed a debt of gratitude to that particular saint.[11]

He married Earl William's third daughter, thus cementing a bond of friendship with his patron. William's name appears as a witness on several charters of Gilbert and Walter Marshall, who were kinsmen of the earl, one of which is dated to 1245. Nothing very much is known about his life or career, but he had clearly died by 1269 when his son Sir Roger de Saint Maur is mentioned as lord of the manor of Undy. We know nothing of this Sir Roger, other than that he married at some point before 1280 and was dead by 1300, by which time he had been succeeded by his son, who was also called Roger. There is no mention of a minority so this Roger must have been of full age when his father died, which dates the latter's marriage to at least twenty years before. Of him we know only that he was alive in 1314 and that he married Joan, the daughter of one Damarel of Devonshire.[12] The date of his death is not known, but he left two sons, John and Roger. John married in about 1340, and died in 1358, leaving a son, also confusingly called Roger, who was of full age when he succeeded. This Roger lived long enough to marry, but when he died at some unknown date he left as his heir an only daughter, who subsequently married one of the Bowlays of Monmouthshire, and conveyed her inheritance of Penhow into that family. Meanwhile John's younger brother became lord of the manor of Undy in succession to his father. However he appears not to have spent much time there, preferring to reside at Evinswinden, or Swindon, in Wiltshire, which was no doubt more convenient for the bulk of his estates. He married Cecilia, the daughter of John de Beauchamp of Somerset, who was also Baron of Hache and a descendant of William Marshall, Earl of Pembroke, whose earlier links with the Seymour family we have noticed. John de Beauchamp died in 1363, and his lands were divided between his two daughters, a fact which greatly enhanced the wealth and importance of the Seymours, although Cecilia long outlived Roger, so he never came into possession of her lands.[13] She died in 1393, by which time she had also outlived her eldest son, William, who died in 1390. This William is mentioned in 1362 as serving the Prince of Wales in Gascony, which presumably indicates a birth date not later than 1340. He resided mainly at Undy and married Margaret, the daughter of one Simon de Blackburn, in about 1365. Their son, confusingly another Roger, was born in 1366 and inherited his grandmother's considerable estates, making him a much more substantial figure than his father. Before 1400 he had married, perhaps as his second wife, Maud, the daughter and co-heir of Sir William Esturmy of Wolf Hall, Wiltshire. When Sir William died in due course Maud inherited Wolf Hall, and Roger appears to have moved his residence there from Undy.[14] Unfortunately we do not know when this occurred, but it was some time before Roger's own death in 1420. The Esturmys had also been hereditary Wardens of the royal forest of Savernake, an office which they had been granted in the reign of Henry III, and this too came to Roger in right of his wife. It is possible that he also inherited the Esturmy patronage of the hospital of the Holy Trinity at Easton near Marlborough, which the family had founded many years before. Altogether the fact that Roger's father-in-law had been the last of the male line of his family brought many benefits to the Seymours. His son, John, who succeeded him, had been born in 1402, and since there is no reference to any wardship, and Roger was certainly a tenant in chief of the Crown, he must have been deemed to be of full age. In the days before birth certificates establishing the age of an heir was largely a matter of testimony, and a determined widow could easily assemble a team who would not know the difference between eighteen and twenty-one, especially if the young man was well grown! Since John was also the heir of his cousin, Sir Peter de la Mere, this was a matter of some importance.

As a result, by the 1420s John was a man of considerable

possessions, and it may have been as a result of this that in 1430, at the relatively tender age of twenty-eight, he was pricked as the sheriff of Hampshire. In 1431 he was elected to Parliament for the county of Wiltshire, and in 1432 served as sheriff.[15] As a result of this he was knighted, an honour which seems to have owed more to his administrative capacity, and possibly the size of his estates, than it did to any service in the field, of which, as far as is known, he was completely innocent. He appears to have been the first member of the Seymour family to have served as a sheriff, and since there is no reason to suppose that Crown policy had changed during the minority of Henry VI, this must have been because of his perceived status in the counties concerned, which was directly connected with his wealth. A series of skilful marriages had transformed John's position from being a middle-ranking gentleman almost to magnate status. In a document of 1434 his name appears first, after that of William Westbury, who was royal justice and a member of the king's council and who would naturally have taken precedence over any local worthy. In that same year he was pricked as sheriff of Gloucestershire and Somerset, which is an indication of the extent of his estates because it was normal to select a leading landowner of the shire in question for this honourable but expensive office.[16] Tracing his career is complicated by the fact that there were other Seymour families around, unrelated to the main branches which we have been considering. One such was a mercantile family in London, where one John Seymour, mercer, made his last will and testament on 31 July 1466, leaving property to his sons John, William and Thomas, who are not otherwise known to the records.[17] Another was John Seymour, 'fishmonger of Banbury', who appears in a document of 1474. Similarly a Thomas Seymour, knight, witnessed a charter in 1462, and appears in various other documents of the period. Presumably a man of some substance, he disposed of the advowson of the church at Pulton in Wiltshire, nor far from the established Seymour property of Kingston Seymour. It is just possible that he was a sibling of John, but if so the genealogy is silent about him. Meanwhile, in 1437 John served again as sheriff of Hampshire, and sat for Wiltshire in the Reading parliament of 1440, although he is not known to have played any part in the proceedings. He was sheriff of Wiltshire again in 1457–8, but did not serve further before his death in 1463. This appears not to have been the result of any falling out with Henry VI's government, but may well have been because of an expressed preference on his part, because he served regularly on the commission of the peace for Wiltshire from 1453 to 1458, and on various other commissions relating to the county.[18] He was a commissioner of oyer and terminer in April 1457 to investigate piracy, with a remit extending, obviously, beyond the county, and in September of the same year was on another 'for beacons'. More significantly he was granted a pardon in 1458 for having allowed a felon to escape during his year as sheriff, which indicates that he was still regarded with favour by the council. As the civil war escalated, in 1457, 1458 and 1459 he was put on the commission of array for the purpose of raising troops for the Lancastrians, but did not, as far as we know, lead any men of his own in such a cause. The nearest he got to partisanship is his place in 1459 on a commission to put down insurrections in the county of Wiltshire, which presumably means any movement in favour of Richard of York. It is probably safest to assume that he was not an active Lancastrian, but was a loyal servant of the king for the time being. The fact that there is no sign of his favour diminishing under the new king, Edward IV, between 1461 and his death in 1463 points in the same direction.

John married in 1424, his bride being Isabel, the daughter of Mark Williams of Bristol. This no doubt enhanced his relations with the mercantile elite of the town, and may well account for the fact that he was able to enjoy 'tronnage' and 'pesage' of the wool traded through the port for several years thereafter, and was able to dispose of those rights to suit himself in due course.[19] This would have been by grant of the Crown, but the king normally listened to those directly involved, and in this case paid attention to a petition from Mark Williams and his friends. Isabel in due course inherited a number of properties from her father, which no doubt made John's life more comfortable, but these properties never came to him as he predeceased his wife by many years. They had one son, also John, who was born in about 1425, and who married about 1448 Elizabeth, the daughter of Sir Robert Coker of Laurence Lydiard in Somerset. This John died a few months before his father in 1463, leaving two sons, John and Humphrey, both underage, whose wardship appears to have been granted to their mother. She lived until 1472, by which time both her sons would have achieved their majority. Humphrey, who was the younger, inherited the property at Swindon, where he settled. He was born in 1451 or 1452, and married in about 1470 Elizabeth, the daughter and co-heir of Thomas Winslow of Burton in Oxfordshire.[20] From him the Oxfordshire Seymours descend, but they play no further part in this story. The elder son, John, received Wolf Hall when he attained his majority, which would have been about 1470 or 1471, as he had been born in 1449 or 1450. Unlike his father, however, he served on no county commissions until after 1480. This can hardly have been because of lack of favour, because he had done nothing to arouse distrust, but must be attributed to his relative youth and lack of experience. After 1480 he served on the commission of the peace and in 1483 was a subsidy commissioner for Wiltshire, although whether this occurred before or after King Edward's death is not known. In 1484, when Richard III was becoming seriously worried about challenges to his power, John was a commissioner of array for the county, and in June 1485, with Henry of Richmond's advent barely two months away, he was granted a survey (or exemplification) of the bounds of Savernake Forest.[21] In the same month, with the warning lights already flashing, he was placed on a commission to deal with riots in Wiltshire, a gesture which seems to indicate that his loyalty to Richard was not in question. Nevertheless he did not respond to the king's military summons in August, and was therefore not involved in his defeat at Bosworth. In fact he received a singular mark of favour from the new king, because in February 1486 he was granted livery and rights of entry to his grandfather's lands. This should have been done in about 1471, but had obviously been overlooked when he attained his majority. He had held possession of those lands since that date, and this omission could have been a serious embarrassment for him. Instead it seems to have been treated as mere technicality.[22] Henry VII does not seem to have entertained any doubts on the subject of John Seymour's loyalty, and the latter made his transition to the new regime without a stain on his honour.

He married twice, his first bride being Elizabeth, the daughter of Sir George Darrell of Littlecote, Wiltshire, whom he wed in about 1473 and who bore him four sons and four daughters. She died, possibly of exhaustion, in the late 1480s, and he remarried Margaret, the daughter of Robert Hardon, who bore him one son, Roger. Roger married, but left only daughters as his co-heirs, and they play no further part in the story. We must concentrate on the sons of his first marriage, because John, the eldest, was the father of Queen Jane. George was sheriff of Wiltshire in 1499, William was made a Knight of the Bath at the marriage of Prince Arthur and Catherine of Aragon in November 1501, and Robert was later a Gentleman Usher of the Chamber. John was well short of his majority when his father died in 1491, and on 26 December 1493 his wardship and marriage were granted to Sir Henry

Wentworth.[23] Rather surprisingly, an inquisition post-mortem was held in May 1492 in order to establish what lands the elder John Seymour had held in Somerset, and the identity of his heir. Why this uncertainty applied in Somerset is unknown, because no similar inquisition was held in Wiltshire, where the inheritance was apparently unchallenged. As a result of being granted the wardship, for reasons which can not now be recovered, Sir Henry married John to his own daughter, Margery, at some time before 1498. Whether he was responsible for introducing him at court we do not know. He seems to have been regularly present there, but his appearances were low-key and his career focussed mainly on Wiltshire, where he was sheriff in 1497–8, and on the commission of the peace for which he served regularly from 1499 until his death in 1536.[24]

2

SIR JOHN AND ROBERT

John Seymour was born in about 1474, and was identified as his father's next heir in Somerset by an inquisition held on 30 May 1492, which dates John the elder's death to a few weeks earlier. However, it was not until 20 December 1493 that his wardship was granted to Sir Henry Wentworth, together with the lands which he had inherited from his mother, Elizabeth.[1] Since issues were granted only from 'Michaelmas last past', this presumably means that the younger John's status had been in limbo for rather more than a year before this issue was settled. We know nothing of his upbringing under Sir Henry's auspices, but he was later literate in English, which indicates a domestic schooling, probably at the hands of one of Wentworth's chaplains. There is no record of his having attended any school, but that would be normal for a gentleman's son at that time. He was, however, trained in arms, with an eye on a military career, which he realised to some extent when he served in the king's army against the Cornish rebels in 1497. It was for valour on that occasion that he received the honour of knighthood, on the field at Blackheath.[2] Meanwhile his uncle Humphrey was also active in the royal service, as a commissioner of the peace for Oxfordshire from December 1485 to December 1493, and of Gaol Delivery for the castles of Wallingford and Oxford in 1486. Another Humphrey, presumably his son, delivered the gaol at Wallingford in February 1496, and served as a commissioner of the peace for Oxfordshire from October 1496 to the end of the reign.[3] John was sheriff of Wiltshire in 1497–8, a commissioner of oyer and terminer for the county in 1502, and a commissioner of the Peace regularly after 1499. John was presumably not that John Seymour of Oxford, 'gentleman', who was pardoned in 1505 for not answering before the justices for a debt of 40 shillings.[4] There were many Seymours around whose relationship to the main family is problematic. Whether the John Seymour, canon of Windsor, who died at the beginning of 1502 was kinsman or not is not known. He vacated prebends both at Windsor and at Salisbury, which is how we know about his death. Or the William Seymour, knight, who served on several commissions relating to Hampshire, Wiltshire, Somerset and Devon in 1503, and appears to have died early in 1506. If he was a sibling of the elder John, then he appears to have escaped the record. Sir John was steward of the Duke of Buckingham's lands in the county of Wiltshire by 1503, and was sheriff again in 1507–8, both of which facts suggest good relations with the Stafford family, which was strong in the area.[5]

He was also a regular attender at court, although this was a low-key aspect of his career. Henry VII liked to keep the gentry of the counties in touch with the centre, and one of his ways of doing so was to create nominal positions for the heads of prominent gentry families, and that seems to have been what happened in this case. Sir John was not a jouster, and appears to have played no part in the revels of the court, but he was still a Knight of the Body by the end of the reign. This was not a position of high confidence, and did not imply much intimacy with the king, but it did mean regular attendance, probably on the shift system which Henry introduced for his less intimate courtiers. He attended the funeral of Henry VII, for which he received a livery grant, and he and Margery both appeared on the pardon roll of the new king.[6] This may well have been to protect him from any comeback from his year as sheriff, although why his wife should also have appeared is something of a mystery. He is described therein as 'of Wolf Hall, Wiltshire, Elvetham, Hampshire and London', the latter designation presumably being occasioned by his occasional residence at court. There was a Seymour family which was prominent in the City, but he is not known to have had any connection with it. The fact that he was neither a jouster nor a reveller cut him off from the more obvious routes to favour with Henry VIII, but he still seems to have been well regarded. Perhaps he was looked on as a kind of father figure for the young king, being by this time thirty-five or thirty-six years old. Limited though his military experience was, he seems to have kept himself in practice, and this no doubt commended itself to the warlike boy. He retained his position as Knight of the Body, and as such was selected as one of the pallbearers at the funeral of Henry's short-lived son on 27 February 1511. He was listed under the mourners, and this is a measure of the confidence that the king had in him, which was exceptional for a man of his status.[7]

Since he came to the throne, Henry had been spoiling for a fight with the French. This was partly because he understood well enough that the quickest way for a king to make an international reputation for himself was upon the field of battle, and partly because France was the ancient enemy and he idolised Henry V. His council, however, most of which he had inherited from his father, were opposed to the idea, pointing out that Louis XII had given him no occasion. They even constrained him in the summer of 1510 to sign a new peace treaty with France, much against his will. However, in 1511 Louis fell out with the Pope, who formed a Holy League against him, and this was too good an opportunity to be missed. So in November 1511 Henry joined the Holy League, and his council, which was dominated by clergy, no longer opposed him.[8] In January 1512 he began to mobilise his navy, and issued instructions to Sir Edward Howard, appointed admiral of the fleet on 7 April, ordering him to proceed to the Trade (the vicinity of Brest) and to keep the seas so that no enemy would dare to appear. For this purpose he was to have eighteen ships and 3,000 men.[9] One of these ships was the *Dragon* of Greenwich, captain Sir William Sydney, and under Sydney served Sir John Seymour with the 100 men whom he had raised in Wiltshire for the purpose. These men would have been his own dependents, as no commission of array was issued to him. Henry was determined not merely to control the seas, but to recover Guienne, and sent the Marquis of Dorset south with 10,000 men for that objective, instructing Howard to escort him as far as the Trade. This expedition set forth on 3 June, and had reached Brest by the 6th, when Dorset proceeded on his way, and Howard turned his attention to the Breton coast. Landing his men in several different locations, he proceeded seven miles into the country, burning and destroying against sporadic resistance, informing those who sought to parley with him that he had come to make war, not peace.[10] After a number of days spent in this occupation, he withdrew his forces and 'scoured the coast' towards Normandy, returning to the Isle of Wight early in July. Sir John Seymour and his men, or what was left of them, were apparently discharged at this point, and played no further part in Howard's actions, which included a confrontation with the main French war fleet at Brest in early August. This was the action in which the *Cordeliere* and the *Regent* were spectacularly lost, although it did not amount to a sea battle.[11] Sir John Seymour and his men were paid off, with the rest of the fleet, on 28 October 1512, when Howard submitted the accounts for his summer's activities.

The following year the fleet was mobilised early, but Sir John was not called upon for further naval service. Howard left Plymouth on 10 April and on the 25th of that month lost his life in a rash attempt to take out the French galleys which were in a defensible position in a bay close to Brest. Deprived of his leadership, the whole English fleet retreated, much to the king's chagrin.[12] However, Sir John Seymour's military services were not dispensed with, because in June he was listed under the 'king's ward' among the noblemen and others who were to serve the king in the Army Royal which he was planning to lead to Picardy. Again he was marked as the captain of 100 men, and features in the same way among the household and other officers in the middle ward, although no office is specified in his case. That is not surprising, as he did not hold one, but is indicative of confidence and closeness to the king's person. When the army was on the march from Calais towards Tournai in August 1513, he appears again as the captain of 100 men, under the command of Lord Lisle, the marshall of the army, and thus indirectly under the king himself.[13] We know that he was present at the siege of Therouanne, and at the Battle of the Spurs which accompanied it, because he was awarded the dignity of Knight Banneret for his valour on the latter occasion. He did not, however, remain in Tournai after its capture, but returned with the king to England in October, and appeared in person when the army was paid off in November. On that occasion he also received the sum due to Sir Anthony Hungerford, which is again a tribute to the confidence reposed in him. On 15 January 1514 he received an additional sum, apparently from the customs of the port of Southampton, as one of the local captains, although this may have been for his naval service in the previous year.[14] It sometimes took a long time for the royal bills to be settled!

By this time Sir John Seymour was a part of the military furniture. In February 1513 he was a muster commissioner for Wiltshire, and in April was granted protection from legal action during his anticipated service overseas, in case he should be sued while he was out of the country. He also received regular rewards. In July 1516 he was granted the wardship of the son and heir of Sir Christopher Wroughton and in July 1517 the keepership of Bristol Castle, which no doubt reinforced the contacts made originally by his great-grandfather. In 1520 he was listed as attending the king at the Field of Cloth of Gold, although he appears as representative of Wiltshire and not among the courtiers. He was allowed eleven servants on that occasion, which indicates his superior status because the average number allowed to a knight was six.[15] There is, however, no sign that Margery accompanied him on that trip; at least she does not appear among the queen's attendants. On 10 July he also accompanied Henry when he went to Gravelines to meet the Emperor Charles V. This was a rather more select band, but there is no indication as to what, if anything, he did during that encounter. His appearance seems to have been purely ceremonial. Nevertheless the invitation was repeated in May 1522, when Charles visited England, and Sir John was summoned to appear at Canterbury on the 27th.[16] It appears that he was sheriff of Wiltshire again in 1521–2, because on 9 June the Earl of Surrey wrote to Wolsey, complaining of the difficulties of finding the money to pay those soldiers who had been raised earlier in the year, and explaining that he had written to the mayors of Winchester and Southampton, and to Seymour as sheriff of the county for the extra £600 or £700 that would be necessary. Whether he was successful is not recorded. In the following year, 1523, Sir John served under the Duke of Suffolk on his ill-fated campaign in northern France, but his role is obscure and he may well have been a staff officer rather than an active commander in the field on account of his age. He was forty-seven or forty-eight by then, which may well have been considered too old for front-line service.[17] It must have been while he was still away on this campaign that he was named to the commission for the collection of the loan in Wiltshire and in the town of Salisbury. Earlier in the year Wolsey had failed to extract from Parliament the subsidy which he had demanded, and had fallen back on this loan as an expedient to cope with the resultant financial shortfall. Sir John's personal contribution had earlier been assessed at £33, which is a fair indication of his wealth at this stage of his career, especially when we realise that as steward of the Duke of Buckingham's land in the county, he was only assessed for an extra 100s.[18] Of course the duke's lands were in the hands of the Crown at this point on account of his attainder, and Seymour was responsible only for that part which had not been already granted away. He made regular reports on the state of his collections, and in November of the following year, 1524, Sir Henry Wyatt, the Treasurer of the Chamber, declared that he and the other collectors for Wiltshire had paid a total of £8,555, which must have been about the whole sum due.[19] In spite of his success in this connection, he seems not to have been troubled over the hefty Amicable Grant tax in 1525, possibly because he was sheriff again in 1524–5.

He continued to receive rewards and in February 1526 was granted the manor of Groveley, in Wiltshire, which would have sat conveniently for other manors which he already held. A year later one William Castell of Marlborough was granted a pardon for having broken into his close at Burbage and stolen two oxen, although whether this was at the suit of John Seymour is not known. Sir John seems to have been prone to this hazard, as there had been an acrimonious correspondence with the Bishop of Salisbury more than ten years before over a similar theft.[20] He may have sat in the House of Commons in the early years of

Henry's reign – that would have been consistent with his status – but unfortunately the returns for those sessions are missing so we cannot be sure. The first parliament which we know about is that of 1529, when he sat for the borough of Heytesbury, along with his brother Robert, which suggests a family interest in the borough. He had lost the county nomination to Sir Edward Darrell and Sir Edward Baynton, which may indicate a falling out with Wolsey, but there is no other indication of such. If he did anything of note during the extended sessions of this parliament, then it was not recorded. In spite of periodic litigation, he seems to have been a peaceable man, and one who was well regarded in his community. His dispute with Sir William Essex is an obscure element in this otherwise placid scene. It surfaced for the first time in 1528, when William Lord Sandys offered arbitration. This was clearly not successful because in 1531 Sir John sought to exploit his contact with Thomas Cromwell, at that time rising rapidly in the royal service, sending him a 'tegg of his own killing', and asking for his good offices in respect of his 'enemy Essex'. What the nature of the dispute was we do not know, nor how Seymour came to be on familiar terms with Cromwell, although it was clearly in his interest to keep in touch with what was going on at court.[21] This may have been connected with Cromwell's defence of Wolsey's position after his fall from favour in 1529, because in July 1530 Sir John served on the commission to assess what lands and goods the Cardinal held in Wiltshire. Wolsey was still alive at that point, and Cromwell's interest in the outcome is obvious. In 1532 he was created a Groom of the Privy Chamber, perhaps at Cromwell's intercession, because we know that he was infiltrating his friends into Privy Chamber positions by that time.[22] Meanwhile the king was running into difficulties in his attempt to secure an annulment of his marriage. This had surfaced as an issue in 1527, when an outraged Catherine had appealed to her nephew Emperor

Charles V to block any appeal which Henry might make to Rome for that purpose. Charles had responded positively, and thereafter used his influence in the curia, which was great, to obstruct every effort made by Wolsey in the king's interest. As a consequence, the legatine court which Wolsey secured in 1529 to hear the king's case in England was secretly instructed by Pope Clement VII to deliver no verdict in the king's favour, and was adjourned to Rome at the end of July. This deceit, to which he was not a party, cost Wolsey Henry's confidence. He was deprived of the Great Seal and charged with praemunire; in the following year he died, leaving Anne Boleyn very much in charge.[23] However, this did not solve Henry's problem, and he was critically short of diplomatic support. It was for that reason that he had signed a new alliance with France in 1527, and joined the League of Cognac against the Emperor. That did not work, as the two arch-rivals made peace at Cambrai in 1529, much to Henry's disappointment. However, he had no option but to continue his alliance with France, war or no war, and in that he was also encouraged by Anne, who because of her background remained consistently pro-French. Since the failure of the legatine court in 1529 she had been urging the king to find a unilateral solution to his problem, and by the summer of 1532 Thomas Cromwell was showing him a way in which this could be done, by utilising Parliament. In the session of 1532 he manoeuvred the Act for the Conditional Restraint of Annates into law, threatening the jurisdictional links between England and the papacy, and thus indicated that he was in earnest.[24] This of course made diplomatic support even more essential, and Henry raised the possibility of another personal meeting with Francis I, similar to that of 1520, but with a more positive agenda. Francis, who was equally keen to maintain the alliance, proved willing, and throughout the summer the preparations were made. The meeting was to be held at Calais during October, and on 1 September Henry created Anne Marquis of Pembroke, probably as a signal of his intentions towards her, and certainly to give her the dignity necessary to meet the French court. Sir John Seymour, newly appointed Groom of the Privy Chamber, was one of those designated to accompany him. He is described as representing the county of Wilshire, rather than the court, although his office must surely have been helpful in securing his selection. What, if anything, he did in the course of this mission is not known. His position may have been purely ornamental, but the king came away from his meeting satisfied that Francis would support him in his continued quest for an annulment, or in his unilateral action if that should prove to be necessary. Anne Boleyn also made a favourable impression upon the French king, and danced with him in the entertainment which followed the talks.[25] Anne's attitude to Sir John is open to question, because he was definitely not a member of the Boleyn faction. If anything his conservative religious tastes would have inclined him to the other side, but his main dependence seems to have been on Thomas Cromwell, who at this point was closely allied to the Boleyns, and he seems to have been happy enough with the Boleyn ascendancy at court. If he wasn't, the king at least does not seem to have noticed, and that was the important thing as far as retaining favour was concerned.

Sir John continued to serve on the commission of the peace for Wiltshire, and in January 1535 was named as a commissioner to collect the subsidy which had been voted the previous year. In June 1536 he owed an unspecified sum of money to the Crown, but this was apparently forgiven a man who was by then the king's father-in-law, and was unconnected with his duties as a subsidy commissioner.[26] How he discharged these duties we do not know, but he did not live long enough to witness his daughter's triumph as a mother. By the latter part of 1536 his health was visibly fading, and he died in early December, being properly mourned by

Jane, whose coronation was allegedly deferred on account of it. Rumours, however, were flying about that anticipated event, and it may well have been put off for other reasons – not least that the king simply could not make up his mind! John may have died intestate, because it was over a year later that Lord Beauchamp, as his son Edward had then become, received livery of his lands, including Wolf Hall, and we do not know what bequests he made to other members of the family. Apart from Lord Beauchamp these would have included his other sons, Thomas and Henry, assorted daughters including Queen Jane, and his younger brother, Robert.

Robert had been born about 1476, and he may have accompanied John against the Cornish rebels in 1497. He would have been of an age to have done so, but he earned no reward in consequence. Nor was he apparently a jouster, but he must have acquired some military experience somewhere, because he served as a captain at the siege of Tournai in 1513 for which he was paid, eventually, at the rate of four shillings a day.[27] In August 1522 he appears again as the captain of a ship called the *Christ*, of 180 men, but did not serve on her because in September he was reported as present at Ardres, and in October 1523 he joined the army of the Duke of Suffolk in northern France. What he may have done in that expedition is not clear, but he is listed among nearly 100 captains who served with his retinue when the army was paid off. He may well have returned to England independently after that fiasco, but it was not held against him. In July 1526 he was granted the stewardship of the hundreds of Amesbury, Winterbourne Earl and Alworthbury in Wiltshire, and in January 1527 the shrievalty of distant Anglesey, which was a part of the Principality of North Wales, and in the king's hands by the death of Owen Holland.[28] The sheriffs of Wales did not follow the English pattern of annual rotation, but were offices granted for life or during pleasure. There is no sign that Robert went to live in North Wales, or even visited

Anglesey, because he would have discharged his responsibilities by deputy. As we have seen, he sat for Heytesbury in the Reformation parliament which assembled in November 1529, having earlier in the year captained the *Christ* again, this time in an expedition led by William Gonson as admiral which involved twelve ships altogether and was apparently successful.[29] By May 1530 he was a Gentleman Usher of the Chamber, a second-grade position which reflected his prominence in Wiltshire rather than any intimacy with the king but was nevertheless a significant gesture of recognition. These promotions of the late 1520s he may well have owed to Cardinal Wolsey, at least in the negative sense that he did not oppose them, but unfortunately we know nothing of Robert's relationship with the Lord Chancellor, nor indeed that of the other members of his family. They appear to have played no part in his downfall, but on the other hand made no move to help him, a risk which Thomas Cromwell took with some enthusiasm. In May 1530, long after Wolsey was in any position to help him, Robert was granted the office of Master Forester of Melchet Forest, which was in the king's hands by virtue of the minority of Peter, the son and heir of Sir William Compton.[30] However, this was limited to the duration of the minority, and whether it was renewed by Peter when he became of full age is not known.

Robert drew his first half-year's pay as a Gentleman Usher of the Chamber on 25 March 1529, and seems to have taken his duties seriously. He claimed two days' riding expenses, presumably for the delivery of letters, in 1532, and is noted in the Privy Purse expenses as playing at Tables with the king at Dover, a game which cost Henry £4 13s 4d.[31] This indicates that Robert had accompanied the king to Calais for his rendezvous with Francis I, although there is no other mention of his having done so. In November 1533, when Elizabeth Barton was confessing that she had shown her various revelations concerning the king to divers persons, among those mentioned were 'Mr Semer and his wife'. Whether this alludes to Robert or not is not clear, but if it does they were not troubled further in the matter. The records are fragmentary, but if this does refer to Robert, it is the only known reference to his being married, and the identity of the lady is not known. From 25 October 1534 he was granted the important military command of the captaincy of Newnham Bridge in the Calais Pale, with a retinue of sixteen men. The intention to make this appointment had been mentioned in a letter from John Hussee to Lord Lisle on the 18th, but it cannot have come as a surprise to the latter because Cromwell always consulted the Lord Deputy carefully before making any such move.[32] Robert was clearly very dependent upon Cromwell. On 10 August 1535 he wrote to him from Calais, reporting that he had delivered his letters and begging to be 'had in remembrance' because he was as much in need as anyone in his position could be. Sir Thomas Palmer had apparently been very reluctant to surrender Newnham Bridge, and it was not until 20 August that he finally wrote in response to the Secretary's peremptory instructions, explaining that he had handed over his charge but not without some qualms as to his successor's competence.[33] Robert kept up his correspondence with Cromwell over the next four years, sending him small snippets of information and constantly reminding him of his suits to the king for some financial reward. Early in 1539 the Secretary reminded himself 'to remember Robert Seymour's suit for Inglechurch', so his efforts were obviously not wasted. The king, however, had had enough. Robert was in debt to the Crown and in March 1539 Henry resolved that that he should pay 100 marks and give up Newnham Bridge, a decision which provoked the plaintive cry from Robert that this was a poor reward for thirty years of service.[34] However he had no option but to defer to the king's pleasure and in December of that year the position was granted to Philip Denys, on the same terms

and with a similar retinue of sixteen men. Cromwell continued to
be his good lord, however, and in January 1540 his preferential
rents on properties in Wiltshire were renewed, and he received the
manor and advowson of Inglechurch.[35] Robert would clearly have
been hard hit by the fall of his patron in June 1540, and apart from
receiving his regular wages from the Chamber he does not appear
again in the records until his death, which appears to have occurred
in the autumn of 1546. Among the grants for November in that
year appears an annuity of £6 13s 4d, payable for life to David
Seymour, a Gentleman Usher of the Chamber. Since this grant was
to be effective from the death of Robert Seymour, it is reasonable
to suppose that David was his son, although nothing is known of
the circumstances of his birth or upbringing. Not even his mother's
name is known, nor the date of his parents' marriage. We do not
know where Robert was normally based, although it seems to have
been on one of the manors which he held in Wiltshire. Of course
he spent quite a lot of his time at court, and must presumably have
lived at Newnham Bridge while he was in post there, although
whether his family joined him is not recorded. In 1536 he wrote
to Cromwell from Wolf Hall, but that must have been courtesy of
his nephew Edward who normally resided there, because there is
no suggestion that that was his usual base and plenty of evidence
that Edward was normally in residence when he was not at court.
So Robert is an elusive figure on the fringes of the court. He exists
mainly in the Chamber accounts and in the correspondence of
Thomas Cromwell. It is not even certain whether he was knighted
or not. Sometimes he is referred to as Sir Robert, but where and
when the honour was conferred (if it was) is not on record either.
He is overshadowed not only by his elder brother, Sir John, but
even more by his nephews, Edward and Thomas, and most of all
by his niece, who became Henry's third queen on 30 May 1536.

3

JANE AND HENRY

We do not know when the king first noticed Jane Seymour. We know only that she was one of Queen Anne's ladies, and that Henry made an approach to her in February 1536. She had been born at Wolf Hall in about 1509, the fifth child but the eldest daughter of Sir John and Margery, who was no doubt very relieved by the appearance of a girl after so many boys. If she lived, Margery would have the rearing of her, and would be able to pass on those domestic skills which she had learned herself at the hands of her own mother. She did indeed live and thrived, but we know very little about her upbringing, other than that it seems to have been at home. The common practice of sending children as young as seven to be brought up in neighbouring households seems not to have been followed by the Seymours, who educated all their numerous brood themselves. Nor do they appear to have hosted any neighbours, it being felt no doubt that the children were sufficient company for each other. Jane was later literate in English, which suggests some schooling, probably at the hands of Sir John's chaplain, and she would have shared her schoolroom with Thomas, who was the nearest of her siblings in age.[1] She did not apparently learn any Latin, which was the gateway to the world of learning, because only the most advanced educationalists thought that such a skill was desirable for females. Chastity was a young maiden's most cherished possession. She would have learned to dance, to wield her needle, and to master those skills of household management that would have been necessary for the housewife which she was destined to become. So her adolescence passed, but no suitor seems to have appeared. This is something of a mystery, and cannot be attributed to any deficiency in the lady herself – unless she was simply unwilling to be courted. The most likely explanation is that Sir John's resources were stretched, and he was unable to offer a sufficiently attractive dowry.[2]

So Jane remained at home, until, at about the age of eighteen or nineteen, a place was found for her at court. What that place was, and how it was arranged, is not known. The most likely explanation is that her father exploited whatever contact he may have had with one of the peeresses in the royal household to take her on. Or it may have been her brother Edward, then a rising man in the royal service, who affected the introduction, except that he would not have been sufficiently senior to have carried weight with so distinguished a lady. We do not know who her first employer may have been, and even her existence is mere deduction. What we do know is that Jane entered Queen Catherine's service in 1529, and that that could scarcely have happened except from an established position within the court. Bearing in mind how difficult a struggle Honor Lady Lisle had just a few years later in placing her daughter by her first marriage, Anne Bassett, in Queen Jane's Chamber, we must conclude that Jane's first patron was a lady of considerable power.[3] It may have been the Countess of Sussex, but the records are silent on the subject. Catherine may even have chosen her herself, because her lack of intellectual training would have been no handicap. The queen was not looking to have learned discussions with her attendants, and Jane's gentle nature, and her virginity, may well have been commendations. She would have been expected to fit in, to go piously to Mass, and to use her needle with the rest of the ladies of the Privy Chamber. The tedium of daily attendance would have been no burden to her, and she no doubt enjoyed the games of courtly love which she would have been constrained to play with those gallants who had no other occupation for their time. Flirtation was not a skill which she would have learned at Wolf Hall, but the basic rules of the game were not difficult to pick up. The lady was always unavailable for whatever reason, and that would have been a stance which came naturally to her.[4] Unlike Anne at a similar stage in her career, Jane had not attracted the serious attentions of any relevant man, and marriage, which was always the prime objective for any unattached lady at the Tudor court, must have seemed a long way off.

The queen was not likely to be any help in that connection. Quite apart from the fact that she had other things on her mind, the Gentlemen of the Privy Chamber, who would have been the natural partners for her ladies, were constrained by their loyalty to the king to give them a wide berth, and that would have reduced the opportunities. Indeed we know very little about Jane's life as a lady of Catherine's Privy Chamber. Presumably she played a part in the court revels of those years, although as Henry's relations with his queen became more and more strained, these were neither as numerous nor as grand as had once been the case, and even the meticulous Edward Hall, who chronicled them all, did not mention her appearance. In the summer of 1531 Henry dismissed his wife from the court, and the revels dried up altogether for the time being.[5] She was still recognised as queen, but kept her establishment separate, and ladies of her Privy Chamber must have become increasingly isolated. Jane may have been protected against that isolation to some extent by her brother's position in the king's service, and by the mysterious relationship with Thomas Cromwell which resulted. In 1532, while she was still employed by Catherine, the latter noted in his remembrances 'to speak with the king for Mr Seymours's daughter for Elderton'. Where Elderton is, and what kind of a grant was in question, is not obvious.[6] This cryptic sentence does not suggest any degree of intimacy, but Jane must be referred to, and a patronage relationship established. Either Cromwell had noticed something special about her or her father had been lobbying on her behalf, because the date is too early for her to have caught the king's eye. It may, however, help to explain the next stage in her advancement. During the summer of 1532 the king finally became convinced that the only solution to his matrimonial problem lay in unilateral action. In September he created Anne Marquis of Pembroke and in October held a series of meetings with Francis I to bolster his diplomatic position in the curia. After the talks, while they were stormbound in Calais, Anne finally agreed to sleep with him, and fell pregnant in consequence.[7] When her condition was recognised in January 1533, Henry was finally constrained to act. It was essential that the child (hopefully a son) which she was carrying should be born legitimate, and the settlement of his marriage problem could be delayed no longer. Towards the end of January he married Anne, and in April persuaded his newly appointed Archbishop of Canterbury, Thomas Cranmer, to declare his first marriage to be null and void, on the grounds that Catherine had first been wife to his brother Arthur, and that the Law of God forbade such unions, which put it beyond the reach of the Pope's dispensation.[8] Anne was therefore his lawful queen, and on 1 June she was crowned as such. Catherine, of course, did not recognise her, but the king's decision left the ex-queen with nowhere to go. During the summer of 1533 the king re-designated her as the dowager Princess of Wales, and reorganised her household. Catherine utterly rejected this new description and insisted that her appeal to the Pope still stood, not being covered by the Act in Restraint of Appeals, which was passed at that time but was not retrospective. The household reorganisation was not as drastic as might be supposed, because she was left with a full domestic staff, but her Chamber was pruned and one of those removed was Jane Seymour. It may be that Jane was thought to be too close to her in her religious sympathies, and was in need of re-education, but someone clearly thought that Jane was worth re-educating. She was transferred to the Privy Chamber of the new queen, Anne Boleyn, who had a much more evangelical agenda than her predecessor.[9]

The responsibility for this easy transfer is not clear. Ultimately, it was the king who nominated Anne's new Chamber, but there is no evidence that he had noticed Jane at this point. Her father was too distant from the court to have any direct influence, and her brother, Sir Edward, although appointed an Esquire of the Body in September 1531, was not sufficiently intimate. It may be that Thomas Cromwell was responsible, or that Anne chose her herself. She was no great beauty, was docile and unlikely to cause any trouble, and since the last thing that the queen wanted was competition from within her own establishment that may be the real answer. Anne was accustomed to getting her own way in such matters, and at this stage was in close alliance with Cromwell. That both of them should have given him the same advice may well have been decisive in Henry's mind. One of her first duties as a lady-in-waiting would have been to take part in the female mysteries of the lying-in. Anne took to her Chamber at Greenwich in August 1533, and thereafter no man was supposed to intrude into her presence until after the birth had taken place.[10] This meant that routine jobs like guarding the door and waiting at table, which would normally have been performed by the Gentlemen Ushers, were now carried out by the queen's ladies, and menial work such as lighting the fires and keeping the place clean now fell to female chamberers. We do not know much about confinement practices in the Tudor court, because the women who took part in them did not discuss their experiences, and the men who wrote the accounts were not admitted. The most responsible job which Jane shared with her colleagues was to sleep on a pallet bed in the queen's bedchamber, in case any crisis arose during the night. However, as her time approached, that role would have been taken by one of the royal midwives, and we have no reason to suppose that Jane lost any sleep over her responsibilities. The birth, when it came on 7 September, was easy, and the only thing that a lady-in-waiting would have been called upon to do was to fetch supplies of fresh water and no doubt wine, when her Majesty needed refreshing after her ordeal. Unfortunately the child was a girl, in spite of the confident predictions of the astrologers, and both her parents were disappointed. Eustace Chapuys, the Imperial ambassador, who was Anne's mortal enemy, by virtue of his role as the defender of Catherine and Mary in his master's interests, could scarcely conceal his glee.[11] The courts of Europe were also amused, because the King of England had broken with the Church, turned the politics of his country upside down and imperilled his immortal soul for the sake of another daughter. Nevertheless Henry and Anne put a brave face on it, and spoke of her youth and fertility. The sons would come in due course. Elizabeth was christened on 10 September at the church of the Austin friars in Greenwich with the muted celebrations due to a princess. Archbishop Cranmer stood as godfather, but the planned tournament was cancelled.[12]

Almost immediately a household was created for the new Princess of England, and a few days later Henry's elder daughter, Mary, had her chamber disbanded and she was placed, along with few personal attendants, in this new environment. Chapuys was outraged by this fresh dishonour to his princess, but his protests were ignored and Henry's motives are quite clear. Mary had followed her mother's lead in rejecting her designation as 'the Lady Mary the King's daughter' and her father's supremacy over the Church, both of which would have implied acceptance of the nullity of his first marriage. This was her punishment. Communication between the two women was supposed to be forbidden, but this ban was slackly enforced and written messages continued to pass, borne usually by Randall Dodd, one of Mary's few remaining servants.[13] Henry's cruelty was more in theory than in practice, and he was saving himself the cost of another establishment. In fact during her time in Elizabeth's household Mary seems to have been a pain to herself and everyone who had dealings with her. Of physical deprivation there is no sign except that she was not allowed to ride abroad in the way that she wanted. The risks of her simply being spirited away were too great. Her mealtimes were adjusted to suit her requirements, and Henry sent his own physicians to attend upon her during her frequent menstrual ailments. However, her refusal to respond to anyone who did not address her as princess caused endless problems. In February 1534, for instance, 'finding herself nearly destitute of clothes and other necessities', she sent a gentleman of the household direct to the king, with orders to return with either cash or clothes, but not to receive any writing in which she was not styled princess.[14] The outcome of this mission is not on record! In March of the same year she refused to cooperate in a routine move of location, and the exasperated Lady Shelton, who was in charge of Elizabeth's chamber, had her dumped in a litter and carried off. This provoked the usual protest from Chapuys, but it is difficult to see what else Lady Shelton could have done in the circumstances.[15] In addition to protecting Mary, Chapuys was concerned to undermine 'the concubine' by all the means in his power, and this involved monitoring the king's behaviour, particularly in respect of his 'amours', by which he usually meant the games of courtly love which Henry was playing. As early as August 1533, while Anne was unavailable to him, the ambassador picked up such a rumour, probably from a sympathetic courtier. Other evidence from the same period flatly contradicts him, and in October of the same year, after the disappointment of Elizabeth, Henry was making extravagant professions of loyalty to his wife. According to the ladies of Anne's Privy Chamber, of whom Jane would have been one, he was declaring that he would beg from door to door rather than give her up.[16] Henry's relationship with his wife was a passionate one, and like most such relationships was subject to ups and downs. There is little doubt that early in 1534 the king was playing courtly love with several ladies of the court, who responded for the most part with enthusiasm. But that does not mean that he had sexual relations with them, and Anne's anger, reported assiduously by Chapuys, was probably misplaced. However in July 1534 Anne had a miscarriage and that changed the situation. Henry had been this way before with Catherine, and his old demons seem to have been aroused. The fact of her pregnancy suggests that there was nothing very much wrong with their relationship up until that point, but now he apparently began to have doubts. Could he have been mistaken in his second marriage? He had made a huge political and personal investment in Anne, but God was clearly displeased, so what had he done wrong? As if to assuage these doubts, in August 1534, Henry seems to have begun an affair. According to Chapuys, writing in September, the king had given up on the prospect of having another child by his wife, and had 'renewed and increased the love that he had previously towards another very beautiful maid of honour'. Anne had reacted savagely, wanting to dismiss the errant girl, but Henry had reprimanded her, reminding her that she owed her position entirely to him, and that he was regretting the indulgence which he had hitherto shown her.[17] A fortnight later he was writing that Jane Rochford had been forbidden the court for plotting with the queen to pick a quarrel with the king's latest fancy and forcing her to withdraw. The new lady was sending encouraging messages to Mary, telling her that her troubles would soon be over, and that the Concubine's influence was diminishing daily, which was what he wanted to believe.[18] Was this new royal paramour Jane? Chapuys does not mention any name, possibly because he did not know it, although that would not be typical of his inquisitive nature. His description of the lady as 'very beautiful' does not suggest Jane, but that was probably based on hearsay rather than first-hand observation. The messages to Mary would have been characteristic of her, but not the confidence which they seem to display in her capacity to change the king's mind.

We might be tempted to explain all this as another of Chapuys's exaggerations, were it not for the fact that the same story had been picked up in Rome, where the Imperial ambassador retailed it. He would not necessarily have been in touch with Chapuys, although his attitude towards Anne would have been equally hostile. According to him the Concubine's arrogance had turned Henry against her, and he had gone in search of alternative company.[19] It must be remembered, however, that all these stories come from Anne's enemies. Chapuys derived his account of her annoyance at Henry's dalliance early in 1534 from Sir Nicholas Carew, who was well known for his support for Catherine, and Jane Rochford, in spite of her close relationship to Anne, was not among her friends. Henry may well have been annoyed at his wife's tantrums, but they soon made up their differences, and his courtly love romances were of no ultimate significance. These were lovers' quarrels, as Chapuys in his more rational moments recognised quite well. Nevertheless Anne was vulnerable in that she did not make the critical move from mistress to wife and mother. As the king's mistress, she was entitled to her fits of pique if his eyes strayed to other women. She might be his darling, but she knew that her position was insecure, and that she might have to fight to maintain it. That she had done successfully for five long years, and she knew all the tricks needed to retain her royal lover's interest. She was entitled to maintain an independent political position, provided that she did not cross him, and to pursue her own evangelical agenda, with the same proviso. She could exercise her influence upon him, and all her tantrums were carried out in the knowledge that, at the end of the day, he would come to her begging her forgiveness. She remained in control of the sexual exchanges between them.[20] As a wife, however, her position was quite different. She was expected to endure his infidelities, as Catherine had done for a number of years, and to be meek and submissive to his will. She was not expected to guide or advise her husband – that was the job of his council – nor to have her own political or religious agenda. This did not suit Anne's temperament at all, and she did not make a good conventional wife. Unfortunately Henry was a very conventional husband, and expected her to make the necessary adjustments. When she failed to do so their quarrels became more serious, and because she had only one way of retaining control in their relationship, these tended to focus on his 'amours', real or imagined, and Henry became increasingly annoyed. He may even have contemplated abandoning her after her miscarriage of July 1534, but if he did, there were cogent factors to deter him, and the most important of these was his ex-wife. Lurking unhappily at Kimbolton, on the edge of the Fens, she showed no sign of surrendering to his wishes, and Henry would have been well aware of the papal sentence of 1533, which had ordered him to return to her.[21] If he should repudiate his second marriage, the pressure to take Catherine back might well have become overwhelming, and he had no desire to face that issue, especially as Chapuys was making it clear that improved relations with the Emperor depended upon just such a change of heart. The ambassador was concerned to drive the king and queen apart, and chose the temporary estrangement of the late summer of 1534 in an attempt to do that, a fact of which Henry would have been well aware. He also sought to use the king's affection for his daughter Mary in his efforts to discredit Anne. If the concubine had her way, he reported, Mary would have been faced with the Oath of Supremacy, and would have been executed as a traitor for refusing to take it. That such a fate indeed awaited those who refused the oath was amply demonstrated by the deaths of Bishop John Fisher and Sir Thomas More in the summer of 1535, but Henry would not allow the oath to be administered to Mary or Catherine, and Anne's malice was frustrated.[22] Meanwhile the king's relationship with his queen continued to be up and down, but if he ever thought of using his affair of the autumn of 1534 as a means of unseating her, then he soon abandoned the idea. The only sign that Jane featured in these calculations at all is that she was allowed to exchange New Year gifts with the king in 1534. This was a sign of exceptional favour for one not on the inward circle of the court, but what provoked it we do not know. It may have been no more than an extension of the support which we know that she had from Thomas Cromwell, although that is equally mysterious. More than two years before Henry is known to have taken any interest in her, Jane was moving quietly into the arc of royal favour.

In the summer of 1535 the king and queen went on an extended progress. They went as far as the Severn, and spent most of September and October in Hampshire.[23] Henry was no doubt glad to get away from London, and from the diplomatic recriminations which followed the executions of June and July. The people of the area gave Anne a cordial reception, and that was also a welcome change from the capital, which had not got over its chilly attitude towards the new queen. Henry had not hunted that part of the world for a number of years, and the sport was good, particularly the hawking, upon which the king spent most of his waking hours. At Winchester on 19 September he witnessed the consecration of three of his favourite clergy as bishops by his own appointment; the preacher Hugh Latimer to Worcester, John Hilsey to Rochester and Edward Fox to Hereford. Latimer was the replacement for Geromino de Ghinucci, who had been deprived as a foreign intruder in March 1533, Hilsey replaced the executed John Fisher, and Fox the innocuous Charles Booth, who had died in May. Latimer was also a favourite of Anne Boleyn's, and she would have witnessed his promotion with satisfaction.[24] Such reports as we have of the behaviour of the Royal couple during these weeks suggests a relaxed cordiality, and that is confirmed by the fact that when they returned to Windsor in late October, she was pregnant for the third time. The progress was a success in more ways than one. In the course of it, in early September they stopped for a few days at Wolf Hall, the home of Sir John Seymour and his numerous brood. Legend has it that it was on this occasion that Jane first caught the king's eye, but it is by no means certain that she was even present, and she was clearly not sitting at home waiting for the royal visitors to put in an appearance. If she was there, it would have been as a lady attendant upon the queen, and unfortunately we do not know how the entourage for the progress was constructed. It is just as likely that Jane had been left behind in London, but her whereabouts in the summer of 1535 is not known. If she remained in London, she was too wise to become involved in the demonstration in Mary's favour, which was staged by a number of citizens' wives, taking advantage of the fact that the court was in Hampshire. Several ladies of the Household were implicated and one or two of them, including Jane Rochford, landed up in the Tower in consequence.[25] Although he may have had difficulty in putting a face to it, the name of Jane Seymour was in any case known to the king. Not only had Cromwell drawn his attention to her in 1532, but he had also made her a New Year's gift in 1534, along with Madge Shelton, Anne Zouche and the other ladies of Anne's Privy Chamber. However, as far as we know, there was no reason why Jane should have been singled out for special attention as 1535 drew to close. Henry's sexual attentions would have been concentrated on his pregnant wife.

Then on 7 January 1536 Catherine of Aragon died at Kimbolton. There were, of course, rumours that she had been poisoned, which Chapuys at first believed, but other contemporary evidence suggests natural causes, probably a series of heart attacks.[26] The king's first reaction was one of relief; 'God be praised that we are now free from any suspicion of war'. The Emperor's attitude was bound to be changed by the death of his aunt, whose appeals he had found increasingly embarrassing over the last few months. Thomas Cromwell's vision of improved relations now seemed more real, a prospect which had profound implications for Henry's ties with France, and might even make Francis more amenable to his wishes. Moreover Catherine's death removed any possibility that he would be forced to return to her, and in a sense made Henry's excommunication obsolete, although there was no sign of it being withdrawn. Anne's position as queen was now unchallenged, except on technical grounds, and there was an upsurge of Boleyn enthusiasm at court. The opinion was even expressed that it was a pity that Mary had not gone the same way as her mother. Most of Catherine's erstwhile supporters now transferred their allegiance to Mary, but that was a long-term prospect. On Sunday 9 January, two days after the news from Kimbolton, Henry and Anne both appeared dressed in yellow by way of celebration, and the infant Elizabeth was triumphantly paraded to Mass.[27] Anne, however, had good cause to be anxious.

If the child she was carrying turned out to be male, and lived, her position would be assured; but if it died, or turned out to be another girl, then she was in serious danger of repudiation now that she was no longer protected by Catherine, lurking unhappily in the background. The stakes could hardly have been higher. Perhaps as a part of his celebrations, or perhaps to advertise his continuing virility, Henry decided to stage a tournament, and in spite of his forty-four years to take part himself. It was several years since he had last jousted, and the decision turned out to be a serious mistake, because during the preparations, on 24 January he had a heavy fall in the lists at Greenwich. He was unconscious for more than two hours and alarm bells started ringing all over the court.[28] Eventually he recovered completely, and was none the worse apart from some nasty bruises, but it was an unwelcome reminder of his own mortality, and he did not attempt to joust again. Such exercises were appropriate for young men, but not for the corpulent, middle-aged figure that he had now become. This was no doubt a blow to his vanity, but it was necessary to yield to reality.

Five days later, on 29 January, disaster struck when Anne miscarried. She tried to blame this misfortune on receiving the news of her husband's accident, but the interval of five days makes that unlikely. The foetus was male, and of about fifteen weeks' gestation. The fact that it could be so described suggests the attendance of midwives, which means that the event was not entirely unexpected.[29] There is remarkably little contemporary evidence for this development, but it was the subject of much speculation later on. Many years later Nicholas Sander wrote that the foetus was deformed and that convinced Henry that he could not be the father, and that consequently his wife was guilty of adultery. While it is true that that was a belief at that time, there is no evidence that it was relevant in this particular case. In the early seventeenth century, Jane Dormer blamed Jane Seymour, claiming that Anne had caught the couple *in flagrante delicto*, with that 'abandoned woman' sitting on the king's knee, and her rage at that discovery had caused her miscarriage.[30] However, Jane was not even born when these events took place, and based her opinion on the words of one of Anne's ladies narrating the incident in old age, when her memory might well have failed her. What we can be sure of is that the king was deeply distressed by the loss of his boy, and began to consider his options. The first was obviously to leave things as they were, and hope for better luck next time, but the second was to get rid of Anne and start again. Chapuys is not entirely consistent on this matter, and it must be borne in mind that he was bitterly hostile to Anne, and all that she stood for, particularly her evangelical agenda and the French alliance. At one point he was writing that Henry had scarcely spoken to her for several months, and at another that, wearied by her expressions of devotion which he was no longer able to reciprocate, he went off to celebrate Shrovetide (28 February) on his own at Westminster instead of keeping her company at Greenwich.[31] There is plenty of evidence that the king was at Westminster at the end of February, but there could have been other reasons for that apart from his annoyance with Anne. The business of Parliament required his urgent attention at about that time, and the queen was still probably convalescent after her miscarriage. What we do know is that there was bad feeling between Henry and Anne at about that time, but what caused it apart from the king's anger at the loss of his son we do not know. Perhaps that is sufficient explanation. According to Jane Dormer, Anne wished to dismiss Jane from her service after discovering her liaison with the king, but that Henry would not permit it. As a result there had been 'much scratching and bye blows between the queen and her maid', but as we have seen such testimony bears all the marks of later hindsight. The king was still referring with all apparent sincerity to his entirely beloved wife in public as late as the end of April, although by then his attitude to her must have been on a knife-edge.

At some point during March he had apparently made an attempt on Jane's virtue. We are dependant on Chapuys for our information concerning this incident, but he cites the authority of one 'Gelyot', who must have been Sir Thomas Elyot, a Gentleman of the Privy Chamber and thus in a good position to know. According to Chapuys the king was at Westmnster at the time and the young lady 'who he serves, Mrs Semel', was at Greenwich, presumably about her usual duties. It is notable that the ambassador had a name to attach to this damsel, which he had not had in 1534, so it is unlikely that the same person is being referred to.[32] 'Gelyot' informed him that the king had sent her a letter and a purse full of sovereigns by a special messenger. We do not know what the letter contained, but the chances are that it was a proposition similar to that which Henry had made to Anne Boleyn in the spring of 1527, before she had made her position abundantly clear. Jane obviously suspected some such thing, because having kissed the letter, she returned it to the messenger unopened, begging him on her knees

> that he would pray the king on her part to consider that she was a gentlewoman of good and honourable parents, without reproach, and that she had no greater treasure in the world than her honour, which she would rather die a thousand deaths than tarnish ...[33]

If the king was minded to send her a present of money then she begged that he would do so only when God had sent her a good marriage. Although Chapuys does not say so, she presumably returned the purse of sovereigns also, otherwise the gesture would have rather lost its point. It is natural to suppose that Jane, like Anne before her, was angling for the big prize, except that there was no sign at that stage that Henry was contemplating abandoning Anne and consequently becoming available on the marriage market. The king was duly impressed by this display of virtue, and declared that henceforth he would speak to her only in the presence of some member of her family. He then set about making her access to him (or his to her) easier, by moving Thomas Cromwell out of his favoured apartments at the court in order to install Sir Edward Seymour and his wife. Sir Edward had just been made a gentleman of the Privy Chamber, and might have commanded such a promotion in his own right, but it is natural to suppose that this was done in order to facilitate his access to Jane, who could visit her brother without arousing any suspicion at the court. A secret passage joined this apartment to the royal quarters, enabling him to come to her whenever she was present. If he was serious about speaking to her only in the presence of some member of her family, then her brother might well have fulfilled that role, although in view of the outcome it is unlikely that he abided by it.[34] Thomas Cromwell, who had by that time fallen out badly with the queen, was no doubt only too willing to support so good a cause. Not only was Anne a serious obstacle to his preferred foreign policy, but they also disagreed about the disposal of former monastic property. Henry, on Cromwell's advice, was gathering the lands and possessions of the smaller monasteries into his own hands, and was already beginning to disperse it among his lay servants, while the queen was of the opinion that such property should only be used for religious purposes, education or the augmentation of poor livings. On 2 April, which was Passion Sunday, John Skip, who was Anne's almoner, actually preached in support of her position in the Chapel Royal. He cited the Old Testament story of King Ahasuerus, who on the advice of his minister Haman was intending to massacre the Jews. However there was good woman called Esther whom the king loved well 'and put his trust in because he knew that she was ever his friend' and she gave Ahasuerus contrary counsel, with the result that the Jews were saved and Haman was hanged. No one who heard the sermon could have been in any doubt about its meaning. Henry VIII was Ahasuerus, Anne was Esther and Cromwell was Haman. The king was not amused, and Cromwell was exceedingly angry.[35] For the time being Boleyn influence remained strong at Court, but by late April Henry's attitude towards Anne, which was the only one which really mattered, was precariously balanced. How far his relationship with Jane had developed by then we do not know, but that is also likely to have been a critical influence in making up his mind. Meanwhile the ever ingenious Cromwell had fed Henry with another notion. If his second marriage was as invalid as his first, how was his long infatuation with Anne to be explained? One possible explanation was witchcraft. She had bewitched her unsuspecting partner. This had the great advantage of absolving the king from all responsibility for what had happened, and also explained her possible descent into adultery, because that was what witches did. This idea was not followed through in the charges eventually brought against her, but undoubtedly influenced Henry's thinking at this critical juncture.[36] More tangibly, on 29 or 30 April Anne had a furious row with Sir Henry Norris, which arose from his slowness to make advances to the girl whom she had looked out for him. In the course of this quarrel, Anne accused him of wanting to possess herself 'if ought but good should happen to the king', and word of what had been said was all over the court in a matter of hours. This not only constituted the treason of imagining the king's death, it also suggested an existing sexual relationship between them. Cromwell reacted swiftly, but not in the obvious way. Later on the 30th he arrested Mark Smeaton, a Chamber musician who had been pining after Anne for some time, and charged him with adultery with her. Under pressure – perhaps physical, perhaps psychological – Smeaton confessed to what was almost certainly a bogus charge, and Cromwell had his case to confront the king, which he presumably did on 1 May.[37] These two events combined to convince Henry that his wife was guilty of adultery, and on 2 May Anne was arrested and taken to the Tower.

There has been a great deal of debate, both at the time and since, about the reality of the charges brought against Anne. She was undoubtedly guilty of frivolous talk, which gave the impression of multiple sexual relationships, but the consensus of opinion is that she was not guilty, and that those who were tried and convicted of adultery with her were framed. This applies particularly to her brother George, who was convicted on no evidence at all of incest with his sister. The real reason why Anne and George had to die is that they were far too formidable as politicians to be shunted aside as Catherine had been dealt with. In other words it was necessary to Cromwell's security that the Boleyn faction should be eliminated, and he succeeded in persuading the king to accomplish this.[38] The only person to speak up for Anne at the time was Archbishop Cranmer, who was effectively kept away from Henry during these days, but expressed his doubts in a letter to the king, which as far as we know had no effect at all. The queen was convicted by the Earl Marshal's court on 15 May, and on the 17th the Archbishop's court pronounced her marriage to the king to be null and void, thus reversing its decision of three years earlier. The papers for this case no longer survive, so we cannot be sure of the grounds for the verdict, except that it cannot possibly have been for adultery. It must have been on the basis of Henry's relationship with her sister Mary, about which it is just possible that Cranmer was ignorant in 1533.[39] The real reason, however, is that the king would have it so, and Anne was beheaded on Tower Green on 19 May.

While Anne was undergoing destruction, Henry was keeping

up his attachment to Jane Seymour. Anne's household had been dissolved by her attainder, and the king had Jane moved to a house belonging to Sir Nicholas Carew which was more conveniently placed for him to continue his courtship. On 18 May Chapuys wrote to Cardinal Granvelle of the king's new lady:

> She is sister to Sir Edward Seymour, of middle stature and no great beauty ... she is over twenty-five years old and has long frequented the court ... she is not a woman of great wit, but may be of good understanding. It is said that she is inclined to be proud and haughty, and has a good affection towards the Princess (Mary) ...[40]

She carried no political baggage, and he added that the king might be only too glad to be relieved of matrimonial trouble. Jane had no agenda of her own, and no desire apart from pleasing Henry, which she was well equipped to do. On 19 May, the very day of Anne's execution, Cranmer issued a dispensation for Henry and Jane to marry 'although within the third degree of affinity'. The reason for this is obscure, because as far as is known there was no affinity between them to require it.[41] At nine o'clock on the morning of the 20th, Jane came secretly by river to the king's apartments and the pair were betrothed, a fact which was reported by Chapuys on the same day. Although Jane was popular, he declared, the king's precipitate action was 'ill taken' of many people, who claimed, reasonably enough, that an understanding had been reached before Anne's death, which they considered to be improper.[42] On receiving the news Mary of Hungary, the Regent of the Low Countries, wrote to the Emperor's brother Ferdinand that the king's new lady was as good an Imperialist as Anne had been a Frenchwoman, and moreover that she was a friend to the princess Mary. Henry had apparently been intending to keep his betrothal secret for the time being, but news of it was all over the court in a matter of hours, and he decided to consummate his union without further delay. They were married in the queen's closet at Whitehall on 30 May, and she was shown to the court as queen on 2 June. Within a few days she had apparently made her first attempt to influence her husband's mind by praising the merits of his estranged daughter, and was told gently to mind her own business. On 3 June Sir John Russell wrote to Lord Lisle, describing the 'showing' of the previous day and commenting,

> I assure you she is as gentle a lady as ever I knew, and as fair a Queen as any in Christendom. The King has come out of hell into heaven for the gentleness of this and the cursedness and unhappiness of the other ...[43]

which was hardly fair to Anne, whose brutal treatment had caused quite a lot of adverse comment. Lisle should write to the king conveying his congratulations as soon as possible, Russell urged, emphasising the joy which this new union would bring him. On 6 June, after Mass, Chapuys was invited to accompany the royal couple to the queen's chamber, where he was permitted to kiss her and to congratulate her upon her marriage, surely a sign of the improved relations which he was anticipating. The Emperor would be delighted, he said, that the king had found so virtuous a wife. The satisfaction of the people with this union, he added mendaciously, 'is incredible'.[44]

Parliament was convened on 8 June, and quickly passed an Act confirming the illegitimacy of both Mary and Elizabeth, and settling the succession on any child that might be born of the present queen, or of any spouse that the king may wed in future. Another statute created the queen's jointure, which consisted largely of lands taken over from the deceased Anne, giving her an income of about £3,000 a year, and a third confirmed the gift of

Paris Garden in London which the king had made over to her a few days previously. On 5 June her brother Edward was created Viscount Beauchamp, and on 1 July he took his oath as a member of the king's council.[45] The rewards of Jane's new position were not far to seek, but it should be emphasised that the Seymours were never a political presence in the sense that the Boleyns had been. This was partly because neither she nor Sir John were leaders in the sense that Anne and the Earl of Wiltshire had been, and partly because of the position now occupied by Thomas Cromwell. When Wiltshire was deprived of the office of Lord Privy Seal at the end of June 1536, he was replaced not by Viscount Beauchamp but by Cromwell himself. He had no intention of allowing so important a fruit of his victory over the Boleyns to fall into any hands other than his own. There is every sign that he was happy with the Seymour ascendancy at court, provided that it did not interfere with his own political influence. He was friendly with Edward Seymour, and with the queen, but did not need to form any alliance with them, and Jane did not offer political advice in the sense that Anne had done. The king's domestic scene remained essentially private.

4

THE HEIR PROVIDED

Henry now had to get his new wife pregnant. One observer in Rome thought that he had already performed that feat, writing that the king had married a woman who was already six months pregnant by him. This may have been simply the result of false information, or it may have been a misplaced memory of his wedding three years earlier to Anne Boleyn. It was, however very wrong, and on 12 August Chapuys wrote to Charles V that the king confessed to feeling very old, and was doubting whether he would have any children by his queen.[1] However, this was in the context of considering what to do about Mary after her submission, and whether she should be included in the succession. It does not therefore represent any serious uncertainty about his potency, and the fact was that he was happy with his new marriage, and enjoying a honeymoon which went well into the autumn. Jane had played a crucial but ill-recorded part in Mary's surrender, which had reconciled her to her father and brought about this new situation. The fall of Anne was critical to this situation, but not in the way that Mary imagined. She believed that Anne was her real enemy, and that her removal would mean automatic forgiveness from the king, who had been unduly influenced against her. In fact it is clear that Anne's presence or absence made no difference to Henry's attitude. A few days before the crisis which removed her, the king had told Chapuys,

> As to the legitimation of our daughter Mary ... if she would submit to our grace, without wrestling against the determination of our laws, we would acknowledge her and use her as our daughter, but we would not be directed or pressed therein ...[2]

In other words her status was entirely a matter for his own determination, and he was looking for an unconditional surrender. This Mary either could not or would not understand, and throughout May she waited in vain for the initiative from her father that would signify forgiveness. This was a misapprehension which was shared, according to Chapuys, both by the ordinary people and by Queen Jane, who did not understand, as Thomas Cromwell did, the king's total commitment to his ecclesiastical supremacy. He would not take any action which compromised that, and accepting Mary's present state of mind would have meant exactly such a compromise.

Consequently the princess waited through May and the early part of June, while her former servants turned up at Hundson, expecting to be reinstated.[3] However, Elizabeth was now equally illegitimate, and the status of her household indeterminate, so Chapuys wisely advised Lady Shelton to take on nobody without the king's express permission. On 26 May Mary wrote to Cromwell, asking for his intercession, now that the woman who had estranged her from her father was gone. He replied promptly, saying that obedience was looked for as a condition of her reinstatement, but Mary did not understand this, and wrote again on the 30th offering only to be as 'obedient to the king's grace as you can reasonably require of me'. Not realising the inadequacy of this response, she then wrote directly to her father, congratulating him upon his recent marriage, and asking leave to wait upon the new queen.[4] She acknowledged her offences, and begged his blessing 'in as humble and lowly a manner as possible'. However, she also made it plain that there were limits to her submissiveness, asking him to remember that she had committed herself to God, and that the ecclesiastical supremacy and her mother's marriage were reserved by that condition. Because she was offering nothing new, the king did not respond to this epistle, but instead went ahead and drew up a set of articles to be presented to her and which would leave no room for equivocation. Cromwell was worried by this new development, because it was no part of his plan to see the princess executed for high treason; he drew up a letter of submission for her to sign and took Chapuys into his confidence. On 6 June the latter reported that he could see an honourable way out of the dilemma, but the nature of that remedy is unknown. It seems to have been short of signing Cromwell's letter, but his false optimism must have communicated itself to Mary, who on the 7th wrote to Cromwell, asking for some token of forgiveness, before she visited the court, and on the 8th to Henry, expressing her joy that he had now 'withdrawn his displeasure'.[5] Sadly this was premature, and on about the 15th the king duly sent his commission, led by the Duke of Norfolk to Hunsdon to demand an unequivocal answer to two questions. Would she accept his ecclesiastical supremacy and the annulment of his marriage to her mother? After a stormy and emotional confrontation, Mary rejected both demands, and thus exposed herself to the penalties of high treason. The council went into emergency session to decide what to do about her, and the crisis which Cromwell and Chapuys had feared was now upon them.[6] It must have been at about this point that Queen Jane intervened, writing to Mary and probably advising her to submit on the grounds that such severe pressure would surely absolve her conscience. On the 21st the princess replied, thanking her for her for her 'most prudent counsel', and begging her intercession for an interview with her father.[7] The following day she signed Cromwell's letter of submission, not making any reservations, and the crisis was over. The relaxation of tension was palpable, and seems to have been as welcome to Mary as it was to the court. Chapuys represented her as conscience-smitten over her surrender, but other evidence suggests a cheerful acceptance of the inevitable. Unfortunately Jane's letter does not survive, but on 6 July the king and queen visited Hunsdon and stayed for two days, during which time the affection between the two women seems to have blossomed. There was only a gap of seven years between them and the relationship seems to have been similar to that between sisters.

Mary was the principal beneficiary from this friendship. Although the rumours that she would be created Duchess of York turned out to be groundless, her chamber was reconstituted in a matter of days. In response to her own suggestion Susan Clarencius and Margery Baynton were appointed, and she was soon surrounded by old friends.[8] Altogether she was granted four gentlewomen, two chamberers, five gentlemen and various lesser servants to a total number of twenty-four – less than half the size of her previous establishment, but Mary was not disposed to complain. On 16 August Sir John Shelton, the controller of the joint household, reported that it was 'served of two sides' equality between the king's two illegitimate daughters now having been established. Even Chapuys described it as 'very honourable'. Mary also re-entered the marriage market. In a fit of enthusiasm on 12 August Henry wrote to his ambassadors in France offering her legitimation and inclusion in the succession in return for an undertaking that the Duke of Angoulême, Francis's third son, would wed her and spend a part of his time in England. How serious he was with this suggestion, which runs counter to so many statements both before and after, we do not know. Mary herself certainly did not take it very seriously, but it signalled her return to the marriage market after three years in the wilderness, and that was what mattered.[9] The Emperor was still keen to match her with Dom Luis, the son of the King of Portugal, but that made no progress either. Meanwhile her place in the succession was highlighted by the death on 23 July of the seventeen-year-old Duke of Richmond. As long as the king had only illegitimate children, the position of his son was bound to be a strong one, and Chapuys was quite clear that Henry intended to name him as his heir in default of issue by Jane. However, there is no contemporary support for such an intention, and his death removed the possibility, leaving Mary in splendid isolation. If the king had died in the autumn of 1536, she would have been bound to succeed him, legitimate or not. Henry did what he could to remedy this situation. On 12 July he instructed Archbishop Cranmer to include the queen in the bidding prayers, and on the 18th Parliament passed an Act vesting the succession in the heirs of her body.[10] His honeymoon extended well into the autumn, and the pair were often noted as being 'merry' together, but there was no sign of pregnancy and by October the gossips of the court were beginning to show signs of anxiety.

By then the king had other things on his mind, because on the 2nd of that month the men of Louth and Horncastle in Lincolnshire rose in rebellion. At least that was the way it looked in London, and as early as 7 October a list was drawn up of about a hundred noblemen and gentlemen who were to go in the king's service against the 'northern rebels'. Viscount Beauchamp figures prominently on this list, and he was supposed to raise 200 men.[11] He may actually have done so, but they did not march against the men of Lincolnshire, who professed the warmest loyalty to the king. They were in their own eyes protesting against evil councillors, particularly Cromwell and Cranmer, whom they claimed were misleading their noble monarch. It was primarily a movement of the commons, stirred up by conservative clergy, but also involved the capture and recruitment of a number of local gentry, because apparently they felt the need for natural leaders. The commitment of these 'leaders' to the cause was more than doubtful, and they would probably have been better off without them. They raised almost 20,000 men in ten days and occupied Lincoln without encountering any resistance. The question then arose as to what to do next, because Henry's initial response had been conciliatory, and it was felt that to go further would have been provocative. It was decided, probably by the gentlemen, to send a set of articles to the king outlining their grievances. These started with the dissolution of the monasteries,

> the suppression of so many religious houses ... whereby the service of God is not well maintained, but also the commons of your realm unrelieved the which we think is a great hurt to the commonwealth ...[12]

This was a protest against the statute of 27 Henry VIII, cap. 28, which Cromwell had steered through Parliament at its most recent sitting and undoubtedly represented the king's intention, whatever the men of Lincolnshire might think. They then proceeded to complain of the statute of uses, the tax or quindene of 4*d* for every beast, which would be an 'importable charge' to the commons, the use of baseborn councillors (notably Cromwell and Richard Rich), and the appointment of several bishops who were held to be responsible for the king's religious policies. On 26 October an anonymous correspondent reported to Cardinal du Bellay, the papal nuncio in France, that the queen had supported this petition, going down on her knees to beg Henry to spare the monasteries, but had been told reasonably gently, to mind her own business.[13] This is Jane's only recorded intervention in the whole business and it was apparently quite ineffectual. The articles were, however, a way of buying time by both sides because by the time that the king's response reached Lincoln the gentlemen had persuaded their followers to go home, and after about three weeks the crisis was over. The gentlemen who had been involved made haste to submit to the Duke of Suffolk, who was in command of the king's camp at Ampthill, and were on the whole well received. This was just as well because the king's response, when it eventually reached Lincoln, was not at all conciliatory, taking the protesters to task for daring to lecture their king about what he should do, or whom he should consult. They were, he pointed out, the inhabitants of one of the most 'brutish' shires in the land, and the gentlemen who had led them were not as 'whole' as they pretended to be.[14] It is doubtful whether this reply reached more than a handful of those at whom it was aimed, but it did not really matter. A number of the original leaders were rounded up, tried and executed, but there was no further trouble from Lincolnshire, and the natural order of gentry authority was quickly restored.

This was just as well because before the Lincolnshire protest collapsed, the word had spread across the Humber into the East Riding of Yorkshire, where the commons also rose, inspired as in Lincolnshire by conservative clergy. This was the so-called Pilgrimage of Grace, and here the agenda was much more radical, starting with complaints about the heresies of Luther and Wycliffe, which they wished to be suppressed, and proceeding to the Royal Supremacy, with the demand that ecclesiastical jurisdiction be returned to the Pope. As if this was not sufficient, these demands were followed by the reinstatement of the Lady Mary as legitimate, and the dissolution of the monasteries, which came in only as the fourth clause.[15] Lincolnshire had not mentioned the Supremacy, nor Mary, so the Yorkshire Pilgrimage, as it came to be known, was a more fundamental rejection of royal policy over the last five years, and stood less chance of meeting with a favourable response. This radicalism it probably owed to Robert Aske, a lawyer and a dependent of the Percys, who quickly assumed a leading role. He is known to have been particularly opposed to the dissolution, which left him on a collision course with the king, whose conscience seems to have been genuinely touched by the behaviour of monks and nuns. This was undoubtedly the most serious defiance which Henry faced in his entire reign. The king needed the money, there is no doubt about that, and he used the lands to reward those of his subjects whom he considered to be the most deserving, including the Seymour brothers, but that was not his main objective. His aversion to the religious orders seems to have sprung from his youthful admiration for Erasmus, who regarded them all as idle and corrupt. The small houses were the worst, because fewer than a dozen inmates left them unable to discharge their liturgical duties properly, let alone carry out their responsibilities in respect of hospitality and education. He therefore supported Cromwell's bill for the dissolution of the smaller houses, which passed in July, in spite of the latter's endorsement of the greater houses 'wherein thanks be to God, religion is right well kept and observed'.[16] Those religious who wished to continue in their vocations could be transferred to one of these houses if they so desired. It is not certain whether this clause represented a concession necessary to secure the bill's passage or a genuine ambiguity in the king's conscience, but if it was the latter then Henry soon abandoned it. Pressure continued to grow on the greater houses to surrender, and they did so individually over the following four years. This would be consistent with the theological ambiguity of the Ten Articles passed by Convocation also during its summer session, which the king seems to have perused with some care, and with the progress made towards the translation of the scriptures into English.[17] As far as we know, Jane made no further protest against these developments, although Luther was to write as early as 20 September that according to Alexander Alesius, a Scot living in England with whom he was regularly in touch, the new queen was an enemy to the Gospel. The state of affairs in England was so altered that Robert Barnes the Reformer was keeping quiet and had gone into hiding. However, Alesius was also of the opinion that she would be crowned at Michaelmas, so his information was not reliable.[18] It is also probable that Luther was using 'the Gospel' as a synonym for his own theological position, which Henry certainly continued to reject without any influence from Jane. Henry's conscience continued to go its own way, and his wife had to accept it.

This was not good enough for Aske and his followers, who were sceptical about the royal conscience, and continued to see Henry as manipulated by Cranmer and Cromwell. As they spread their message around Yorkshire, they swept together a number of disparate and spontaneous protests, ranging in their motivation from bad landlords to border tenures. However, religious discontents were general, and appealed to all these various constituencies, so that he may have had as many as 30,000 men under his leadership when he advanced to Pontefract early in December. Although these protesters were ostensibly united in a single cause, in fact they were riven by disagreements and divided both in their leadership and in their objectives.[19] Consequently, when the king's lieutenant, the Duke of Norfolk, turned up at Doncaster in December, he had a rather easier task than might have been anticipated. He had been authorised by the king to negotiate because he had only about 7,000 men under him, that being as many as Henry was able to raise. The Earl of Shrewsbury was already in the north with a rather smaller force, but even if they had worked together they would not have been strong enough to defeat the protesters in the field, so negotiation was the only option. After the first encounter Norfolk sent a conciliatory message to the Pilgrims Council at York intended to reassure them that the king would address their grievances and that they could go home. Aske, however, was not deceived, and kept his host in being in spite of all the difficulties while he and his colleagues debated earnestly over the articles which they should present to the duke. Realising that two long and complex documents would not produce a quick response, they concentrated their demands on two points; a free general pardon and a parliament to meet in the north to resolve such matters as required legislation.[20] These Norfolk was empowered to concede, and when he had done so Aske took off his Pilgrim badge of the five wounds of Christ, and vowed that henceforth he would wear no sign but 'the badge of our sovereign lord' the king. On his instructions the Pilgrims then dispersed, and the immediate crisis was over. Aske took himself off to court to complete the negotiations which had been so hopefully begun.

It is not known exactly what Norfolk had conceded because his report to the king does not survive. There may have been some understanding on the fate of the monasteries, but basically the king was buying time while he built up his own forces, which he continued to do after the Doncaster agreement. It seems to have been his intention to reduce the north by force, but his dissimulation, if such it was, was justified by the outbreak of fresh risings in Yorkshire and Cumberland in February 1537. Sir Francis Bigod, who was a religious reformer whose agenda had nothing to do with the original Pilgrimage, raised a force and attacked Hull, while the commons of Cumberland and Westmorland laid siege to Carlisle.[21] Neither of these movements remotely resembled the power of the original Pilgrimage, and both were suppressed without difficulty. However, they gave the king an excuse to renege on his promise of a pardon. By mid-May Norfolk had descended on Yorkshire again, and executed a number of the original protesters on the grounds that the king's pardon was now null and void. Lord Darcy and others of the original leaders were rounded up, tried and executed also. Meanwhile the international implications of the rising were becoming obvious, because Henry stood under sentence of excommunication and the Pope was looking for any possible means of unseating him. As soon as news of the rebellion reached Rome Pope Paul III created Reginald Pole a cardinal and sent him on a mission in support of the rebels.[22] This he was to do by mobilising either the King of France or the Emperor (or both) against Henry. It was a forlorn hope because each was more concerned to retain English friendship than they were to end the schism, and in any case it was February before Pole even reached northern Europe. The main rising was long since over, and the cleaning-up operations were well under way. Since Pole did not have the resources to raise troops of his own, there was nothing that he could do, beyond retreating to Italy. All that he had achieved was to convince the king that he was a double-dyed traitor.

Mary had featured largely in the articles originally drafted at Pontefract, but nobody suggested that she had consented to the use of her name. All through this time she remained quietly at court, occupying second place among the ladies, after Jane. Lord Hussey, her former Chamberlain, was executed for his share in the rising, but there was no suggestion of her involvement.[23] Her friendship with Jane clearly developed further at this point, and the queen may have been responsible for the letter which she wrote in March 1537 to the Emperor, asking him not to use her as a means of applying pressure to her father, as he had done through Chapuys. She was, she professed, completely reconciled to her father's religious supremacy, and to her own illegitimacy, as had been demanded of her. There is no proof that Jane had any share in the writing of these letters, but it would be entirely consistent with the role which she had played in Mary's surrender in June 1536, and with her own irenic nature. The Emperor was not pleased, and a certain chill entered into his relations with the princess, but he had no intention of doing anything else about it. Instead he concentrated his attentions on pressing John III of Portugal to make a firm offer of marriage on behalf of Dom Luis, and John gave his ambassadors in London full powers to negotiate such a match.[24] Nothing came of this initiative, probably because Henry was unwilling to concede either Mary's legitimacy or her place in the succession. The negotiations dragged on until June, when Henry finally suggested that any resulting treaty would have to be confirmed by Parliament, a notion altogether strange to the Portuguese, who went away disgruntled. We do not know how disappointed Mary may have been by this outcome, nor whether Queen Jane had played any part in the process. It would have been typical of her to be concerned for her friend's happiness, but the most that could be said for a Portuguese marriage is that it would have avoided disparagement. Mary had never set eyes on Dom Luis.

However, Jane concerned herself with finding a peaceful end to the Pilgrimage of Grace. She played her part in welcoming Robert Aske to court over the Christmas, and in early December ventured to tell the king that God had permitted all this trouble to happen because of the number of churches which had been razed.[25] This must refer to the monasteries, because as far as we know no parish church was touched, but the result, as before, was an admonition to mind her own business, which was of course the production of an heir. In this connection the absence of any sign of pregnancy by January 1537 was causing dark murmurings among the people, and the oddest of rumours. On 18 January it was reported from Rutland that it was being said that the king had had too many women to be able to get a child on his queen. The connection here is hard to grasp, but Henry obviously had a sexual reputation which did not correspond to the facts.[26] As far as we know he never looked seriously at another woman throughout his marriage to Jane, and even his games of courtly love seem to have been curtailed. As early as July 1536 public prayers were being offered for the birth of a prince, and in October there were rumours that a child had been conceived. It is possible that Henry was still thinking of linking this happy event to Jane's coronation, because on 31 December John Hussee reported to Lord Lisle that the crowning would take place after the parliament which was due to be held in the north, and that it would be at York. Since Henry had not fixed a date for this parliament, he was possibly thinking of linking the two events together, although when the pregnancy happened he did not follow up this line of thought.[27] Whatever had been promised in early December, no parliament was to meet in the north. Jane's pregnancy, which was eventually confirmed at the end of March, must have come as a huge relief to the king. He was, at forty-six, still able to 'do the deed', and his wife was as fertile as her background had led him to suppose. As spring turned into summer in 1537, Henry was at peace with the world. He had punished the Pilgrimage to his satisfaction; Cardinal Pole's mission had turned out to be a fiasco; he was in no danger of interference from France or the Empire; and his queen was expecting a child.

Jane's pregnancy dominated the small talk of the court that summer. John Hussee's correspondence with the Lisles is full of allusions to it. The queen had apparently taken a fancy to fat quails and dotterels as an aspect of her diet, and Lady Lisle had undertaken to supply these as needed. In May, in writing about one consignment which had gone astray, Hussee conveyed Jane's good wishes, and added optimistically, 'God send her a prince.'[28]

At the beginning of June she felt the child's first movements, and the rejoicings intensified. This 'quickening', which proved that the infant was alive, was a significant moment, and on 1 June William Lord Sandys, the Lord Chamberlain, wrote that he had arranged suitable celebrations, including the singing of *Te Deum* in the Chapel Royal. A few days later the Duke of Norfolk announced that similar festivities were planned for York, and Jane was no doubt suitably gratified by these manifestations of traditional piety.[29] As early as the previous July she had persuaded her husband to licence the foundation of a new chantry by the executors of John Baily of Tamworth, to pray for the good estate of King Henry and Queen Jane as well as for the souls of Henry VII and Elizabeth, and of Baily himself and Agnes, his wife. Sceptical as he might be about the doctrine of purgatory, the king was quite willing to tolerate this form of piety, especially when advocated by one so near to him. In December 1536 she also added her name, and a handsome donation, to the chantry originally established at Guildford by Eleanor, the queen of Henry III.[30] Whatever doubts Henry may have had about the value of such endowments, Jane clearly had none, and invested her money in requiem Masses. Two things, however, marred these tranquil summer months. The first was the infliction of punishments on the Pilgrims of the previous autumn. The pretext for this was the rising briefly engineered by Sir Francis Bigod, who had attacked the town of Hull, which gave the king the right, in his own eyes, to ignore the pardon which he had issued in December. The Duke of Norfolk returned to the north, reaching Doncaster on 1 February, where he found the gentlemen too nervous to go about arresting the leaders of these 'new commotions' until inspired with confidence by his arrival at the head of 7,000 men. Within a few days the first trials by martial law had taken place, and the executions swiftly followed.[31] On 7 February he reached York and began swearing the gentlemen of the county to accept the pardon which they had received before Christmas. He appears to have experienced no difficulty and no duplicity was suspected. Moreover, it was at this same time that the commons of Westmorland were threatening Carlisle, and that gave the gentlemen the perfect opportunity to display their loyalty to the Crown. By the time that the duke arrived at the head of 4,000 Yorkshire horsemen, the rising had in any case been dispersed by Sir Christopher Dacre and Thomas Clifford. Some 700 of the rebels were taken, of whom one in ten was executed by martial law.[32] The confidence which this success inspired then encouraged Norfolk to proceed against some of the leaders of the original Pilgrimage, even when there was no evidence of subsequent disaffection. Aske, Lord Darcy and Sir Thomas Constable were caught in this trap. They were travelling with the duke, confident that their pardons would hold, and even presented themselves voluntarily at court in March and April. On 7 April the council wrote to the Duke of Norfolk to inform him that, owing to new evidence which had emerged relating to the recent insurrections, all three had been committed to the Tower.[33] What this evidence may have been is not apparent. That which was produced at their trials a few weeks later was manifestly absurd, alleging conspiracies in places where the defendants had never been and with people that they had never met. However the intention was to create a general impression of guilt, and was not to be taken literally. In all eighteen people were tried for their involvement in these disturbances, the majority having been indicted by a commission of oyer and terminer issued to the Duke of Norfolk and his council on 28 April. The indictments were then transferred to London, where the trials were held on a separate commission between 15 and 22 May. The evidence offered was largely circumstantial, and the most innocent correspondence construed as malicious. The actual trials were a formality, the king having already decided on a guilty verdict, and none of the jurors venturing to dissent. The punishments followed quickly; Sir Thomas Tempest and some others were hanged, drawn and quartered at Tyburn on 25 May, and another batch which included Bigod were executed on 2 June. Lord Darcy, who had been tried by his peers, was deprived of his Garter (as was customary with members convicted of treason) and beheaded on Tower Hill on the 30th. A few were taken north for execution as an example to the country; Sir Thomas Constable at Hull on 6 July and Robert Aske at York on the 12th.[34] A few died in prison, and Norfolk remained in the north until October, although he was not asked to carry out any further investigations. Henry clearly regarded the death of Aske as drawing a line under the whole episode, and the parliament promised for the north was quietly forgotten. It would not be true to say that the north was pacified in any very positive sense, but the commons were sufficiently intimidated as to cause no further trouble.

The second thing which marred the summer months was an outbreak of plague. It was common for this scourge to surface during the warm weather, but 1537 was unusually bad. Henry was notoriously nervous when that infection came anywhere near the court, and Cromwell routinely forbade access to anyone who had been in contact with the disease.[35] In this case Jane was exceptionally jumpy, and on 11 July Sir John Russell wrote to the Lord Privy Seal reporting that he had felt bound to tell the king about his wife's extreme nervousness, 'considering that she is with child'. This casts an odd light on the relationship between the royal couple; did Henry not know of his wife's apprehensions? Or was Russell being exceptionally officious with his information?[36] The fact that Cromwell did nothing further about it suggests the latter. John Hussee obviously had good sources of information within the queen's Privy Chamber, and on 21 July he wrote to Lady Lisle, 'You would not believe how much the queen is afraid of the sickness'. This was in spite of the fact that the mortality had actually been less than in the previous year, when she had expressed no concern, so it must have been her pregnancy which was making her so worried.[37] The king was certainly anxious, although for other reasons. As early as 21 June he had written to the Duke of Norfolk, putting off his anticipated progress to the north to another year on account of his wife's condition. This was a major decision and had not been taken, he went on, through any representations from her, but because his council had urged him not to travel more than 60 miles from her, in case any emergency should arise. What he could have done in such a situation is not clear, but the council felt that he should be within reach, and he accepted that.[38] How the queen was occupied during these months is uncertain. She seems not to have interceded for any of the victims of the northern rising, although Sir Robert Constable had felt it worth his while to seek such intercession. Writing to his son Sir Marmaduke on 16 May, he had begged him to get the queen to speak for his life, but if she did so, it did not work and has escaped the record. Chapuys was withdrawn in March, and his replacement Diego de Mendoza was instructed to present his credentials to the queen as well as to the king, because she was felt to be a useful ally in persuading the king of the benefits of a marriage between Mary and Dom Luis, and might even induce him to restore her in the order of succession. Cromwell, of course, knew of these approaches and did not respond. Instead he instructed Sir Thomas Wyatt, the ambassador with the Emperor, to stall on all such suggestions until the outcome of the queen's pregnancy was known.[39] Jane meanwhile confined her efforts to maintaining a good relationship between Henry and his daughter, and remained a benign presence as her condition advanced. On 28 June she instructed the Keeper of Havering Forest to supply two bucks to the Gentlemen of the Chapel Royal, probably as a reward for their share in the celebration of her quickening, which had taken place a week or two earlier, and on the 23rd John Hussee commented upon the fit of her clothes, and upon her craving for fat quails.[40] Honor Lisle meanwhile was engaged in a delicate ongoing negotiation to get one of her daughters by her first marriage, either Anne or Katherine Bassett, accepted into the queen's Privy Chamber. The problem lay not in any chill in the relations between Jane and Lady Lisle, nor in the inadequacy of the girls, but rather in the absence of a vacancy. However, by early August the Countess of Sussex had persuaded the queen to take one of them, and on 3 August Hussee passed on the countess's instructions that both girls should present themselves at court 'before the queen takes her Chamber' so that she could make a choice. On 1 September he wrote again with some urgency; Jane now wished to see the Bassett girls as soon as possible, because she was due to retire to her Chamber in three weeks and wanted to choose before then.[41] On 26 September Sir Thomas Palmer reported to Lord Lisle that Anne had been the successful candidate, and had been sworn on 15 September into the 'room of a yeoman usher'. This was perhaps not quite as grand as had been anticipated, carrying a fee of only £10 a year, but it was a start. Katherine meanwhile was being 'entertained' by the Countess of Sussex until Lady Lisle's will in respect of her was known; in the event she remained with the countess for the time being.[42]

At the end of September Jane retired for her confinement at Hampton Court, which suggests that she expected to give birth in late October. At the same time she ordered some changes to Anne's apparel, which was apparently too French for her taste. On 2 October John Hussee reported that these changes had been effected by Lady Sussex, but that Lady Lisle was expected to supply the additional garments before the queen's churching, which would follow the birth of her child, and was expected to be almost a month away.[43] Henry seems to have kept discreetly away from all this feminine activity. He joined Jane for a few days in early October, but even the king was not welcome at a confinement, and he had departed again by the 6th, on which day Norfolk reported to Cromwell (who was also keeping his distance) that the king had virtually shut down Hampton Court apart from the 'queen's proceedings'. He had departed himself and ordered that no outsiders were to be admitted on account of the strength of the plague in London. Altogether her pregnancy had been normal and easy, apart from the fear of the plague, which was held at bay by the king's precautions, so there would have been considerable optimism among her attendants as the day of birth drew near. The astrologers had confidently predicted a boy, because they knew that was what the king wanted. They had a 50 per cent chance of being right, or rather better considering the number of times they had been wrong in the past! What no one had predicted, however, was how hard that birth would be. Jane went into labour at some time on 9 October, and when the baby had still not appeared by the 11th special prayers and intercessory processions were ordered in London.[44] It was reported many years later that the delivery had been by caesarean section, but that operation was not known in the mid-sixteenth century. There was a surgical practice of a similar nature, but it invariably sacrificed the mother's life, and would not have been contemplated in this case. The royal physicians who were in attendance do not seem to have been called upon, and the midwives struggled on their own through two days and three nights to induce the infant to appear. What went wrong we do not know, but it was in the small hours of the morning of 12 October before the birth eventually took place, leaving Jane completely exhausted by the ordeal. The child, however, was normal and healthy, and above all it was male. In the words of the subsequent official announcement,

By the provision of God, Our Lady St Mary and the glorious martyr St George, on the 12th day of October, the feast of St Wilfrid and the vigil of St. Edward which was on the Friday, about two o'clock in the morning, was born at Hampton Court Edward, son to King Henry VIII.[45]

Henry's decade-long struggle, which had cost him enormously both in personal and political terms, now seemed justified. 'God,' the court preacher Hugh Latimer declared, 'is English.' The rejoicings were thunderous.

Incontinent after the birth *Te Deum* was sung in Paul's and other churches of the city, and great fires in every street, and goodly banqueting and triumphant cheer with shooting of guns all day and night, and messengers were sent to all the estates and cities of the realm ...[46]

The same day someone wrote on Jane's behalf to Thomas Cromwell, announcing the birth, and she managed to sign the letter. He wrote immediately to Sir Thomas Wyatt, instructing him to inform the Emperor of the happy event, and promising him a personal letter from Henry. At the same time the King of France was informed by similar methods and in the same terms. Within England the news spread verbatim with great rapidity, and by the time that the courtiers got around to informing their country cousins, the latter for the most part already knew that Henry had an heir at last. The king was understandably gratified. This time the stall which he had thoughtfully provided in the Garter Chapel at Windsor would not be wasted!

The prince was christened the following Monday, 15 October, in the chapel at Hampton Court, with the Duke of Norfolk and Archbishop Cranmer as godfathers and the Lady Mary as godmother. The Lord Chamberlain's department must have worked overtime to get everything ready, because it was a full-blown court ceremony, and no detail was spared to make it impressive.[47] Fear of the plague had receded with the advent of cooler weather, and all the officers of the household were there, with their retinues. The procession was led by certain gentlemen of the Chamber bearing unlit torches which were to be ignited at the ceremony itself. There then followed the choristers and clerks of the Chapel Royal, led by the Dean, and the royal chaplains two by two. After them came such bishops and abbots as could be assembled at short notice, and the members of the king's council, then such peers as were not members of the court or the council, and the ambassadors and envoys of foreign states. The Lord Privy Seal and the Lord Chancellor then preceded the godfathers, who were followed by the Earl of Sussex and Lord Montague carrying a pair of covered basins to be used at the ceremony. They were followed by the Earl of Wiltshire bearing the taper of wax which would be lit to symbolise the child's emergence into the light of the Christian Church, and by the Lady Elizabeth carrying the chrisom oil for the anointing. Because of her extreme youth (she had just turned four), Elizabeth was carried in the arms of Viscount Beauchamp; a gesture demonstrating the high confidence in which the queen's brother was held. Then followed the prince himself, carried under a canopy by the Marchioness of Exeter, who was supported by her husband and the Duke of Suffolk. The prince's robe was carried by the Earl of Arundel, accompanied by the nurse and the midwife, who were no doubt kept close to their charge in case of any mishap. Happily, their services were not required as Edward appears to have slept soundly throughout the proceedings. The canopy under which the prince was borne was carried by another select group of Gentlemen of the Privy Chamber, including Sir Thomas Seymour, and was followed by the Lady Mary, whose train was borne by Lady Kingston. The other ladies of the court then brought up the rear, walking 'in the order of their degrees'. When the moment of christening arrived, all the torches were lit, and the Garter King of Arms proclaimed Edward's style and titles. He was recognised as Duke of Cornwall and Earl of Chester from birth, but not as Prince of Wales. Although that was the traditional title of the king's eldest son, and he was often to be referred to in that way, it was also by tradition conferred separately at a distinct ceremony.[48] Henry decided to wait until his son had acquired a few more years, and in fact he was still waiting when he acceded to the throne almost ten years later. After the baptism, according to custom, he proceeded straight to confirmation, and the Duke of Suffolk took over as godfather 'to the bishop'. Following which the company was refreshed with wafers, spices and wine, and the rest of the congregation was given bread and sweet wine. 'The going homeward was like the coming outward, saving that the salt and the basin were left and the gifts of the gossips carried.' These gifts, which must have been taken to the chapel in advance, consisted for the most part of the same type of plate as the king usually gave as New Year gifts. The Lady Mary received a cup of gold, and the duke and the Archbishop each 'two bowls and two great pots of silver and gilt'. The trumpets then sounded as the company withdrew to the palace, and the prince was borne to his father and mother to receive their blessings. The king then gave a 'great largesse', which no doubt reflected his triumphant state of mind.[49]

The person who is almost invisible in all this celebration is Jane. Henry watched the proceedings from his gallery, but she seems to have sat in the antechapel, receiving the gifts and congratulations of her well-wishers. She was still weak, and a more positive role was ruled out by that fact. Cromwell later blamed her servants for allowing her to catch cold, but this seems not to have been the problem, as she was warmly wrapped for this appearance.

Nevertheless her health soon began to give cause for alarm, and three days later she developed puerperal fever. This was a condition little understood in the sixteenth century, even by learned medics, and the necessity for hygiene was simply ignored.[50] So it is likely that the disease was transmitted by her servants' failure to wash either her or themselves after dressing or attending to her wound. By 23 October she was very ill and was becoming delirious. On the 24th the Earl of Rutland, whose source of information was his wife, wrote to Cromwell that the queen had been very ill all the previous night, and that her confessor had administered the last rites. The same day the Duke of Norfolk also wrote to say that, for their mistress, 'there is no likelihood of her life', and he feared that she would be dead before his letter came to hand.[51] His fears were justified because Jane died later that same day, which was a Wednesday. The news was not at first made public, and on the 26th Sir Thomas Palmer wrote to Lord Lisle that although there was a rumour to that effect, he hoped that it was ill-founded. If good prayers could save her 'she is not like to die for never was lady so much [pitied] with every man, rich and poor'.[52] This was a fitting tribute to her popularity, but unfortunately the news was true. Jane was dead, and as a direct result of her greatest triumph, the birth of Prince Edward. Henry was not apparently with her at the end, for reasons which are now obscure; perhaps her attendants had been anxious to spare him the experience. Rutland and Norfolk had, after all, written to Cromwell when things got desperate, not to the king. He was, however, informed almost at once, and took the news hard. Richard Gresham, writing to Cromwell on 8 November, when the dust had settled a little, reported that

of none of the realm was it more heavilier taken that of the king's majesty himself, whose death caused the king immediately to

remove into Westminster, where he mourned and kept himself close
and secret a great while.[53]

Within a few days letters had been written on his behalf to the
Emperor and the King of France, informing them of his loss, and
Cromwell had followed these up with letters of his own, warning
them that although the king had taken his wife's death with
Christian resignation, he was not disposed to marry again.[54]

Queen Jane's body was prepared for burial in the usual way by
evisceration and partial embalmment. She lay in state for several
days in the chapel at Hampton Court, watched over by her ladies
and the other servants of her household, and by 1 November the
king had decided upon Windsor as her place of interment. Monday
12 November was named as the date, and the arrangements were
entrusted to the Duke of Norfolk and Sir William Paulet. Their
main task was to assemble a suitable cortege, because Jane was
the first Queen of England to die 'in good estate' since Elizabeth
of York in 1503, and on 1 November they wrote to Cromwell
outlining the state of their researches into that occasion. At the
interment of Elizabeth of York, they reported, there had been
present seven marquises and earls, sixteen barons and sixty knights,
in addition to numerous members of the king's household. They
thought that they could do better than that. Starting with the Duke
of Norfolk himself, they had summoned the Duke of Suffolk, the
marquises of Dorset and Exeter and the earls of Surrey, Oxford,
Rutland, Wiltshire, Sussex, Hertford and Southampton. These,
together with the Lord Privy Seal (Cromwell himself), the Lord
Chamberlain, and a supporting cast of barons and knights, would,
they thought, do sufficient honour to the deceased.[55] According
to Richard Gresham, Norfolk had ordered on his own authority
1,200 Masses to be sung for the repose of her soul. He was also
of the opinion that a dirge at St Pauls would be appropriate, and

asked Cromwell to ascertain the king's pleasure in that respect. Apart from determining the date, Henry seems to have left all these details to his servants, which, given the fact that he was punctilious about ceremonies, is probably a measure of his distress. Custom forbade his appearance at the actual burial, so he was spared a trip to Windsor, the Chief Mourner being, appropriately enough, the Lady Mary. Mary had been too 'accrased' to attend the first phase of the obsequies, the translation of the body from her chamber to the chapel at Hampton Court, but was sufficiently recovered to take her place in the funeral procession on 12 November. This moved by easy stages from Hampton Court to Windsor, being welcomed at each stage of its journey by the clergy and civil dignitaries and accompanied by five carriages bearing the ladies and gentlewomen of her household, forty-five in number. These last were escorted by noblemen, including the Earl of Hertford, and by the officers of arms. The cortege arrived at Windsor at about eleven o'clock, where, in a vault beneath the Garter Chapel, Queen Jane was laid to rest with full royal honours. The interment was completed by noon, whereupon the mourners withdrew to the castle for refreshment. The emphasis throughout had been on Jane's status as queen, and her family were not greatly involved. The court mourning extended over Christmas, which was kept with 'small joy' that year, and it was February 1538 before the king brought that phase to an end. When his own time came, nine years later, it was with her that he chose to be interred rather than beside his own parents in Westminster Abbey, which was surely a sign of the special regard which he had for Jane.[56]

The following day Bishop Cuthbert Tunstall of Durham informed Cromwell that he had written a letter of condolence to the king, but had kept it brief lest he 'press too sore upon a green wound'. Similar letters arrived from the courts of Europe, those from the Emperor and the King of France containing delicate hints that the king would now be looking for a new wife, in spite of Cromwell's disclaimer. The council shared this concern, but for the time being the king was not interested. He had his son, and he had his memories. At forty-six years old he was probably doubting his capacity to father more children, which was the main point of marriage, and at the beginning of 1538 the question of a foreign alliance did not appear urgent. The rituals of courtship could wait until he had come to terms with his grief. Meanwhile, for those who had not been emotionally involved with Jane, there was a lot of tidying up to be done. Anne Bassett, so recently recruited to the queen's Privy Chamber, was now unemployed again, and took temporary refuge with the Countess of Sussex until her future could be determined.[57] An inventory of the queen's jewels was prepared, which is remarkable mainly as a record of what was given away. Many of the items listed are shown as given to Lady Mary, Lady Lisle, and to numerous ladies of the court with whom she is not known to have been particularly familiar. She must also have received gifts of this nature, but these are not so listed in the inventory, and unless there was a second list which does not survive, she seems not to have been particularly interested in personal adornment. In this, as in so many ways, she was a contrast with her predecessor, who loved finery.[58] A valuation was also drawn up of the lands 'lately parcel of Queen Jane's jointure and dowry, and now reserved unto the King's Highnesses own hands', which showed estates and manors in nine counties, and the names of the stewards and other officers responsible for their management. In addition Cromwell prepared a summary of debts owed to the queen, which gives us an idea of how she conducted her business. For instance, she appears to have paid a sum due to her brother Henry 'Receiver of Berkamptead and Kings Langley' by one Richard Warren of Beaconsfield, and his debt was duly recorded. Who Richard Warren may have been, and what claim he had on her generosity, we do not know, but he clearly had difficulty in raising money, and that may have continued because as far as we know the debt was never discharged.[59] Other money was owed for routine business transactions, from farmers of various lands and for a wood sale at Kingsdown in Kent, although how long it had been outstanding is not apparent. All these debts would have fallen due to the Crown after Jane's demise, which was why Cromwell was interested in them, but no strenuous effort was made to extract them.

Jane's household retained a shadowy existence until most of it was absorbed into the establishment created for Anne of Cleves in December 1539 instead of being dissolved as was customary. It appears to have been paid from the Chamber account. Her lands were kept in the king's hands, whether for practical or sentimental reasons, and were not used to form the jointure of Queen Anne, as had been the case with previous royal wives. These arrangements suggest again that Jane occupied a special place in Henry's affections, and that he wanted to retain a memory of her for as long as possible.

5

EDWARD SEYMOUR

Edward Seymour, the future Duke of Somerset and Lord Protector, was born a second son. John Seymour had married Margery Wentworth at some point in 1497 or 1498, and their eldest son, named for his father, was born at some time in 1499. Nothing is known about this younger John, except that he had died unmarried before 1520, and it seems likely that he deceased in infancy. Edward was born in 1500, and a third, called Henry, in about 1504. A fourth, Thomas, was born in 1508 or thereabouts before the first girl, Jane, appeared in 1509.[1] This tendency to father sons provoked a humorous exchange with the new king early in his reign. Sir John was not a great courtier, but he was sufficiently close to Henry for Edward to be named as a page 'to do service to the queen' on 12 October 1514. The queen was Mary, Henry's sister, who was to be married to Louis XII as part of the peace settlement with France, but what prompted young Edward's inclusion on this list, along with the sons of lords Roos and Cobham, is a mystery, unless he was already known around the court.[2] He cannot have stayed long in France because within a few days of their wedding Louis sent most of his wife's English attendants back home on the grounds that they were disrupting their relationship. Apart from this episode, we know nothing about Edward's upbringing, which presumably took place at Wolf Hall under the supervision of his mother. He is not known to have attended any school, and his early lessons would have been administered by one of Sir John's chaplains, that being the normal practice for an aristocratic youth at that time. He must have been able to read Latin, because after his return from France he is alleged to have spent some time at the universities of both Oxford and Cambridge, although he left no trace in the records of either and certainly did not take any degree. This, however, would also have been normal practice, it being customary for aspiring courtiers to spend some time bringing their education up to scratch for progress in an institution where a modicum of learning was appreciated by both the king and the queen.[3]

In December 1516 he was listed among the gentlemen attendant in the king's Privy Chamber, which suggests a jousting companion, although he is not known to have taken part in any of the 'feats of arms' of these years. Perhaps he was considered to be too young for such public exposure. However, his father was clearly looking ahead, and on 15 July 1517 secured for him the constableship of Bristol Castle, in survivorship with himself.[4] This would have been a purely honorific title, as he would not have been expected to discharge any of the duties of the office, which would have been undertaken by his father's deputies. It would, however, have strengthened his position in the royal favour. For the next five years or so he presumably busied himself with his duties about the court, although he did not attract any attention in the course of doing so. Then in August 1523 he appears among the gentlemen intended to accompany the Duke of Suffolk to France, and he took part, along with his father, in that abortive campaign. He must have distinguished himself in some unrecorded battle during that operation because the duke knighted him 'in the field' before returning to England in December.[5] In January 1525 Sir Edward Seymour was named to the commission of the peace for Wiltshire, a position which he continued to occupy thereafter. Meanwhile, King Henry's mistress, Bessie Blount, had borne him an illegitimate son in July 1519, who had been immediately acknowledged and named Henry Fitzroy. On 18 June 1525 the king decided to ennoble this child, and created him Duke of Richmond, much to the queen's annoyance. Cardinal Wolsey's intention seems to have been to use this infant duke to reinforce the king's government in the north of England, and shortly after his creation he was despatched with a suitable council to Middleham in Yorkshire to carry out the nominal responsibilities of king's Lieutenant in the North. This, of course, necessitated a suitable household as well, and that was duly constituted on 24 July, with Sir Edward Seymour as Master of the Horse, on a fee of £60 a year, which was a senior and responsible position.[6] When Richard Colan, the duke's Clerk Comptroller, drew up his accounts for the first half-year of his responsibilities on 31 December, he registered Seymour's expenses at £91, which indicates a high level of activity. How he divided his time between Middleham and the court is not apparent, but he must have spent some part of it in and around London, because he had been an Esquire of the Household since 1524, and that must have involved some attendance. Then in July 1527 he was given his first taste of foreign service when he was named on the mission of Cardinal Wolsey to France.[7] This was intended to take advantage of Clement VII's temporary imprisonment in the Castel de San Angelo, following the sack of Rome by a mutinous Imperial army at the end of May, to set up an interim government for the Church which would be under Wolsey's control, and thus give the king the annulment of his marriage which Clement had refused. The mission was abortive, and Seymour was not in any sense in Wolsey's service, but it would have given him a reasonable experience of diplomatic life, experience that would serve him well in the future.

In July 1528 a dispute seems to have arisen over the disposal of certain offices lately held by Sir William Compton, who had died of the sweat shortly before. The king apparently wrote to the Duke of Richmond, asking that certain stewardships which were in his gift be bestowed upon Sir Giles Strangeways and Sir Edward Seymour. The offices in question were the stewardship of Canford and Corfe, which was worth 100 shillings, and that of 'my Lord's woods in Somerset', the fee for which was £6 13s 4d. Neither of them wealthy preferments, but ones to which considerable perquisites were attached.[8] Sir Edward insisted that both were intended for him, but when Sir Thomas Magnus replied on Richmond's behalf by writing to Wolsey on 22 July, he pointed out that it was already too late. Canford had been bestowed upon Sir William Parre and the Somerset woods upon one George Cotton. Presumably both were closer to the young duke (or possibly to Magnus) than was his Master of the Horse.[9] Eventually, in March 1529, Sir Edward was granted the stewardship of the manors of Henstage and Charlecote in Somerset, which had also belonged to Sir William Compton, with the power to appoint bailiffs and other officers, probably in compensation for his failure to secure Canford. In the autumn of 1529 Wolsey fell from power, as a direct result of the failure of his legatine court to secure an annulment of the king's marriage, and as a consequence of the praemunire charge which brought him down all his vast possessions were forfeit to the Crown. On 14 July 1530 some of these lands were reassigned, Sir Edward Seymour and his brother-in-law Sir Anthony Ughtred receiving manors to the value of £123 12s 8d.[10] None of the Seymours are known to have played any part in the fall of Wolsey, nor to have been supporters of the Boleyn party. Given their religious conservatism their sympathies were probably on the other side, but Sir Edward at least was close to Cromwell, and it was perhaps through that relationship that his sister Jane was placed in the queen's service in 1529. The Earl of Northumberland was in debt to the king at about this time, having pledged certain lands to Sir Edward Seymour, who seems to have been acting for Cromwell in this matter. In September 1531 he redeemed his pledge at a cost of £1604, which was paid by Cromwell.[11]

In February 1532 Sir Edward embarked upon a complex transaction with Arthur Plantagenet, Lord Lisle for the purchase of the reversion of Cheddar Norton and other lands in Somerset. These lands had come to Lisle from his first wife, and consequently he had only a life interest in them. They also seem to have been subject to an arrangement called an enfeoffment to use in the interest of James Bassett, Honor Lisle's son by her first marriage, which complicated the question of the sale of title. On 23 February an indenture was made whereby Seymour agreed to pay Lisle a rent of £140, until the sale was completed.[12] However, this never seems to have become effective, and in July 1533 Edward Windsor, who was one of Lisle's men of affairs, wrote to say that his counsel had held several meetings with Seymour

> about the bargain of the lands which he bought of your Lordship, but Master Denzil and Master Morgan (Edward's counsel) say that you have not kept covenant with him in entering your lands again, and that he was bound to make your Lordship a lease for the term of your life of £140 ...[13]

Edward was insisting upon having possession, and no agreement had been reached. An action for debt was being taken out against Lisle for the non-payment of the £140, and Lisle's officers, particularly his auditor John Smith, tried to put pressure on

Seymour to abandon this suit, but without success. In November 1533 Lisle lodged a complaint against Sir Edward on the grounds that he had got him to sign an indenture to his own prejudice, in which some kind of fraud seems to have been implied. The legal tangle was one of peculiar density, and in February 1534 an arbitration was agreed, with Cromwell as the chief arbitrator, but that was by no means the end of the matter.[14] Naturally Lord Lisle's correspondence of the later part of 1533 is full of this matter, and his men of business kept a careful eye on Sir Edward Seymour's other transactions, particularly those involving Sir John Dudley from whom he also seems to have purchased lands. The source of Edward's wealth at this time is not apparent. At one point he borrowed £1,000 off Cromwell, probably for the purchase of Eastham manor in Somerset from Lord Braye, but this would have needed to be repaid in strict instalments. He did not enter into his inheritance until his father's death in December 1536, and his annuity of fifty marks as an Esquire of the Body would have gone nowhere near meeting his requirements. Perhaps a series of royal grants and preferential leases were responsible. There seems to be no doubt about his favour with Henry at this juncture; he even exchanged New Year gifts with the king in 1532 and 1533, which was by no means common with courtiers who were not part of the inner establishment.[15]

Meanwhile Edward had married. His bride, who he wed at some point before 1518, was Catherine Fillol, the daughter and co-heir of Sir William Fillol, who had lands in Dorset and in Essex. Given his youth at the time, this was almost certainly an arranged match for which his father was responsible, and in spite of producing two sons it was not a success. At some point after 1530 he repudiated her, alleging adultery. This did not affect the legitimacy of their children, but they played no part in his subsequent career, and had no claim to his titles. John, who was the elder and who had been born in the mid-1520s, was MP for Wootton Bassett in Wiltshire in 1547 and died comparatively young in 1552. Edward, the younger, who was born in 1529, served in the Scottish campaign of 1547 and at the tender age of eighteen was knighted by his father at the Battle of Pinkie Cleugh. Apart from serving on various commissions for Wiltshire and Dorset, neither of these had a career of any distinction, although Edward lived until 1593.[16] Both were children when their mother was repudiated, and were brought up by her until her death in 1535, at which point their care reverted to their father. However, he remarried on 9 March 1535 and his second wife, Anne Stanhope, wanted nothing to do with the boys, who were consequently educated by servants responsible for Edward, but at a distance from the court, where neither of them put in an appearance. They were provided for out of their mother's inheritance, and in 1538, probably on Anne's insistence, were excluded from their father's properties and titles by Act of Parliament. His future was reserved for his children by Anne, and although at that stage it was not envisaged that he would die attainted it was Edward, the eldest son of that marriage, who was restored to the earldom of Hertford in 1559. His sister Jane, for all her gentle nature, never showed the slightest interest in her nephews.

1534 seems to have been occupied largely with Seymour's dispute with Arthur Plantagenet, Lord Lisle over the Somerset lands. Each seems to have been convinced that Cromwell favoured him, which must have made his task as an arbitrator invidious. In the autumn the case was before the Lord Chancellor, and was discussed in the king's council. According to John Gayneford, writing to Lord Lisle in October, Mr Secretary had offered to buy off Seymour by paying him all the money that he had paid to Dudley, who as we have seen was a part of this quarrel, plus £100. He would also pay Lisle £1,000 in full settlement of his claim in the case.[17] However, this does not seem to have worked, and the dispute was to drag on for another two years. Meanwhile Sir Edward continued to dun Lisle for the £140 rent which was due, according to him, and in 1536 his agent, one Hollys, refused to grant any respite on the payments. John Hussee then persuaded Cromwell to write to Seymour on Lisle's behalf, but even this appeal was apparently unsuccessful. This was possibly because he also owed Lisle money, which he had agreed to pay through Cromwell as an intermediary, but according to other letters of Hussee during November, that had not worked either and at the end of that month they were still trying to get the money out of him.[18] To be fair to Sir Edward, his own affairs were not in the best of shape at this time, and on 21 July he features in a list of lords and ladies who had defaulted on the last payment of the subsidy, which was not the best of ways to retain the royal favour.

Seymour's position was transformed by his sister's success. In September 1535 Henry and Anne had visited Wolf Hall towards the end of their summer progress. It cannot be proved that Jane was actually present at this encounter, but it was undoubtedly set up by Sir Edward, who was high enough in the king's favour to be listened to in such a context. Sir John, whose health was failing, must have issued the formal invitation, but he was remote from the court and would perforce have left such an important matter to his son. The visit was a great success, and Henry thought better of the whole Seymour family in consequence. Whatever the effect on Jane's career, it certainly enhanced that of her brother, who from this point on may be classed as an intimate of the king. In January 1536 Catherine of Aragon died, and Queen Anne's position became exposed. If for any reason she displeased the king sufficiently, she could now be replaced without any pressure being brought upon him to return to his first wife. Then, at the end of January, Anne miscarried of a son. Henry was devastated, and in addition to his other reactions began to pay his attentions to Jane.[19] In February he sent her a rich present, and was intrigued by her response. She became the third corner of the triangle of royal romance and Thomas Cromwell, who had fallen out with Anne for a number of reasons, began to sense an opportunity. As the king became suspicious of his wife's fidelity, Cromwell began to work on his fears, until on 2 May Anne was arrested and taken to the Tower. At the same time he moved out of his quarters at Greenwich in order to facilitate Henry's access to Jane, and the affair between them began to flourish.[20] Anne, however, was too formidable a politician to be shunted aside; she and all her family-based faction must be destroyed, and in the first fortnight of May the secretary devoted himself to that task, creating a case which was sufficient to convince the king. A group of her Privy Chamber familiars was rounded up, tried and executed. This left the queen with nowhere to go, and on 15 May she was tried as well by the Earl Marshal's court, and in spite of an impressive defence, was convicted also. The charges included one of incest with her brother, George, which no one apart from Henry actually believed. However that was sufficient to secure his conviction also, and the pair were beheaded on 17 and 19 May.[21] Cromwell's task was now effectively complete, and Henry was free. On the morning of 20 May he proposed marriage to Jane, and was accepted. Chapuys, who was obviously well informed, wrote to Cardinal Granvelle, the Emperor's chief minister, of this betrothal on the same day that it happened. The speed of the king's reaction wrong-footed just about everyone at court, and when he married her in the queen's closet at Whitehall just ten days later it was widely believed that she was responsible for her predecessor's death. She was first shown as queen on 3 June, and on the 5th her brother, Sir Edward, was raised to the peerage as Viscount Beauchamp.[22] There were soon rumours that he would replace the Earl of Wilshire, Anne Boleyn's father, as Lord Privy Seal. Wiltshire had not been involved in his daughter's alleged misdemeanours, but when he was replaced in office on 29 June, it was by Thomas Cromwell himself, Lord Beauchamp being compensated with the position of Governor and Captain of Jersey. Then on 16 August he was appointed Chancellor of North Wales. He seems to have taken his duties in the Channel Islands seriously, and visited the island several times, although he did not set up a base there, and there is no suggestion that he ever went to North Wales. His duties there were discharged entirely by deputy. These preferments he owed to the Secretary, who as early as 12 May, while Anne Boleyn was still alive, had noted in his remembrances that he owed a duty to Sir Edward Seymour, whose debt repayment of £300 he acknowledged in the same document.[23]

On 8 June, as a result of his recent elevation, two Acts of Parliament assured his lands to Viscount Beauchamp and the Lady Shelton his wife, and to the heirs of their bodies, excluding the children of his first marriage. This clearly reflected his, or perhaps her, will, and was unprecedented, attracting quite a lot of comment at the time. In the same month he was granted extensive lands in Wiltshire, including the manor and hundred of Amesbury, the site and grounds of the late abbey of Holy Trinity Exeter, and the manor of Caverly formerly in the possession of Streetly Abbey. All these properties were carefully granted to his wife, the Lady Shelton, and to the heirs of their bodies as well as to him, bringing these grants into line with the statutes.[24] At some time during June Beauchamp was also sworn of the king's council, to which he was summoned along with other peers on 1 July. A degree of intimacy is suggested by Chapuys's report that on 22 September immediately after dinner the queen's brother was summoned to the king's chamber, but we do not know the occasion of the invitation. In October Lord Beauchamp was named, along with other peers, to lead 200 men in the king's service against the Pilgrimage of Grace, and we can presume that during the autumn he was occupied with military matters connected with the rising, although in exactly what way is not clear.[25] Most of the references to him in the correspondence of this period relate to his financial dispute with Lord Lisle, and the efforts which were made to persuade the Lord Privy Seal to resolve it. Credit was apparently hard to obtain, perhaps because of the Pilgrimage of Grace, and Lisle had no security to offer, so the matter was one of peculiar difficulty. Cromwell was eventually able to secure a reconciliation, but only because Beauchamp was willing to forgo part of the sum to which a strict interpretation of the law would have entitled him.

At the end of March 1537 Jane's pregnancy was confirmed, and Henry decided that he wanted his brother-in-law closer than his residence in Kew would permit, so he wrote to Bishop Rowland Lee of Coventry and Lichfield, asking him to exchange his house on the Strand for that in Kew in the interest of Lord Beauchamp. On 2 April the bishop responded, lamenting the fact that the house in Kew which he was being offered was not convenient, and asking for some better residence in compensation.[26] The following day Lee's servant John Packington wrote to Cromwell to the same effect, describing his master as 'very sad' and asking the Lord Privy Seal to arrange some better exchange. On 5 May Lee himself wrote to Cromwell, expressing his willingness (of course) to gratify his prince, and his surprise that his reservations should be taken so lightly. He trusted that the Lord Privy Seal would secure adequate compensation for him. Where that might have been is not clear, but a couple of months later Lord Beauchamp was in occupation of what was later to be known as Somerset House (in the Strand), which in due course he was to spend a fortune in rebuilding. On 8 May Beauchamp received a communication from Sir Richard Bulkeley, who was doing the actual work of the chancellorship in North Wales, complaining of his endless quarrels with Dr Glynn, the Dean of Bangor, who wanted no Englishman interfering on his patch. He suggested a special commission to look into the matter, presumably as a means of getting Glynn off his back, and confessed to a debt of 600 marks to Beauchamp, of which he undertook to pay 200 by midsummer.[27] Then on 14 May Lord Beauchamp was named to the commission of oyer and terminer for the trials of the 'northern rebels' and to the Earl Marshall's court of peers for the trial of lords Darcy and Hussey. These appointments were confirmed on the 17th and indicate that Beauchamp, in addition to his other qualities, was considered to be a safe pair of hands; one who could be trusted to see these cases in the way that the king intended. Meanwhile Anthony Ughtred had died, leaving his sister Elizabeth as a widow, and Thomas Cromwell decided to cement his alliance with the Seymours more closely by marrying her to his only son, Gregory. News of this impending arrangement was conveyed to Lord Lisle by John Hussee on 17 July. Hussee's sources of information were as accurate as usual, but Lisle's reaction is not known, although the news did not bode well for his ongoing dispute with Beauchamp, which was then reaching a rather messy conclusion.[28] The pair appear to have been married in early August, and on 2 September Beauchamp wrote a friendly letter to Cromwell, welcoming him into the family.

Meanwhile Lord Beauchamp had become involved in another legal tangle, this time a dispute with Lord Dawbeney over some lands in Gloucestershire. These were worth £100 a year, but the details of the quarrel are unknown, because we lack a sequence of letters such as we have for the Lisle–Seymour dispute. All we know is that at the end of May 1537 the issue was still uncertain at law, and it seems likely that Beauchamp used his influence at court to get it resolved in his favour. Perhaps a bargain was struck because we know that Dawbeny's subsequent creation as Earl of Bridgewater was carried out on the intercession of the

Earl of Hertford (as Beauchamp had then become), and there was no other obvious reason for it. In August 1537 Beauchamp was granted a couple of manors in Wiltshire worth £159 a year, although whether these were a gift or a purchase is not clear.[29] As we have seen September was largely taken up with preparations for Jane's lying-in, a matter in which Lord Beauchamp is likely to have been much concerned, although not much involved. At the beginning of October, as her time drew near, another promotion for him was clearly being considered, and on the 16th Sir Thomas Palmer wrote to Lord Lisle that he was likely to be created Earl of Salisbury, but this was mistaken as the title was then held by Margaret Pole. In the event he was advanced to the earldom of Hertford on the 18 October, a title which had been vacant since the death of Gilbert de Clare in 1314, and was consequently available. He was presented by the Lord Great Chamberlain, the Earl of Oxford, and Thomas Cromwell read his patent of creation before the king girded him with the sword which signified his new dignity.[30] At the same time his assets were assessed to ensure that he had sufficient wealth to support his new status. His lands were valued at £1,034, of which £430 was listed as his inheritance from his father, who had died in the previous December, and £604 of the king's grants. His total gross income, including the annuities given him with his titles, was given as £1,107 6s 8d. Against this was to be set £91 15s paid in fees to bailiffs and stewards, £60 for his mother's jointure, £120 to Lord Lisle, which presumably marks the final resolution of their dispute, and various other small sums, leaving him with a net disposable income of just over £811.[31] This did not, apparently, include the fees of his numerous offices, such as the captaincy of Jersey, and his true income was probably well in excess of £1,000. A later estimate of £1,700 would probably be a more accurate reflection of his actual prosperity which was, in any case, deemed to be sufficient for an earl. In January 1538 he exchanged New Year gifts with the young prince, which was considered to be a mark of singular favour, and his sister's death does not seem to have diminished his standing at all. He was later described as being 'of small power', but that seems to reflect an unwillingness to do any more for Mary than any diminution of his authority.[32]

At the New Year gifts ceremony in 1538, Hertford stood beside the king and Thomas Cromwell, which was a fair reflection of his status. In the same month he was granted the site, manor, churches and advowsons of the recently dissolved monastery of Mochelsey, in Somerset, together with all the property of the house. No purchase price was named, so presumably this was a gift from the king, in reward for his agreeable company, good council, and service on the commission of the peace for Somerset and Wiltshire which had continued over many years.[33] Meanwhile his dispute with Lord Lisle rumbled on, and in March 1538 John Hussee reported to Lisle that he had complained to Thomas Cromwell of Hertford's victimisation of one of Lisle's agents, named Wykes, writing of the earl's 'ungodly proceedings'. Cromwell had professed himself willing to speak to the king on Wykes' behalf, but it is not clear that he ever did so, because it was his policy to keep on the right side of the Earl of Hertford, whose favour with Henry was almost as great as his own. Lisle himself wrote to Cromwell in February denying that he had ever sold the lands in question to Hertford, claiming instead that they had been pledged to Sir William Holton, merchant of London, acting on the earl's behalf, for £400. He had missed his repayment date, and Holton had refused a late payment, saying that he would 'meddle no further' in the matter, which presumably left the lands in Hertford's hands.[34] That is the last that we hear of the matter until the reconciliation which took place in the following year. In the early part of 1538 Hertford was signing council letters, which indicates his attendance at meetings, not otherwise verifiable. In early April one Wolfe, described as the earl's servant, fought a duel with a master of fence at St Martin's in London, and killed him. Wolfe took sanctuary at Westminster, but it is not known what became of him. Probably his master's influence was sufficient to get him pardoned on the grounds that the deed was committed in self-defence. 1538 also saw the so-called Exeter Conspiracy. This was Henry's revenge upon the Pole family for Reginald's tract on the unity of the Church, which had attacked the king's ecclesiastical policy comprehensively in 1536. That, the king decided, made the cardinal not merely an ungrateful subject but an arrant traitor, and anyone who stayed in touch with him was in danger of the law. Reginald's brother Geoffrey was arrested in September 1538 and, threatened with torture, disclosed a great deal about the loyalty of the Pole family and of their close allies the Courtenays. It is very doubtful whether these letters and other contacts amounted to treason, but they did disclose a high level of disaffection with the king's actions, and that was sufficient for Henry.[35] Geoffrey's elder brother Henry, Lord Montague and his close friend the Marquis of Exeter were detained together with various servants and dependents, and Reginald's mother, the Countess of Salisbury, was placed under house arrest. On 3 December the Earl of Hertford was named to the Earl Marshall's court for the trial of the two peers, and on the 4th to the commission of oyer and terminer which was to deal with the others. All were found guilty by unanimous decision of the courts, which means that the earl had done his duty as the king understood it, and that he was regarded as both loyal and effective.

Edward Seymour was primarily a soldier, and he spent much of 1539 raising and training troops for the king, who was much exercised by the fact that peace had broken out between France and the Empire. The treaty of Toledo of January 1539 committed each of the signatories to make no fresh deal with England without the other's consent, and this not only heralded diplomatic isolation, but appeared to threaten a joint campaign to enforce the excommunication of three years earlier, which Henry had hitherto ignored.[36] He mobilised his fleet and caused musters to be held right across the country. The aristocracy were called to the colours, and for six months or so England resembled an armed camp. In February, at the height of the crisis, Hertford was sent with 600 men to fortify the Calais outpost of Guisnes and in the following month served on the commission which was sent to examine the whole question of the fortification of the Pale, an assignment which was completed by 7 April, when Richard Lee reported to Cromwell that he needed 120 bricklayers from the works office to complete the repairs which had been recommended.[37] On the 14th Hertford wrote a friendly letter to Lady Lisle thanking her for her hospitality during his recent visit and offering to 'entertain' her daughter Katherine, presently with the Countess of Rutland, until Lady Lisle should make up her mind about how to deploy her. On the 16th there was a rumour circulating in London that Hertford was to be made Governor of Calais in Lisle's place, but John Hussee was quick to scotch such reports, writing to Lisle that the earl had instead 'offered me his assistance in your Lordships affairs at any time'. This signalled that as far as Hertford was concerned, their feud was at an end, and on 10 May this was confirmed by a friendly letter from Lady Lisle to the earl, thanking him for the trouble which he had taken over Katherine, and saying that she would leave her with the Rutlands for the time being.[38] Later that same month the Council of Calais wrote to Archbishop Cranmer referring to Hertford's recent commission from the king, which had also covered an assessment of the religious situation in the Pale, and sending the 'evil' preacher Adam Damplip, whom the earl had detected, to the Archbishop for examination. On 16 September he was named, at the king's suggestion, to the reception committee for the Count Palatine of the Rhine on his visit to England, and on 21 November was one of several earls designated to attend upon Anne of Cleves. The following day his wife, Anne, was nominated as one of Anne's ladies-in-waiting, along with the Duchess of Richmond, in an obvious attempt to honour the king's choice of bride.[39]

Cromwell's accounts for 1538–9 present further evidence of his intimacy with the Earl of Hertford. He repaid £100 which 'my lord had lent him', in an interesting reversal of their earlier relationship, and paid out £18 5s 3d for a cup which he had given at the christening of the earl's son Edward, which had taken place in May 1539, and at which he had stood as godfather.[40] In spite of this evidence of a close relationship, Hertford seems to have been in no way implicated in the fall of Cromwell, an event which occurred in June 1540, and which has been blamed unfairly on the failure of the Cleves marriage. In fact the Lord Privy Seal could have extricated Henry from that disastrous entanglement as easily as he had got him into it, on the grounds of non-consummation, which was eventually done. The fact is that Henry chose to blame him for the wave of evangelical preaching which was stirring up London in the early months of 1540, and for the activities of Adam Damplip in Calais, developments which left Cromwell fighting for his political life. In April it seemed that he had won, when he was created Earl of Essex and Lord Great Chamberlain, but this was a deceptive victory. Perhaps influenced by Henry's infatuation with Catherine Howard, the religious conservatives on the council, particularly the Duke of Norfolk and Bishop Stephen Gardiner of Winchester, convinced him that Cromwell was responsible for the dissention which they so much deplored. In early June they succeeded in turning the king against him, and he was arrested at a council meeting on the 10th.[41] Hertford was a member of the council, and was probably present on that day, but he made not the slightest attempt to help his friend, realising that any such would be futile and would run the risk of forfeiting that favour upon which he depended. Unlike Cromwell's other known friend, Thomas Cranmer, he did not, as far as we know, write subsequently in his defence, not choosing to venture himself in what was clearly a lost cause. Cromwell was executed on the 28 July and during August Hertford served on a number of royal commissions, including his usual ones of the Peace for Somerset and Wiltshire. In fact his favour does not seem to have been diminished at all by his former patron's demise, and although he cannot have been happy with the Howard ascendancy which followed Henry's marriage to Catherine, he was prepared to live with it, and it turned out to be of short duration.

Hertford was a regular attender at council meetings in the later part of 1540, and although his wife is not known to have transferred her service from Queen Anne to Queen Catherine, his position at court appears to have been unaffected. In January 1541 he was sent back to Calais, to lead a commission for ascertaining the exact boundaries of the Pale, and particularly the status of Ardres. His instructions were to consult with the French king's commissioners, because Ardres was thought to be within the precinct of Guisnes, and thus part of the Pale, a claim which the French denied.[42] On 4 February Hertford wrote for additional evidence to support his case, and was rewarded with a copy of a letter dating from the reign of Edward III which showed that shortly after the conquest Ardres was definitely considered to be within the Pale. On the 13th Hertford and his companion Sir Edward Carne were able to report good progress, and on the 19th that the French had conceded. They were then able to turn their attentions to the other matters contained in their instructions, the investigation of religious dissent in the Pale, and the conduct of Sir John Wallop, the Lord Deputy.[43] Wallop had replaced Hertford's old sparring partner,

Lord Lisle, in January 1540, when the latter had been recalled and placed under arrest on suspicion of secret dealings with Reginald Pole. However Wallop's own performance had been less than satisfactory, and he was now about to be recalled in his turn. The commissioners who were responsible for this action were recalled on 10 March, and filed their formal report on the 19th. This covered their secondary as well as their primary commitments, and reveals Hertford to have been a tough negotiator. Although described by Marillac, the French ambassador in England, as being respected for his 'goodness, sweetness and grace' rather than for his experience of affairs, he did well enough on this occasion, and the king was pleased.[44] He was rewarded with a strange grant made to him in June 1541, when he was given livery of the lands of Sir William Esturmy, as the great grandson of that John Seymour who had been the son of Matilda, 'daughter and heir of the said Sir William Esturmy'. How these lands had come into the hands of the Crown is something of a mystery, and they should in any case have descended to his father or grandfather. However, they had not been mentioned when he had been granted livery of his father's lands four years earlier, and had somehow skipped about four generations. The Earl of Hertford's lawyers must have come upon them, and he solicited their restoration, because it is hard to see Henry making such a gift without being asked for it. It is nevertheless an extraordinary example of the favour in which the earl was held at this time.[45] His fortunes were also enhanced by the failure of the Howard ascendancy, which came about as a result of the disclosure of Catherine's infidelities, in the autumn of 1541. The entire Howard clan, apart from the Duke of Norfolk, were indicted for misprision of treason, and although they were subsequently pardoned, their power at court was broken. The feckless Catherine was condemned by Act of Attainder in February 1542, and executed along with Jane Rochford on the 13th.

With the Bishop of Winchester away in France this left the route open for Hertford to become dominant in the council, and the indications are that he took his opportunities with both hands. He had served on the commissions of oyer and terminer which condemned Catherine's alleged paramours, as he had served on many such commissions in the past, but the queen was not tried, perhaps out of a desire to spare the king's feelings. There is plenty of evidence that he was deeply distressed by her misdemeanours, which reflected adversely upon his own manhood. With all the puissance of his crown he was not able to retain the affections of a fickle wench.[46]

In June 1542 Henry signed a new treaty with the Emperor, committing him to war with France in 1543, and mindful of what had happened in 1513, he decided to deal with the Scots first. To this end he sent the Duke of Norfolk with instructions to find some pretext for an intimidating raid into the Scottish lowlands. The duke did this by making impossible demands of the Scottish commissioners who had come to York to negotiate about border infringements, and when they prevaricated he launched 10,000 men across the border in a brief but immensely destructive operation. The Earl of Hertford was the actual commander of this foray, which took place during October, and he was rewarded by being appointed Warden General of the Marches.[47] The Duke of Norfolk was recalled on the grounds that he would need to begin preparing himself for the campaign in France. Hertford protested his own unsuitability for such a position, and Henry seems to have been genuinely uncertain what to do. On 8 November he yielded to Hertford's petition and sent John Dudley, Viscount Lisle to replace him. Dudley was an experienced soldier and a friend of the earl's, so the appointment must be deemed a suitable one, but he missed the only significant action which was to take place on his watch. Unable to resist the pressure to respond to Hertford's provocative action, James V launched 20,000 men into the West March via the debateable land in early November, and on the 25th, while Lisle was still on his way north, they were defeated by a smaller but much more effective English force under the command of Sir Thomas Wharton, the Warden of the West March.[48] The Battle of Solway Moss was not a bloodbath like Flodden, but a number of Scottish lords were captured and sent south. This defeat may have contributed to the death of the ailing King of Scots, which occurred just over a week later. This left the crown of Scotland in the hands of James's week-old daughter, Mary, and meant that Lisle, who took up his responsibilities on 1 December, had to deal with an uncertain situation north of the border. On 1 January the Council of Scotland appointed James Hamilton, Earl of Arran to be regent, but he did not command universal support and the exercise of authority in Scotland continued to be confused.

Meanwhile the Earl of Hertford appears to have served a brief term as Lord Admiral, a position which he is mentioned as holding on 28 December, but on 26 January he was replaced in this office also by Lord Lisle, who for the time being continued to double the duties with his responsibilities in the north.[49] This made sense in a way, because his main Admiralty duties during these months related to the north-east. At the end of June the French ambassador was given an ultimatum which amounted to a declaration of war, which was just about all that Henry achieved to honour his treaty with the Emperor. Meanwhile negotiations with the Scots continued, and in these the Earl of Hertford was deeply involved. In July, by the Treaty of Greenwich the king obtained his main objective, a commitment to marriage between the infant Queen of Scots and his own six-year-old son, a marriage designed to unify the kingdoms to England's advantage.[50] Henry was much concerned by the fragility of Arran's position in Scotland, unacceptable as he was to some of the nobility, and in the autumn offered to send troops to his support. However, such a gesture was made pointless by the fact that in September Arran changed sides, and began supporting the French interest represented primarily by Cardinal Beaton, whom he had previously held under arrest. Partly as a result of this defection, in December 1543 the Scots parliament repudiated the Treaty of Greenwich, much to Henry's rage. It appeared that the fruits of Solway Moss had been dissipated to no good effect, and the English party in Scotland was reduced to the earls of Angus and Lennox, who acted as much out of antipathy to Arran as from any commitment to Henry's interests.[51] The king was committed to war with France in the summer of 1544, and this was an obligation which could no longer be evaded, but he could not allow the rejection of his treaty to go unpunished, so he decided upon an early but fierce campaign in Scotland. This was to take the form of an amphibious raid on Edinburgh, and by the end of January he had appointed the Duke of Suffolk to lead this operation at the head of 15,000 men. Suffolk accepted this commission, but asked that the Earl of Hertford and Viscount Lisle should accompany him, no doubt with an eye on their recent military experience. However, the king changed his mind. He intended to campaign in France in person, and wanted his old friend at his side, so that at the end of February Suffolk was withdrawn from his northern command, and replaced by the Earl of Hertford.[52]

This inevitably led to some delay, and it was not until 21 March that Lord Lisle set off for Harwich to muster the ships needed. Bad weather disrupted their sailing, and at the end of March Hertford reported from Berwick that, although he had almost all the troops that he was supposed to have, hardly any of the ships had arrived, and his men were consuming victuals at an alarming rate. It was not until 20 April that the majority of the vessels reached the Tyne, sixty-eight in number, of which eleven were warships and the other fifty-seven had been taken up to provide the troop transports. On 28 April Hertford issued his instructions to the captains of his fleet, and on the 1 May they began to struggle out of the Tyne.[53] Thereafter the operation was conducted with exemplary efficiency. They landed at Inchkieth about two miles from Leith on the 3rd, and brushing aside a token Scottish resistance took and plundered the town, which they found unexpectedly rich. This, however, was rather the result of English perceptions of Scotland than of exceptional wealth. While he was in Leith, Hertford received a deputation from the city of Edinburgh, offering to surrender on terms, but he rejected it on the ground that his instructions were to destroy, and on 8 May he blew in the principal gate with a culverin. There was some fierce resistance, but this was swiftly overcome and the town was burned. No attempt was made to take the castle, whose garrison inflicted a number of casualties upon the invaders which are glossed over in the English accounts. Meanwhile, Hertford's warships were attacking places on the Firth of Forth, meeting slight opposition, and his horsemen were raiding as far as the gates of Stirling.[54] Having accomplished their mission, the English retreated on 15 May, the army going this time overland because their ships were so loaded with plunder and captured ordnance. By 18 May the men and the fleet were back at Berwick, and Hertford began to implement his supplementary instructions. The foreign ships were paid off, while Lisle and the remainder of the fleet were redeployed to the south to join the navy which was assembling for the campaign in France. Most of the troops were similarly despatched, but about 4,000 were reallocated to the border garrisons to guard against any Scottish reprisals. On 19 May the earl submitted his final report to the king, especially commending the service of Lord Lisle, who had commanded the vanguard at each stage of the operation. His final account was rendered with exemplary speed on 8 June, in which the campaign was deemed to have lasted for fifty-three days, and the naval expenses to have come to £2,000, exclusive of the cost of hiring the foreign vessels.[55] Hertford had thoroughly earned his reputation for efficiency, and the king's confidence in him was fully justified.

In the summer of 1543 Henry had taken his sixth wife, the evangelically minded Catherine Parr, Lady Latimer. It may have been her religious orientation which persuaded Hertford, or he may have come to such a position spontaneously, but by 1544 the earl was the leader of that group in the council known as the evangelical faction. They took their religious tone from Archbishop Cranmer, but Hertford was the political master, in opposition to the conservative faction led by the Duke of Norfolk and the Bishop of Winchester. It is therefore of great significance that when Henry decided to campaign personally in France in the summer of 1544 he left his queen behind him as regent, and named the Earl of Hertford as Lieutenant of the Kingdom.[56] It is not quite clear what he did in this capacity, but he would have had plenty of opportunity to observe Prince Edward's education at close quarters, and this would have confirmed him in his evangelical orientation. There would clearly be many changes when the old king died, and his health was giving constant cause for concern. Hertford began to manoeuvre himself to secure control of the minority government when that happened, as it now seemed increasingly likely given Edward was only seven years old in 1544. In spite of his responsibilities in England, Hertford was present when Boulogne surrendered in September, and even won a battle in the Boulonnais against a French army in January 1545, at which he seems to have been present merely as the leader of the reinforcements which had been sent over for the safeguard of the town, because he was not at any time part of the regular management structure of the conquest. His role of the lieutenancy would in any case have come to an end with Catherine's regency on Henry's return from the Continent, and he returned to his function as the king's most intimate adviser. Not as visible as Thomas Cromwell, nor as effective, but cast in the same mould. He had been Lord Great Chamberlain since the summer of 1543, a promotion which may have been connected with the king's marriage, and his voluminous correspondence passed to the Crown with his attainder in 1551. Consequently, as with Cromwell, we have a complete record of the letters which he received from the king, the council and numerous other officials during these particularly active years from 1542 to 1545.[57]

Meanwhile the Emperor had signed a separate peace with France at Crespy, on the same day that Henry entered Boulogne. Angered by the king's failure to cooperate in his intended campaign against Paris, he decided that Henry could defend his conquest on his own. Francis had no intention of letting go on Boulogne, so the king faced a difficult year in 1545, and the French mobilised an army and a large fleet to retake the town in the summer of that year. This was supposed to be achieved by launching an attack upon Portsmouth to take the English navy out of the equation and prevent the supply of the Boulonnais by sea. The result was a confrontation in the Solent, in the course of which the *Mary Rose* was lost, but this did not amount to a French victory, because Lisle was ready, and the battle never developed.[58] Instead plague broke out on the French ships, and after landing a few troops to help with the siege D'Annebaut, the French admiral, was compelled to retreat and demobilise. Lord Hertford had been at the king's side during the preparations for this confrontation, in his accustomed role as military adviser, but at the end of May he was sent back to the north, with instructions to prevent any Scots action in support of the French. This he did largely by mobilising the English party among the Scottish aristocracy, and on 10 June he wrote that it would be easy to invade Scotland with 8,000 men because the Scottish army was stranded without victuals. This would be the most effective way of impeding the French men's efforts but it did not happen because Hertford's plan failed to secure the king's approval. Henry had no desire to be fighting on two fronts unless it was unavoidable, and this was an optional initiative.[59] Frustrated for the time being in his main intention, Hertford turned instead to working in collaboration with the English party, notably Lord Maxwell, and to strengthening the defences of the border. Then in August he got his own way, and the king consented to a border raid in some force, which did considerable damage without provoking a response. This was done on the pretext of border grievances, which were always a fruitful source of conflict, and cost the king about £15,000, which was considered to be good value for money. Hertford appears to have quitted the north on 19 August, a move which may have been connected with the death of Charles Brandon, Duke of Suffolk earlier in the same month. Suffolk had been Henry's brother-in-law, and although an erratic councillor had been close to the king to the very end, and the latter may well have felt as his own health deteriorated that he needed his younger friends around him. Hertford continued to interest himself in border matters, however, and on 1 October was instructed by the council to discharge part of the border garrisons, which he presumably did from a base at court.[60]

His presence there was necessary because the conservatives had not given up, and they scored a notable victory in the summer of 1546 with the execution of Anne Askew for heresy. Anne had been close to a number of ladies in the circle around the queen, but even torture did not elicit from her any confession to that effect. Anne was a lady of considerable strength of character, and even the fact that some of them sent her money while she was in prison did not result in charges against them. It was a limited victory because she was a sacramentarian, and that was a doctrine which the king was known to abhor, so no member of the evangelical party embraced it, but it was a success nonetheless.[61] Judging the king's mood was essential to the outcome of these internecine battles, as is demonstrated by a story told by John Foxe nearly twenty years later. According to Foxe, Henry had become irritated by the theological discussions which Catherine occasionally held with her privy chamber and at which he was sometimes present. Noting this irritation, Stephen Gardiner seized the opportunity to convince the king that she was a heretic, and drew up a sequence of articles against her which the king signed. Realising the danger, some evangelical councillor obtained a copy of these articles, which he then conveniently dropped where the queen would be bound to find it.[62] We do not know who this councillor was, it may even have been the Earl of Hertford himself, but the effect was immediate. Catherine sought out her husband and cast herself on his mercy, protesting that the whole point of the discussions had been to learn from his great wisdom. 'And is that so, sweetheart,' Henry had responded, 'and tended it to no other end? Then are we as great friends as ever.'[63] He was as good as his word and when the Lord Chancellor turned up the following day, expecting to escort Catherine to the Tower, he was sent away with a fearful ear-bending. We have no other authority for this story, but the observation of the king's mood changes is accurate. It may well be true, and if so it was a victory for the evangelicals.

As Henry's health continued to decline in the latter part of 1546, he became increasingly concerned about the future of his 'master work', the Royal Supremacy. Rightly, it would seem, he became suspicious that the conservatives would do a deal with the papacy as soon as he was dead, and that his son would never be acknowledged as Head of the Church. He therefore inclined increasingly towards the Earl of Hertford and his allies, who by this time included not only Archbishop Cranmer, but also Lord

Lisle and the king's secretary, Sir William Paget. It may have
been as a result of the machinations of this group that Henry fell
out decisively with Stephen Gardiner in October. Ostensibly this
was over an exchange of lands with the king, but the ideological
difference between them was probably more important, and
Gardiner, who had survived the execution of his secretary and
nephew, Germaine Gardiner, for popery in 1544, was now excluded
from the council. He was also cut out of the list of executors of the
king's will, which was being drawn up at that time, on the grounds
that he was a 'masterful' man whom only Henry could manage.[64]
It was obviously felt that if he had remained an executor, he would
have taken over the minority government in a way which neither
the king nor the Earl of Hertford wanted. Even more significant
of the evangelical ascendancy at the end of 1546 was the fall of
the Howards. The Duke of Norfolk's son, Henry, Earl of Surrey,
as well as being a poet of note, was a wild and ambitious young
man. He had been recalled from Boulogne in disfavour earlier in
the year, and made no secret of the fact that he despised the 'foul
churls' with whom Henry surrounded himself. These included
Wolsey and Cromwell, and probably the Earl of Hertford as well.
The best men to manage the minority government would be the
ancient nobility, among whom he ranked his father and himself.
In preparation for such a role, he adopted the arms of Edward the
Confessor as part of his blazon, and thereby raised suspicion that
he aimed at the crown himself. His father could hardly profess
ignorance of these pretensions and the pair of them were arrested
on charges of treason in December 1546. They were subject to
hostile interrogation at the Tower by their ideological opponents,
and tried by the Earl Marshall's court in January 1547. Both
were found guilty and Surrey was executed on the 19th. Norfolk
remained in the Tower and was reprieved by Henry's own death
on the 28th. The fate of the Howards was very much the king's

own doing, rather than a victory for the evangelical party, but it left them in undisputed control of the body of executors who took over the government of the country as soon as the king was dead. The Earl of Hertford was set up for a distinguished future.

6

THE LORD PROTECTOR

When Henry VIII died on 28 January 1547, the Earl of Hertford was very much in control of the situation. This was not because he was the leader of an evangelical party, but because he was a blood relation of the young prince, and the king trusted him. When he came to create the body of executors who would administer his last will and testament on 30 December 1546, Henry was particularly anxious about the future of the Royal Supremacy in the hands of a child, and took what he considered to be appropriate precautions. The majority of the sixteen members of that group should probably be described as religious neuters, and the king had turned his back on the religious conservatives, simply because he did not trust them.[1] Of the executors named Sir Anthony Denny was probably the most radical, but it would be a mistake to describe even him as a crypto-Protestant. Archbishop Thomas Cranmer was obviously the religious leader among them, and he was a reformer, but he had always been very careful to stay within the parameters which Henry had marked out. The Earl of Hertford was in control because he was the most experienced leader among them, and because of his proven competence. He was also closely in alliance with Sir William Paget, the king's principal secretary and the best informed of the executors, although the initiative for this relationship is not clear. Probably Sir William, with an eye to the main chance, decided to back the man who was the natural leader, and it was quite possible that they had already decided on the protectorate even while the breath was still in the old king's body. Paget later reminded the earl 'of what had passed between them when they walked in the gallery outside Henry's chamber during those fraught hours'.[2]

How many of the executors were physically present at that time is not known, but it was probably a majority because they took a collective decision to delay any public announcement of the king's death until his heir had arrived in London. Consequently the routine of the court continued for the time being without a break. Even meals were solemnly borne into the privy chamber with the sound of trumpet, as though Henry was eating normally. Meanwhile at about 3 a.m. on the morning of 29 January the Earl of Hertford set out, accompanied by Sir Anthony Browne, the Master of the Horse, to bring Edward to the capital.[3] When they arrived at Hertford, the prince was under the impression that he was being summoned in connection with his creation as Prince of Wales, an event which he had long anticipated, and he was not at once disabused. It was not until they reached Enfield on the return journey, where Elizabeth was then living, that the truth was made clear to both of them. We are told that they wept copiously, but that would have been expected of them, and in fact neither of them had been particularly close to their father. On the return journey also, Seymour is alleged to have 'opened' to Browne the question of the protectorate, and won his consent to that as the surest form of government for the commonwealth, which is an indication that the remaining executors were not at that time in on the secret. On the morning of Monday 31 January, Edward reached London, and was taken at once to the Tower where the royal apartments had been prepared for him, and where he was greeted with a great shot of ordnance.[4] Meanwhile the old king's death had been made public, the Lord Chancellor, Thomas Wriothesley, making the formal announcement in the parliament that morning, thus dissolving the session. At the same time a popular announcement was made from an improvised stage at Westminster, and Edward was duly proclaimed king as Henry's 'only son and undoubted heir' to the great comfort of the people. Paget had read a part of the king's will to the parliament that same morning, presumably as much as was deemed good for them to hear, and relating particularly to the succession. The same morning, before Hertford's return, he had met with the remaining executors and secured their agreement to the earl's nomination as Lord Protector and Governor of the King's Person offices which were created and filled officially later the same day.[5] This involved breaching the terms of the king's will, which seems to have envisaged a collective responsibility, on the grounds that a single person was necessary to head the government. It could be justified, however, on the grounds that the will itself contained a clause empowering the executors to take whatever steps they deemed to be necessary for the security of the state. This confusion over the king's actual intentions probably indicates that the will signed or stamped on 30 December represents the king's thinking at that date rather than a definitive statement of purpose. In other words, Henry's thinking was still in progress when it was thus frozen in time.[6]

The following day, 1 February, Edward VI was brought from his apartments in the Tower, where he had been lodged in accordance with tradition into the presence of the assembled nobility at Westminster, who solemnly took their oaths of fealty to him. The will was then read by the Lord Chancellor, who also disclosed that the executors had appointed the Earl of Hertford as

Lord Protector and Governor, decisions which were unanimously endorsed by those present. The king consented at the same time and a commission was issued under the Great Seal giving legal effect to the new order of government.[7] The executors, and some of the assistant executors, then constituted themselves as the Privy Council of King Edward VI, and wrote formal letters to various heads of state announcing the change of regime. No letter was sent to the Pope, indicating that the new government in England intended to carry on where the old one had left off. Van der Delft, the Imperial ambassador in England was under no doubt that all this resolution and purposefulness sprang from Sir William Paget, whom he described as having 'great authority' in the kingdom. The ambassador was aware, probably because Paget had told him, of the long hours which Sir William had spend closeted with the old king in the days before his death, and formed the judgement that the Protector would depend on him heavily.[8] Hertford himself he dismissed as a 'dry, sour opinionated man' who owed his position rather to his blood relationship with the king than to any qualities which he possessed.

So what sort of a man was he, this Protector, the Earl of Hertford, shortly to become Duke of Somerset? He was soon to be known as the 'good duke' because of his alleged sympathy with the insurgents of 1549, and to be classed as a tolerant liberal by some twentieth-century historians. However, liberal in the twentieth-century sense he was certainly not, nor would he have understood what that meant. He was a man of action, particularly military action. Knighted in the field in 1523, he had been largely responsible for the successful actions in Scotland in the latter part of Henry's reign and had burned Edinburgh in 1544. He could be quite ruthless when the occasion seemed to demand it, and was obsessed with maintaining his position in Scotland after the victory at Pinkie Cleugh in 1547. Nor was he as interested in education as has been alleged. He had no intellectual training himself, and owned few books. Most of the dedications which he received owed more to his position as Protector than to any known sympathy with the causes maintained by the works concerned. Admittedly one of the reasons alleged for the dissolution of the chantries in 1547 had been for the 'erecting of grammar schools to the education of youth in virtue and godliness, the further augmenting of the universities, and better provision for the poor and needy'. However the income thus gained went into the coffers of the Crown, and only those lands already designed for the maintenance of schools was actually preserved.[9] In general Somerset and his circle were not distinguished for their interest in education. He arranged for both the universities to be visited in 1548, but that was more for the purpose of eliminating popery than out of any concern to reform the curriculum. He did attempt to establish new centres for the study of civil law in both Oxford and Cambridge, but allowed these efforts to be frustrated by vested interests, and by the need to maintain the study of God's word, as was pointed out by Bishop Nicholas Ridley. Similarly, his desire to reform the Church seems to have owed more to his objective of supporting the Royal Supremacy than it did to any deep-rooted Protestant commitment. His royal visitation of the summer of 1547 was dominated by laymen, and his adoption of the 1549 Prayer Book was carried out in Parliament without reference to the clerical assemblies of convocation. On the other hand he was closely associated with Coverdale, and appointed known Protestants to positions in his household; notably his physician William Turner and one of his chaplains, Thomas Becon.[10] It was probably the political uncertainties of the time rather than any sympathy with his doctrine which caused him to offer the hospitality of his household to the firebrand John Hooper on his return from exile in 1549, although one contemporary observer thought that it was owing to Somerset that Hooper was nominated to the see of Gloucester in the following year.[11] The fact that he was the recipient of no fewer than twenty-four dedications of reforming books during this period says no more than that he was the person in power, and was deemed to be sympathetic. The suspension of censorship during the first eighteen months of his period in office is better evidence for his toleration, but it belongs in the same category as the repeal of the Henrician treason laws, and control of preaching was reintroduced in 1548, when freedom of expression was in danger of getting out of hand. Somerset's religious position is probably best summed up as Erasmian; moderately Protestant because it suited his political agenda. The real Protestant in his household was his duchess, Anne, who had been involved with Anne Askew, although that had not come to light at the time. It was owing to her influence that their daughter Jane was given an academic education, or, as Thomas Becon put it in dedicating the revised edition of *The Goveranse of Virtue* to Jane Seymour in 1550, she had been brought up in 'good literature and in the knowledge of God's most holy laws'. By 1549 the duchess was widely recognised as a woman of radical religious views, a view which undoubtedly rubbed off on her husband, in spite of the fact that his own intellectual and spiritual observations were of the most moderate. Somerset was not therefore 'a Protestant patron and man of letters'; indeed he was scarcely a man of letters at all, and some of the dedications which he did receive were from known conservatives such as Henry Parker, Lord Morley, who was one of the first to jump on the opposition bandwagon when the crisis came in October 1549.

On 2 February the new Privy Council sent out formal letters to the sheriffs, the Wardens of the Marches, the Lord Deputy of Ireland, and the governors of Calais and Boulogne, announcing the succession and the structure of the new government. In these early days also the king was knighted by Seymour, which was a necessary formality before Edward could bestow that dignity upon others. In these early days, while the old king still lay unburied, and possibly in response to the council's invitation to submit claims for the coronation, various noblemen and others began to put themselves forward for grants and promotions of various kinds, alleging the late king's intention to reward them. Consequently, on 5 February, the council called before them Sir William Paget, Sir Anthony Denny and Sir William Herbert, who had been most intimate with Henry in the last days of his life, and asked them what they knew of these intentions. Paget testified that the king had indeed been intending to replenish the nobility following the fall of the Howards, and had marked out a number of creations, together with grants of land to support their new dignities. The Earl of Hertford was to be made a duke, either of Somerset, Exeter or Hertford, with £800 worth of lands, and the Earl of Essex was to be Marquis of Northampton, with £300 in lands. Viscount Lisle was to be Earl of Coventry and Lord Wriothesley, the Lord Chancellor, to be Earl of Winchester, each with an appropriate grant.[12] In addition several knights were to be made up to barons, the most notable being Sir Thomas Seymour, the new Lord Admiral, who was to become Lord Seymour of Sudeley, with the generous grant of £500. On the king's instructions, Paget had then spoken with each of the intended beneficiaries, some of whom had expressed reluctance to be advanced, and others that the proposed grants were too small. No one seems to have doubted Paget's testimony, backed as he was by Herbert and Denny, and by the memories of other members of the council who had been close to the old king. He also had a reputation for honesty, and had been wise enough not to propose any enhancement for himself. The council deliberated this information for several days, and then on 15 February resolved on the following promotions:

the Earl of Hertford was created Duke of Somerset, and the Earl of Essex Marquis of Northampton, as had been proposed. Lord Wriothesley was to be Earl of Southampton, rather than Winchester, and Viscount Lisle Earl of Warwick in preference to Coventry, probably at his own suggestion. Sir Thomas Seymour became Lord Seymour of Sudeley as intended, Sir Richard Rich Lord Rich of Leighs, Sir William Willoughby Lord Willoughby of Parham, and Sir Edmund Sheffield Baron Sheffield. The grants of land in support of these dignities seem to have been taken mainly from the forfeited Howard estates.[13] Time now became a factor because it was important that these new dignities should be in place before the king's coronation, which was scheduled for the 20th, and the old king's funeral was due to take place at Windsor on the 16th. In the event the formal creations were made at the Tower on the 17th, the new Duke of Somerset taking precedence, as was appropriate. Supported by the young Duke of Suffolk and by the Marquis of Dorset, with the Earl of Arundel bearing his sword, Seymour made his obeisance to the young king sitting in his chair of state, and then knelt before him while Sir William Paget read the charter of creation. That done, he was girded with his mantle and sword, and the ducal coronet was placed on his head. He then stood beside the king while the other creations were carried out.[14]

Perhaps because of these preoccupations, the councillors of the new regime were not prominent in the obsequies of the old. Edward did not attend his father's funeral, but that was a custom sanctified by centuries of usage, and the chief mourner was the Marquis of Dorset, who was the next-nearest thing to a male blood relation that Henry had possessed, being the husband of his niece, Frances. The old king had been prepared for burial after laying in state in his chamber for several days before being moved to the chapel at Hampton Court on 3 February, where the mourners had assembled 'in order after their degrees' to hear a requiem Mass. There he continued until the 14th, watched over night and day by relays of his servants. On the 14th the cortege set out with great solemnity for Windsor because it was intended to lay him beside his third and favourite wife, Jane Seymour, in accordance with his own instructions. He was duly interred beneath the chapel of St George on the 16th, the pallbearers having some difficulty in lowering his massively heavy coffin into the grave. The courtiers who had been present then retired to the castle for refreshments, and the councillors hastened to go back to London, where much business awaited them.[15] According to the council's own accounts, the funeral cost them the relatively modest sum of £1039 9s 7d. The majority of the peers and others attending had presumably done so at their own expense.

The business which drew them back was partly, of course, the peerage creations which took place the next day, but it was also partly the ongoing preparations for the coronation. On 12 February the council had already approved a somewhat shortened form of the traditional service, out of regard for the king's youth, in order not to tire (or bore) him unduly. It was, however, nearly forty years since England had last enjoyed the coronation of a ruling monarch, and much searching of precedents was called for. This included claims for service, which had been solicited on 4 February, and ranged from such activities as the Earl of Arundel (butler at the coronation banquet) to one Nicholas Leigh who demanded that he be permitted to make for the king 'a mess of potage called Digeront'. This last claim was allowed on the condition that the king's chef created the actual dish![16] On Saturday 19 February, 'all things being prepared', the king passed through London from the Tower to Westminster in a joyful pageant which gave ordinary Londoners a chance to show their enthusiasm for the boy who was now their king, and perhaps their expectation that his government would be more lenient than that which they had recently endured. As suited the occasion he was magnificently dressed in a gown of cloth of silver 'all over embroidered with damask gold' and with a white velvet cap 'garnished with pearls and stones', trappings which he appears to have enjoyed. He was escorted by the Lord Protector and council, and followed by the nobility and senior clergy, the whole procession being guarded by men-at-arms.[17] At various points along the route the king was greeted with pageants, songs and salutations, but the most spectacular was reserved for the precinct of St Pauls, where a Spanish acrobat performed various feats on a cable stretched from a steeple to an anchor near the dean's house, descending at last 'like an arrow from a bow', to be suitably rewarded by an enthralled king who had allowed his retinue to be halted for some time by this performance. A peevish Imperial ambassador, who refused to attend the coronation, remarked that there had been 'no very memorable show of triumph or magnificence', but this is not supported by other evidence, and may have been occasioned by the knowledge that the City of London had reused the pageant sequence originally written by John Lydgate for Henry VI's entry in 1432, rather than commissioning a new set.[18] This had been occasioned by the shortness of the time available for preparations, and seems in no way to have detracted from the happiness of the occasion.

The following day the attendance was limited to the court circle, the nobility and the senior clergy, who were warned to be in their places at the abbey by seven o'clock in the morning. Edward walked from the palace, and arrived between nine and ten. The rite followed the fourteenth-century *Liber Regalis*, with intervals interposed so that the king could rest. The first part consisted of the showing, the presentation of the king to his people by the Archbishop of Canterbury, who invited them to show their approval in the traditional way. The assembled nobles thereupon responded by shouting, 'Yea, yea, yea, King Edward, King Edward, King Edward', and the king solemnly took his coronation oath, wherein he promised to uphold the laws and customs of England, and to defend its Church and people.[19] The second and most important part of the service was the blessing and anointing of the king, for which Edward discarded his elaborate robes and donned a crimson satin surcoat, which would enable him to be anointed on the breast, shoulders and back. While the king was changing, his coronation pardon was declared, which on Somerset's advice was issued in his own name, in spite of his youth, on the grounds that the new king needed all the gratitude that he could get. The anointing was performed by Cranmer, under a canopy held by Sir Anthony Denny and Sir William Herbert. Edward then put on rich garments of crimson satin, and offered his sword on the altar. Finally the king was crowned, the Archbishop and the Duke of Somerset putting on his head in turn the crown of Edward the Confessor, the Imperial crown of England, and a special lightweight crown which had been made for the occasion. The orb and the sceptre were then presented to him, he was enthroned and a solemn *Te Deum* sung.[20] The Archbishop preached a sermon, urging the king to use the powers of the supremacy, which God had granted specifically to him, to preserve the unity of the Church, and the boy acknowledged his willingness to do so. He must have been weary by this time, because the ceremony had been going on for several hours, but his task was not yet done. Still wearing his light crown, he was brought into Westminster Hall for the traditional banquet, where his table was apparently shared by the Lord Protector and the Archbishop, the other lords being 'sat at boards in the hall beneath'. The marshall of the feast was the Duke of Somerset, but it was his deputy who took on the onerous (and invidious) task of making sure that there was somewhere for everyone to sit which did not offend their sense of precedence. In this he was not altogether successful and the Imperial ambassador, who had not been present at the coronation itself, later complained that he was compelled to sit among the gentry, no place having been reserved for him.[21] However, everyone being settled, the king's champion, Sir John Dymocke, then made his appearance to issue his traditional challenge, and the king drank to him, presenting him with the cup from which he had drunk as a reward. Since it was made of silver, this was no trivial matter, and Dymocke would have been well satisfied with his day's work. Soon afterwards Edward was allowed to withdraw to the palace, where no doubt he was soon in bed. But the night being young, the festivities continued with jousts and foot combats, presided over by the Lord Protector. The next day order was taken for all the servants who had been with his father and himself as prince 'and the ordinary and the unordinary were appointed'. Presumably it was a matter of protocol to leave this establishment until after the coronation.[22] Meanwhile the Londoners continued their rejoicings, reflected in the ballad sung in the streets

> Sing up heart and sing no more down,
> But joy in King Edward that weareth the crown[23]

If there was any anxiety that this was a minority government, it was not allowed to appear on this occasion.

In spite of the pre-eminence which he had achieved, the Lord Protector was not altogether satisfied with the terms upon which he held his office. He was bound by the original grant to act only with the consent of the rest of the council, and he was not given any power to appoint councillors, which meant that, in spite of appearances, his control was only partial. He consequently began to press for an augmentation of his powers, and this was granted in Letters Patent which were sealed on 12 March, and recorded in detail in the council register the following day.[24] The clause requiring him to seek the consent of his fellow councillors for any action was quietly dropped, and he was specifically given the power to recruit new councillors as circumstances might dictate. It is obvious that these changes met with the approval of the majority of the other councillors, but there was one dissident voice, and that was the Lord Chancellor, the Earl of Southampton. Wriothesley was an irascible man and an acute politician, who could have made a considerable nuisance of himself had he remained in post. A subterfuge was therefore adopted to get rid of him. He was a keen advocate of the civil law, and two days before the coronation issued a commission to a team of four civil lawyers to discharge his duties in Chancery while he concentrated on his work in the council. This provoked an immediate protest from the common lawyers, firstly on the grounds that it would undermine their position, and secondly that the Chancellor was not entitled to issue such a commission without the council's authority. The council took these representations seriously, and having consulted 'the best learned men in the laws of the realm' decided to deprive him of his office. In a hearing which was accorded to him, Wriothesley allegedly argued that he was entitled to issue such commissions *ex officio* and used unseemly words both of the council's legal advisers and of the Lord Protector. On 6 March the council confirmed its decision against him, and condemned him to such imprisonment and fine as the king might impose.[25] In the event he was not imprisoned and his fine was remitted. A few months later he was quietly readmitted to the council, but as an opponent of the Protector his teeth had been temporarily drawn. Sir William Paulet, Lord St John took over as Keeper of the Great Seal until Richard Rich was appointed Chancellor in October.

Meanwhile the reform of the Church continued. Cranmer had

set the tone for this by issuing fresh commissions to all the bishops at the outset of the reign. This was normal with royal servants on the demise of the crown, and emphasised their dependence on the king's supremacy. There were of course no precedents for this situation, and Stephen Gardiner objected on the grounds that he was an ordinary, and that his episcopal authority derived from his consecration and not from his appointment, an argument which the council rejected.[26] At the same time there was a surge in the publication of evangelical tracts, which the Protector did nothing to suppress, less, it would seem, out of toleration than out of a desire to signal impending changes. Then on 1 July a set of injunctions was issued and a metropolitan visitation was announced. These injunctions were based on those used by Cromwell in his visitations of 1536 and 1538, and urged the preaching of the Royal Supremacy by bishops, and restraint in the use of images in worship. They were not therefore particularly original, and were seemingly intended mainly to emphasise the king's authority. As such they were also concerned to insist upon the use of a new set of homilies issued and partly written by the Archbishop, which Gardiner rightly objected were heretical on justification and offended against the Act of Six Articles.[27] It was partly this consideration which inspired the repeal of that Act when the parliament met in the autumn. Gardiner also apparently objected to the suspension of his own visitorial powers for the duration of the metropolitical operation, but in that he was on much less secure ground. It would be an exaggeration to describe the English Church in the summer of 1547 as being Protestant, but it had certainly moved in that direction, and the Duke of Somerset was largely responsible for that development. The reforming movement, which had been foreshadowed by the education given to Prince Edward, was now beginning to work itself out in the actions of the minority government.

In August 1546, just four months before Henry VIII died, Sir William Paget had drawn up a document on the state of England's foreign relations, perhaps with a view to those religious reforms which he could see were coming. The Emperor, he argued, was an uncertain friend because of his relations with the papacy, which he saw as meaning more to Charles than the friendship of England. An alliance with the Protestant princes of Germany and the Baltic was a possible answer to this problem, but that had been tried before without success, because England was not a Lutheran state, and was not likely to become one. Charles had also made it clear that he would not be drawn into offering a defence of the 'new conquest' of Boulogne, which was not covered by the existing treaty of 1542.[28] Boulogne was also the key to relations with France. Although Francis had surrendered the town for eight years by the treaty of Camp earlier in 1546, Paget suspected that he had not really given up hope of recovering it by military action, which was what made an understanding with the Emperor so important. However, the real lesson of these deliberations was that England must be united within itself, and gather its resources 'by knitting to us the surest and most sincere friends that we can get', wherever they might be found. Rather surprisingly, Paget did not include Scotland in his assessment, because Scotland was a country with which England was still technically at war. It had been included in the treaty of Camp only in the negative sense that England renounced any intention of attacking it unprovoked, but Scotland remained tied to the French interest. When French policy towards Boulogne became increasingly hostile after the death of Francis I and the accession of Henry II in April, Somerset began to contemplate a strike to the north. During May he had himself appointed Lieutenant General of the Kingdom and began to gather men and munitions. Then nothing happened, because during June the Protector seems to have been considering his options, including reopening negotiations for the implementation of the Treaty of Greenwich. At the end of July Leo Strozzi, with a French galley force, took St Andrews Castle, where the murderers of Cardinal Beaton had been in residence since the previous year, and that aggravated the situation.[29] Nevertheless, negotiations continued, and Somerset may even have offered the French the cession of Boulogne in return for a free hand in the north. If this was the case it did not work and at the end of August the Protector prepared to launch himself into the lowlands. On the 27th, accompanied by Lord Grey and Sir Ralph Sadler, he reached Newcastle, and mustered his men on the 28th. They numbered about 15,000, and the estimated cost of a thirty-day campaign was nearly £25,000, which gives us a fair idea of how long the incursion was intended to last. In 1544 the army had been seaborne, but on this occasion it was to go overland, with the fleet under Lord Clinton in logistical support. It crossed the border on 2 September, and almost at once the nervous gentlemen of the Scottish borders began to 'come in' and commend themselves to Somerset, who received them graciously enough.[30] It was part of his purpose to build up the English party in Scotland, so only those places which offered resistance were attacked in the course of this march. Opposition on the whole was slight until the English came upon the main Scottish host deployed upon Fauxside Bray near Musselborough, on 10 September. The Earl of Huntley having offered single combat to the duke and been politely rebuffed, the battle was joined. At first the advantage lay with the Scots, who deployed their artillery to advantage, until

by the policy of my Lord's grace, and the diligence of every captain and officer besides, were so opportunely and aptly applied in their feat that where this repulse by the enemy and retire of us were doubted by many to turn to the danger of our loss, the same was wrought and advanced, according as it was devised, to our certainty of gain and victory.[31]

William Patten's account of the battle is very full, and particularly praises the Earl of Warwick for his skill and courage. The result was an overwhelming English victory, the pursuit continued long into the night, and although Patten's counting of 13,000 Scottish dead must be an exaggeration the casualties were undoubtedly very heavy. The day following this battle, normally known as Pinkie Cleugh, the Lord Protector rode to Leith, and found the place almost deserted. Meanwhile Lord Clinton's ships had been raiding along the Firth of Forth, as far as Blackness, recovering the *Mary Willoughby* and the *Anthony*, two ships taken by the Scots earlier in the year, and burning the remainder.[32] On 18 September Andrew Dudley was knighted and installed in command at Broughty Crag, a garrison created near Dundee on the north shore of the Firth of Tay, and the army set off homeward. It reached the border on the 23rd, and was soon thereafter disbanded, certain men being held back to form the core of the garrisons which it was the Protector's policy to establish in the border country for the purpose of registering an English presence.

As a result of the defeat at Pinkie Cleugh, which saw the destruction of its field army, Scotland was well nigh helpless for several months, but Somerset, who had many other things on his mind, did not pursue his advantage. He reached London on 8 October, leaving his command in the north to Lord Grey. Grey was not in a position to take any initiative, and concentrated his attention on establishing the garrisons which the Protector had determined upon before his departure, from Inchcolm and Haddington in the east to Dumfries and Cockpool in the west.[33] The obvious thing to do was to rebuild the English party in Scotland, except that it consisted of unreliable characters like the

Earl of Bothwell and Sir George Douglas, whom neither Grey nor Somerset trusted. It would have been better to link the growing power of the religious reformers to English interests, except that they did not at this stage include any of the noblemen who were deemed to be necessary for such a party. Shielded as they were by the Protector's preoccupations from further military intervention, diplomatically the Scots remained intransigent. The infant queen was removed into a secure hiding place, and an appeal was made to France for urgent military assistance. The French had been sparring with the English over the harbour works at Boulogne throughout the spring and summer of 1547, but the Scots' request put them on the spot, and their initial response was equivocal. An agreement was reached with the English over the mutual grievance of privateering, restoring normal commercial links from 30 October, and it began to look as though the Scots would be disappointed. Somerset then made a mistake. On 16 November he offered the return of Boulogne in exchange for the cession of Marquise and Fiennes (two places on the border of the Calais Pale) and French support for the marriage of Mary and Edward. Henry II was clearly offended by this proposal, and offered in return French support for the marriage at the price of the surrender of Boulogne, Calais and Guisnes, which Somerset denounced as an insult to his master.[34] The duke then responded by offering Boulogne in exchange for 2 million crowns in gold and support for the marriage as before. No negotiations followed, but rather a strong French raid into the Boulonnais, which resulted in a number of casualties. Somerset, however, did not want war with France, and strictly forbade any reprisals. Then, on 3 January 1548, Sir Andrew Dudley, in requesting money and reinforcements for his garrison at Broughty Crag, also disclosed that fifty French officers had arrived in Scotland to assess the aid which was needed.

For the time being the weather made any further military

Right: 2. John Seymour, father of Edward, Thomas and Jane.

Below left: 3. Edward Seymour, Duke of Somerset and Lord Protector of England (1547–9). He was also appointed Governor of the King's Person to Edward VI, his nephew.

Below right: 4. Sir Thomas Seymour, Lord Seymour of Sudeley. After Henry VIII's death Thomas would marry the king's widow, Catherine Parr.

5. Jane Seymour. She was not a great beauty, but carried little political baggage and had no agenda of her own. She was greatly praised for her sweet disposition.

ANNA BOLLINA VXOR HEN VIII

Right: 6. Anne Boleyn, the wife whom Jane displaced. Her feisty sexuality left her vulnerable to political attack by those she had offended in the course of her rise to power.

Below: 7. The Field of Cloth of Gold, an opulent celebration shared between Henry VIII and Francis I of France in June 1520. Sir John Seymour was privileged enough to accompany Henry to this event.

Bottom: 8. A distant view of Greenwich Palace, from a drawing by Anthony van Wyngaerde of about 1550, in the Ashmolean Museum at Oxford. Henry installed Edward Seymour and his wife in a suite here in March 1536, a sign of the growing favour of the Seymours.

Above left: 9. From the title page of the Great Bible. Archbishop Thomas Cranmer receives the Word on behalf of the clergy. On the day Anne Boleyn died, Cranmer granted Henry a dispensation to marry Jane Seymour despite their consanguinity.

Above right: 10. From the title page of the Great Bible. Thomas Cromwell, Viceregent in Spirituals, receives the Word on behalf of the laity. After Jane's death, Cromwell would push his king to marry again; the subsequent marriage would result in his execution.

Below: 11. Whitehall Palace, acquired by Henry VIII on the fall of Thomas Wolsey. Jane and Henry were married in the queen's closet here on 30 May 1536.

12. Prince Edward, Jane's son by Henry VIII (later King Edward VI) as an infant, by Hans Holbein. Edward was born on 12 October 1537, and this drawing was made at some time before Holbein's death in 1543.

Above left: 13. Thomas Howard, 3rd Duke of Norfolk. The Lord Treasurer, and uncle to queens Anne Boleyn and Catherine Howard, he was a leading councillor and rival to Thomas Cromwell. Having survived the fall of both his nieces, he was convicted of high treason in January 1547, and saved from execution by the death of Henry VIII on the 28th of the month. The fortunes of the Howards often rose at the Seymours' expense, and vice versa.

Above right: 14. Henry VIII's will, dated 30 December 1546. The fact that the will was signed with a stamp rather than the sign manual complicated the succession.

Below: 15. Lucas de Heere's *Allegory of the Tudor Succession*, from around 1572, painted as a gift to Queen Elizabeth. The painting shows Henry VIII sitting on his throne and passing the sword of justice to his Protestant son Edward VI. On his left is the Catholic Mary I, with her husband Philip II of Spain, followed by Mars, the god of war. To the right of Edward VI is Elizabeth I, holding the hand of Plenty and followed by Peace.

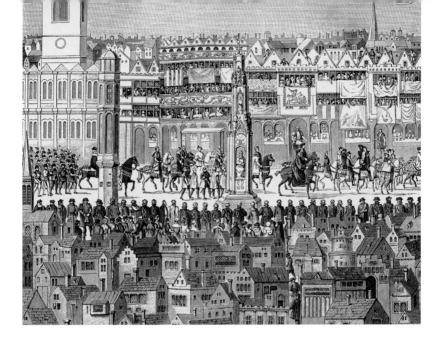

Above: 16. The coronation procession of Jane's son Edward VI in February 1547, passing Cheapside Cross on its way to Westminster Abbey. The windows and rooftops are crowded with spectators, suggesting the enthusiasm of the citizens for their new king.

Below left: 17. Edward VI's 'device' for the succession, naming Lady Jane Grey as his heir. The amendments are not written in Edward's hand.

Below right: 18. The unfortunate Lady Jane Grey. Edward VI had recommended her as his successor, but Princess Mary made a triumphant procession to London on his death in 1553 and Lady Jane Grey was thrown in the Tower, being executed the following year.

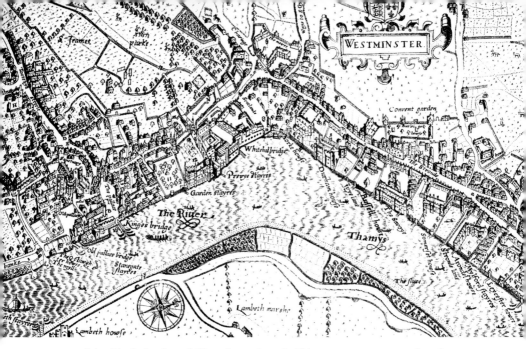

19. John Norden's plan of Westminster (1593). This near-contemporary plan shows Westminster as Jane would have known it. The palace was the centre of government, and was surrounded by other palaces and homes belonging to nobles, courtiers and royal servants. The City was close enough to London for the two to be seen as a single unit.

20. The White Tower of the Tower of London, from a mid-fifteenth-century illumination. The Tower was a palace and fortress as well as a prison, and monarchs traditionally passed the night before their coronations here. Both Thomas and Edward Seymour would be held in the Tower, each being executed on Tower Hill.

operations on the Scottish borders impossible, and Somerset concentrated his efforts on a propaganda campaign. In February he issued an 'Epistle or Exhortation' to the people of Scotland, which was widely circulated north of the Tweed. In this he argued the merits of the proposed marriage between Edward and Mary and the benefits which would accrue from the union of the crowns which would follow, which would include a reformation of the Church.[35] We do not know what impression this made on the people as a whole, but it would have meant the end of the dominance of the turbulent Scottish nobility, and was therefore unwelcome to them. Moreover the reform of the Church was anathema to the powerful Queen Mother, Mary of Guise, and to most of those who were advising her, so although it represented a genuine attempt on the Protector's part to be positive, it had little impact on the political situation. The same is true of the work of James Harrison, a Scot who also wrote in defence of the marriage treaty, and who advocated not only a reform of the Church but a thoroughgoing social reformation as well. This was aimed not merely at reducing the military power of the Scots nobility, but at the founding of almshouses and schools in parishes, and at the reform of the universities.[36] All this would follow, he argued, if the senseless antagonism between the two realms could be brought to an end, and the peoples united under the name of Britons. The thought of Harrison and Somerset had much in common, but their idealism did not much appeal to those in power at that time. Instead, Lord Grey reported on 12 June a French fleet standing off Dunbar. These ships evaded the screen which Lord Clinton had placed about the Firth of Forth, and on 18 June landed 6,000 French veterans at Leith. The arrival of these troops transformed the military situation in the north, enabling a full siege to be laid against Haddington, which was the principal English garrison in the eastern Marches and Lord Grey's chief headquarters from

April to June. Strenuous efforts were made to reinforce the place before the siege closed in, and Grey moved his base back to Berwick. Haddington was eventually relieved by a large army led by the Earl of Shrewsbury, but not before the French and the Scots had signed a treaty at d'Esse's camp, which is known as the Treaty of Haddington. By the terms of this agreement Mary was to be betrothed to the Dauphin and shipped at once to France, the laws and liberties of Scotland being guaranteed in the event of a union of the crowns.[37] The French meanwhile pledged their wholehearted support for Scotland's military position. Before the end of July Mary had departed by the western route from Ayr, and Somerset's whole strategic position in Scotland lay in ruins. However, for the time being England's relations with France were unaffected by this debacle. Skirmishing continued around Boulogne, but during the latter part of 1548 diplomatic relations between the two powers, although frosty, remained normal. This was largely because Henry was uncertain of the Emperor's intentions, and Charles, whose power stood high at that time, was not anxious to enlighten him. He allowed Edward VI to recruit mercenary troops in his realms, but was not prepared to go further than that. That, nevertheless, was sufficient to deter the French from indulging in direct hostilities, and to restrict themselves to intervention in Scotland. In Scotland itself relations with the local inhabitants became surly, and Henry began to wonder whether his investment of money and troops was worthwhile. For the time being, however, the Treaty of Haddington was sufficient reward, and even Somerset's attempt to revive English claims to suzerainty over the northern kingdom did not alter that situation very much. The French held on, and some of the English garrisons were abandoned as the Lord Protector considered his options.[38]

Meanwhile Somerset had met his first parliament on 4 November 1547, and proposed two important bills. The first repealed the early fifteenth-century heresy laws, and most of Henry VIII's treason legislation, on the grounds that such severe laws were no longer necessary. 'So we have seen,' the preamble ran,

> Divers strait and sore laws made in one parliament, the time so requiring, in a more calm and quiet reign of another prince by like authority and parliament repealed and taken away; the which most high clemency ... the king's highness of his most tender and godly nature most given to mercy and love of his subjects [is willing to exercise] ...[39]

This Act must be seen against the background of ongoing religious reform, because it was under the statutes of Henry IV that the persecution of heretics had been carried out by the previous regime, and with the repeal of those Acts it was, or should have been, unlawful to have burned anyone. Henry's comprehensive treason laws were replaced with a simple statement to the effect that the denying of any of the king's titles, including that of Head of the Church, remained treason on the third offence. The Lord Protector turned out to be rather too optimistic in his appraisal of this situation, and most of these abrogated treasons were restored to the statute book later in the reign. The second important bill was that dissolving all chantry foundations and colleges, and vesting their property in the Crown. This was in fact a repetition of the Act of 1545, which had granted all such lands and other goods to the king on the grounds that he had urgent need of the money. This time, however, the reason given was the 'superstitious practices' of the chantries; in other words it was part of the reforming agenda. The bill, when it became an Act, gave the king an additional £600,000 worth of property, and struck traditional religion far harder than the dissolution of the monasteries. Many parishes had been unaffected by the disappearance of monks and nuns, but almost every church had its small pieties, memorials and charitable endowments which were confiscated under the terms of this Act.[40] It was widely and deeply unpopular, as it came to be implemented over the next year or two, but since it did not affect the Mass, which lay at the heart of popular religion, it was not resisted in any systematic way. More important than this Act in stirring up opposition was the English version of the liturgy which Cranmer was permitted to introduce at Easter 1548. He had been working for several years on this project, but it was not made mandatory at this stage, and most parishes went on using the traditional Latin rite, a fact which kept the opposition within bounds. Only those incumbents who already had reformed credentials took advantage of the Archbishop's initiative.

During the summer of 1548, while the Lord Protector was preoccupied with his diplomatic relations with Scotland, France and the Empire, there were ominous signs of social discontent, particularly in Cornwall where the unpopular Archdeacon William Body was murdered. Most of these riots were stirred up by land-use issues, which had been stimulated by preachers and pamphleteers of the so-called 'Commonwealth School'. There is no evidence that these writers were working together, or that they had an agreed agenda, but they tended to be hostile to the propertied classes, who they represented as enclosing land for their own profit and engrossing the common land which should have been open to the whole community. The enclosure of arable land for sheep farming was not really an issue by the mid-sixteenth century. It had reached its zenith over a hundred years before, when the population had been much lower, and had caused little comment. By the mid-1540s, however, the rural population had expanded to the point where there were far more potential tenants than there were holdings available, and this caused even old enclosures to be regarded as a grievance.[41] Aware of his royal responsibility to safeguard the interests of the poor, and of the precedent set by Cardinal Wolsey in this respect, in the summer of 1548 Somerset set up a number of royal commissions to investigate the situation, and this aroused expectations of speedy remedies which were never part of his intention. Disappointment led to riots, and the Protector's policy was attacked even from within the Council, most notably by John Dudley, Earl of Warwick. The risings were put down, and Somerset was not deterred by the opposition, but nevertheless in the light of what was to happen in the following year they look ominous. The Protector was regarded as being altogether too sympathetic to the propagandists of the Commonwealth School.

Towards the end of 1548 Somerset also became concerned over the behaviour of his brother, Thomas. Thomas had made no secret of the fact that at the beginning of the reign he thought that he should have been granted the office of Governor of King Edward's person. The barony and the office of Lord Admiral, which he did receive, were no compensation when his brother became a duke. He married the queen dowager, Catherine Parr, and that also was source of friction between the two brothers, the Protector being firmly opposed to any such move.[42] While he might have been expected, as Lord Admiral to have commanded the fleet which went against Scotland in the autumn of 1547, Thomas decided to stay at home, and delegated his authority to Lord Clinton. During the summer of 1548 he was more than suspected of colluding with the pirates whom he was supposed to suppress, and of paying his attentions to the Lady Elizabeth who was residing in Catherine's household. He had already quarrelled bitterly with his brother over his wife's jewels, which the Protector claimed were Crown property, and in August 1548 the latter had written to him advising him to be less abrasive in his relationships.[43] Seymour had persuaded the Marquis of Dorset to entrust his daughter, Jane Grey, to him on the grounds that he could arrange a marriage for her with the king, which it was not within his power to do, and could be interpreted as treason. Then in September 1548 his wife died in childbirth, and her significant contribution to his household expenses came to an end. Within a month he had returned to the Princess Elizabeth, this time speaking of marriage, which he must have known was treason without the council's consent, a consent he was never likely to obtain. Lord Seymour was a loose cannon, and when he began to plot against his brother, he seriously overstepped the mark. He spoke indiscreetly to several peers about raising a party in the House of Lords to annul the Protector's patent by statute, and conspired with Sir William Sharrington to defraud the Bristol Mint of several thousand pounds, which he used to stockpile arms at Sudeley and to build up a retinue in the West Country.[44] Most of this was vaguely known to the council, and then at the beginning of January Sharrington was arrested and the treasonable nature of their conspiracy became clear. The Protector had no alternative but to investigate and Seymour's liaison with Elizabeth came to light. Kate Ashley, the princess's mentor, was removed from her position, and Elizabeth herself was interrogated. She was pardoned on account of her youth, but a search of Sharrington's home at Lacock Abbey on 6 January produced further incriminating evidence, and Seymour was summoned to a private interview with the Protector. This he declined on the grounds of convenience, and by so doing probably forfeited his only chance of escaping from the mire in which he was now trapped. On 17 January the council resolved on measures 'for the stay and repressing of the said Admiral's attempts', and Seymour was arrested, along with Sharrington, Fowler (who was Lord Seymour's contact in the Privy Chamber) and several of Elizabeth's household.[45] The investigation was very thorough, and lasted more than a month. A list of thirty-three articles of accusation was drawn up. Several of the depositions were very telling against him, particularly those of Sharrington and Fowler, but more importantly the testimony of the young king himself demonstrated the nature of his ambition. Early in February Somerset had written to Sir Philip Hoby, even before the depositions were complete, to say that it was clear that his brother had tried to take control of the king and to move 'plain sedition' in Parliament. When the examinations were considered by the council on 22 February, it was unanimously agreed that Thomas Seymour was 'sore charged of divers and sundry articles of high treason ... against the King's Majesty's person and his royal crown'. It was therefore agreed that all the available members of the council, and that included the Lord Protector, would go to the Tower and read the articles to Seymour, inviting him to defend himself.[46] This was duly done on the 23rd, but Seymour declined to make any answer unless or until he was brought to trial and his accusers were produced against him. This result was then reported to the king, and Somerset declared how sorrowful a case this was to him. However, his duty to the king must take precedence over any family feelings which he might have for his brother, and he therefore had no alternative but to endorse the council's report. In reply the king agreed that the charges against the Lord Admiral amounted to treason, and that in spite of the fact that he was his uncle, he willed that they should proceed to justice against him.[47]

The council determined to secure an Act of Attainder against him rather than bringing him to trial before the court of peers. This was allegedly to spare the Duke of Somerset's feelings, but the truth is probably that they were apprehensive as to what kind of defence he might be able to mount in open court so close had he been during his earlier interrogations. The bill of attainder was introduced into the House of Lords the day after the king's declaration. On 25 February, the record of the depositions was read and the judges gave their opinion that they amounted to manifest treason. Two days later, in the absence of the Lord Protector, the bill passed unanimously, and proceeded to the Lower House on the 28th. At first some members of the Commons wanted Seymour to be summoned to give his defence, but on 4 March the king scotched that idea, saying that if further evidence was required, the Lords would provide it. The measure passed its third reading later that same day, and on 10 March the council waited upon the king to know his pleasure concerning the carrying out of the sentence. Edward replied that they should proceed as they desired without further troubling him or the Lord Protector.[48] On the 17th the Bishop of Ely was sent to Seymour to prepare him for death, and the execution was carried out at the Tower on the 19th. The Duke of Somerset later acquired an evil reputation for permitting the death of his brother, but at the time all the evidence suggests that the council was both sympathetic and supportive. Seymour was a wild and irresponsible man, and although there may be some doubt as to whether his actions actually constituted a danger to the state, there is no doubt that they were technically treasonable, and that the former Lord Admiral deserved his fate. Hugh Latimer later denounced him as a godless man, and W. K. Jordan has cast doubt upon his mental stability, but neither of these considerations affected his conviction at the time.[49] Sir William Sharrington, who after an abject confession was convicted by attainder at the same time, was nevertheless pardoned later in the same year and was able to buy back his lands including his house at Lacock, where he was to die in 1553.

The Lord Protector was not out of the woods. Inflation, resulting from the debasement of the coinage in the last years of Henry VIII's reign, was making the economic situation worse and causing social unrest. At the same time he had become haughty, ignoring the advice of his fellow councillors, insulting his friends, and abusing those who disagreed with him. On 8 May, his old friend and ally William Paget wrote to him,

If I did not love you so deeply I might hold my peace as others do, but I am forced to say that unless you show your pleasure more quietly in debate with others and graciously hear their opinions when you require them, there will be sorry consequences and you will be first to repent ...[50]

Unfortunately Somerset ignored this advice, and handled the troubles of the summer of 1549 without reference to the wishes of the council. He had committed himself to a major offensive against Scotland and was most reluctant to divert the troops he was gathering on the border. The disturbances of the summer of 1548 had been swiftly contained, but those of 1549 were altogether more serious and widespread. In May and June there were riots in most of the counties of lowland England, which were put down by the local gentry and nobility. In Lincolnshire and Cambridgeshire these could have been serious, except that the Bishop of Ely moved smartly against them, and in West Sussex the Earl of Arundel used his prestige to affect a reconciliation. In Wiltshire and Hampshire there were riots which were contained with difficulty, and in Oxfordshire things got completely out of hand until Lord Grey arrived in July with mercenary troops on his way to the West Country.[51] As the king put it in his journal,

The people began to rise in Wiltshire, where Sir William Herbert did put them down, overrun them and slay them. Then they rose in Sussex, Hampshire, Kent, Gloucestershire, Suffolk, Warwickshire, Essex, Hertfordshire, a piece of Leicestershire, Worcestershire and Rutlandshire, where by fair persuasions, partly of honest men among themselves, and partly by gentlemen, they were often appeased ...[52]

Somerset was extremely reluctant to use force against these troubles partly because he did not have much available, and partly out of a genuine sympathy with the protesters' demands. He therefore issued a series of proclamations promising redress and ordering all those who had assembled to return to their homes. This attitude disgusted many members of the council, particularly the powerful Earl of Warwick, who put it down to mere spinelessness. They wanted a more robust defence of the gentry position, which was everywhere under attack, and had no time for the sympathies of their leader with his commonwealth views.[53] Only in three places did the Protector act with belated resolution. The first of these was the south-west, where the commons of Bodmin, stirred up by conservative clergy, began a wholehearted assault on the government's religious policy. The Cornishmen were not especially motivated by dislike of the gentry, and were led in a sense by one of their number, Humphrey Arundell. At the beginning of June they spilled out into Devon and joined forces with the formidable rising which had been occasioned at Sampford Courtenay through an attempt by the local parish priest to obey the royal injunctions and introduce the English Prayer Book in the Whit Sunday ritual. He had been compelled to revert to the traditional Latin Mass, and a local gentleman who had attempted to pacify the mob had been murdered on the following day, 9 June.[54] This violence was widely welcomed in the county, and the riotous assembly, which was mainly motivated by religion and led by conservative clergy, produced a series of demands which were forwarded to the council before settling down to besiege Exeter. The local gentry were swept aside, and the noble family which might have exercised a restraining influence had been removed with the execution of the Marquis of Exeter in 1538. The Courtenays were sadly missed in the south-west at this juncture, and a major rebellion was under way.

At first Somerset tried to address this situation in his accustomed fashion with conciliatory proclamations, but this, as the demands had made clear, was a wholly different situation. Meanwhile

Cranmer had replied to the rebels' demands, pointing out to them the error of their ways and not promising anything very much by way of concession.[55] There was, however, a substantial Devonshire gentleman at court at that time in the person of Sir Peter Carew, and Somerset decided to send him to negotiate with the dissidents, to see what could be done. Carew made a mess of his mission when his men set fire to some barns at Sampford Courtenay, and was forced to retreat in some disorder. After another unhelpful memorandum to the justices of the peace for the county, on 26 June, Somerset was at last compelled to act and sent Lord John Russell, who had received much of the Courtenay lands, to confront the rebels with a substantial force, most of which had been retrieved from the Scottish borders. John, Lord Russell was an elderly and cautious man who advanced only slowly, and sent repeated requests to the council for reinforcements. His instructions did not help very much. These, which were issued about 25 June, urged him to recruit local troops in Wiltshire and Hampshire, which he was most reluctant to do on account of their unreliability.[56] In fact the council sent him what few mercenaries could be spared, and these arrived in dribs and drabs during the first days of July. After an interval spent at Mohuns Ottery, during which Russell sent out probing attacks against Arundell's forces besieging Exeter, he received the reinforcements for which he had been pressing. At the beginning of August Lord Grey joined him with the 2,000 or 3,000 men who had been mopping up in Oxfordshire, and at long last he felt himself strong enough to move against the main rebel army. For two or three days, from 3 to 6 August, he fought to dislodge them from their entrenched positions before Exeter, until at last Arundell broke off the engagement and retreated towards Clyst St Mary, his forces having taken a terrible mauling from the royalists' greater firepower.[57] On 10 August Russell made his formal entry into the city, whose sturdy resistance had made all the difference to the outcome, because if Exeter had fallen the whole situation in the region would have been transformed. A few days later he broke the remaining rebel force at Clyst St Mary and the rebellion was over. Having fought cautiously, Russell now permitted himself the indulgence of executing the large numbers of prisoners who had been taken during the battles of the last week or so, and thus earned for himself a fearsome reputation in the south-west. The council instructed him to deploy most of his forces along the south coast for defence against the French, who had just declared war, and Russell did this with his local levies, but not with his German and Italian mercenaries, whom he kept together for their own safety in returning slowly towards London.[58]

The second rebellion of the summer of 1549 was in the totally different circumstances of East Anglia. Here the issue was not religion but land use, particularly the enclosing of common land by the gentry, and the enemy was not the council in London, or the Lord Protector, but the local commission of the peace. The enclosure of land was a symbol rather than a real cause of this discontent, because the throwing down of hedges was an easy gesture to implement, while the misuse of common land was much harder to demonstrate. Norfolk was an area of rich agriculture, with many small landholders and much old enclosure. It was also an area, like Devon, where the principal peer had been eliminated, and there was a consequent power vacuum which the local gentry were quite unable to fill. The Duke of Norfolk was in the Tower under sentence of death and his estates in the county had been redistributed. Princess Mary had received the bulk of these, but she was in no way involved in these disturbances, and the local gentry, who had also received a proportion, proved quite unable to organise themselves when faced with the threat.[59] On the night of 20 June the commons of Attelborough, near Thetford, removed some recent enclosures, and a few days later the disturbances spread to nearby Wymondham, where the target was a lawyer named Flowerdew. In an attempt to divert the attention of the rioters he then drew their attention to some similar enclosures which had been made by Robert Kett. Kett then, to everyone's astonishment, joined the protestors, destroyed his own enclosure and assumed the leadership of the movement. He was a man of some substance, and not at all associated with commonwealth ideology, but he now found himself at the head of several hundred men who encamped at Bowthorpe a few miles from Norwich on 9 July.[60] There the sheriff, Sir Edward Windham, visited them and ordered them to disperse, an order which they ignored. Kett's force had by now been augmented to several thousand drawn from all over the county, and on 12 July he set up his camp on Mousehold Heath, overlooking the city. From there he entered into negotiations with Thomas Codd, the mayor, who vainly urged him to disperse, and sent a list of demands to the council. These were mostly concerned with minor agrarian grievances, and with the misdeeds of the gentry and clergy. Unlike in the negotiations with those from the south-west, religion was scarcely mentioned, and the whole movement gives the impression of having been engendered rather by the slowness with which Somerset's reforms had been implemented than any dissatisfaction with the reforms themselves.[61] The Lord Protector responded with the offer of a pardon on condition of dispersal, an offer which Kett treated with contempt, and the government realised that a military effort would be called for. At the end of July Somerset scraped together 1,800 mercenaries, and appointed the totally inexperienced Marquis of Northampton to lead them. Ignoring instructions, he entered Norwich on 30 July and was driven out by rebel forces on the following day. Hastily regrouping in the field, he then fell back to London, leaving Kett in complete control of Norwich, where he set up an auxiliary camp in the cathedral grounds.[62]

On 3 August, the council met to consider the significance of this rebuff and decided that only a military victory would redeem the situation. Somerset originally intended to lead this second force himself, but was persuaded instead to appoint John Dudley, Earl of Warwick to this role. Warwick was in the north at the time, but acknowledged his new instructions on 10 August. The garrison of Boulogne was reduced and the north was drained of forces to give him an estimated army of 6,000 foot and 1,500 horse. Moving with great speed and efficiency, he then entered Norfolk, setting up his headquarters at Intwood, three miles south-west of Norwich, on the 23rd. Warwick's first move was to attempt negotiations on the basis of a conditional pardon, which Kett was retrained by his own men from accepting.[63] The fact is that Robert Kett, who had organised his camp brilliantly and administered justice with an even hand, was no soldier, and his men were not under military discipline. On the 26th, cut off from supplies out of the city, he moved from his fortified camp to a nearby valley, where he was attacked and his men slaughtered by the highly organised royal forces. Kett fled the field and on the following day was captured about eight miles away. Warwick then began his mopping-up operation, hanging several of those who had been taken in the battle. However he resisted pressure from the local gentry to carry out a bloodbath by martial law. 'There must be measure kept,' he declared, 'and above all things in punishment men must not exceed.' He was only too well aware that this pressure arose from a sense of guilt at not having done more to resist the rising at an earlier stage.[64] In the event Robert and William Kett, his brother, were sent to London for trial and were eventually returned to the county for execution. On the 29th Warwick and his retinue joined the citizens of Norwich for a service of thanksgiving in St Peter Mancroft church before returning to London where he was soon involved in the intrigues which would lead to the fall of the Protector in October.

By the end of July 1549 the Duke of Somerset was unpopular with his council colleagues, whom he had slighted, and with the gentry and nobility as a whole. They felt that he had been unduly lenient with protestors against what they considered to be their lawful rights, and had not defended their interests in the way which they expected. He was arrogant and aloof, ignoring the good advice even of friends like Sir William Paget, and had taken his duty to defend the poor altogether too seriously. They also objected to the money which he was spending on his houses, at Syon and at Somerset House in the Strand, and to the way in which he was demolishing redundant monasteries to supply the building stone for his projects, although this was a normal practice. Some of this trouble was attributed to his wife, who was, if anything, more unpopular than he was himself, and who had taken Sir Thomas Smith to task for the 'gorgeous apparel' in which his wife had appeared, a reprimand which Sir Thomas had taken personally.[65] The duke was also accused of enriching himself at the cost of the state; a reference to the 8,000-mark salary which he had been allocated as Lord Protector in May 1547. His gross annual income by July 1549 was of the region of £12,730, which was a lot for a subject but by no means excessive for a head of government. By the beginning of August these discontents were being reflected in clandestine discussions among members of the council aimed at limiting the Lord Protector's powers, or even removing him from office altogether. The protagonists of these discussions appear to have been the earls of Arundel and Southampton, who were inclined to be conservative in their religious views, and this has led to the description of their activities as a 'catholic plot'.[66] They do indeed seem to have approached Princess Mary for her support against the Protector, but to have been told that she had no desire to become involved, and the fact that they were joined in their deliberations by the Earl of Warwick in early September would seem to kill that interpretation. If there was one thing that Warwick was not it was religiously conservative. Friction was evident in relations between Warwick and the Protector in mid-September, after the former's return from Norfolk, but that can be attributed to his failure to disband his forces as instructed, and does not necessarily imply that the duke already knew that a conspiracy was afoot against him. It was not until the end of September that Somerset's letters to Russell, returning with his forces from Devon, indicate any awareness of the crisis which was soon to engulf him.

On 30 September the Protector issued a proclamation instructing all soldiers to go to their place of posting, and to avoid the City of London, which is the first sign of such an awareness, and on 3 October eleven of the original executors of Henry VIII's will gathered in London.[67] The Protector was with the king at Hampton Court, but only a handful of the council were with him, and the signs were now distinctly ominous. Then on 5 October Somerset made a serious mistake. He issued a proclamation calling upon all subjects to assemble at Hampton Court to defend the king and his 'entirely beloved uncle' against a most dangerous conspiracy which was levied against them.[68] This allowed the London Lords, as they were now known, to denounce him as a populist, and thus rally the city authorities behind them. With no response from Russell or Herbert and having only 500 household troops at his disposal, Somerset realised that his position at Hampton Court was untenable, and on the evening of the 6th he moved the court to the greater security of Windsor Castle, giving young Edward a bad fright (and probably a cold) on the way. Over the next few days a propaganda battle then ensued between the London Lords and the Protector for the allegiance of the city, where a strong popular party favoured the duke but could not prevail against the mayor and Common Council. On the 7th the Lords addressed the king directly, professing their allegiance and complaining that the

Duke of Somerset would not listen to their good advice, but insisted upon following his own councils. The decisive letter, however, was sent by Russell on the 8th, in which he cast in his lot with the London Lords and thus deprived Somerset of his last hope of effective military assistance.[69] On the 9th Sir Philip Hoby, who was trusted by both sides, was engaged to try and broker a deal. Warwick wrote to Cranmer and Paget, who had remained with the duke at Windsor, urging them to persuade him to see sense. At the same time, Somerset wrote to Warwick exhorting him to remember their long friendship. Deprived of all other resources, he gave way on the 10th, stepping down from his office as Lord Protector and withdrawing his men from the king's presence.[70] It would be interesting to know exactly what bargain was struck between Warwick, Cranmer and Paget which finally persuaded him to this course of action, but it is reasonable to suppose that the earl undertook to preserve the religious settlement which Somerset had worked so hard to put in place and which obviously meant a great deal to him. Later that same day, Sir Anthony Wingfield was ordered to go to Windsor and to detain the Duke of Somerset and his chief associates in custody, and early on the 11th he arrived with 500 horse to carry out his mission. Along with the duke were detained his eldest son, Edward, his younger brother, Sir Henry, and Stanhope, Smith and Cecil, but Wingfield was able to report that the king was quite safe, although desperate to get away from Windsor. On the 13th the London Lords made their own way to the castle, and held a very full meeting of the council. Having briefly interrogated Somerset, they decided to send him to the Tower, where he was taken under heavy escort on the 14th. Edward returned to Hampton Court, and the Privy Council assumed responsibility for directing the nation's affairs. A highly coloured version of the *coup d'état* was then prepared and sent to ambassadors abroad, where the general reaction appears to have been one of relief.

7

THE END OF THE DUKE OF SOMERSET

The Earl of Warwick did not immediately emerge as the new leader of government. Towards the end of October Van der Delft believed that power in the council lay with the earls of Arundel and Southampton, and was at a loss to explain the continued presence of Cranmer, or why the Mass had not been restored.[1] It was only later, with the advent of the Marquis of Dorset and one or two other reformers onto the council, that the true nature of the new regime began to become apparent, and the Protestants led by John Hooper began to breathe more easily. Warwick was not concerned with the trappings of power, and did not assume the title of Protector, partly because that title was now discredited, and partly because he wished to distance himself as far as possible from Somerset's policies. He called himself Lord President of the Council. He was, however, concerned with the realities of power, and was aware that the council's existing mandate might be invalidated by the removal of the office of Protector, and consequently caused a new commission to be drawn up in the king's name, authorising its continued exercise of power. The king recognised 'how much unable yet for a time we are for want of perfect knowledge and experience to take unto our own [hands] the direction of affairs'[2] and authorised the new commission, but it is not certain that it was ever enrolled. It did, however, have the effect of confirming past actions, including the deposition of the Duke of Somerset, and gave a legal basis for the continuation of the council's power until Edward came of age.

Somerset, meanwhile, was in the Tower along with several of his associates, and the undertaking given at the time of his surrender that he would not be harmed either in his person or his estate was beginning to look distinctly fragile. He was interviewed in a hostile fashion by councillors among whom the earls of Arundel and Southampton featured prominently, and a series of twenty-nine articles was drawn up against him. By the end of November it was clear that a power battle was developing in the council over his fate. The Earl of Arundel wished to use Somerset's earlier friendship with the Earl of Warwick as a means of discrediting them both. 'Traitors ... and worthy to die by my judgement,' he is alleged to have said.[3] Warwick therefore became committed to securing the release of the duke, and forced a showdown shortly before Christmas where, 'with a grim visage' and his hand on his sword, he accused his opponents of seeking the execution of Somerset as a means of getting rid of him also.[4] Dudley enjoyed majority support on the council by this time, and the issue was not in doubt, but it was sealed a few days later by the removal of Arundel, Southampton and Sir Richard Southwell from the board. Arundel and Southwell were incarcerated on fictitious charges, and Southampton was ordered to keep his house. It was soon communicated to Somerset that his submission to the charges against him would be the price of his release, and he agreed to submit. The articles seem to have been based on propaganda notes kept by the London Lords while the tension was at its height. Only half a dozen of them touched the real nature of the case against him, and in accepting them he confessed to having been arrogant and insensitive while in power, hot-tempered and stubborn on political issues.[5] None of them touched the treason of which he had been wildly accused during the crisis, and therefore amounted to no more than a confession of ineptitude, which was an acceptable price for him to pay. On 14 January 1550 he was formally deprived of the office of Lord Protector, and on the 27th he signed the articles of submission, which he had previously agreed to do. A few days later he was released on a recognisance of £10,000, and on the condition that he reside with his family at either Syon or Sheen, and remain within four miles of his chosen residence. On 18 February he received the royal pardon for whatever offence he was deemed to have committed, and his estates were restored to him.[6] For about six weeks the duke remained under house arrest, being barred from access to the king or the council. However, he was not without friends. On 25 March the Duchess of Suffolk wrote to Sir William Cecil in response to a letter from him inviting her to try her intercessionary powers on the Earl of Warwick, saying that it would not be necessary as she understood that Somerset was shortly to be restored to the council. The duchess's information was entirely correct, and after dining amicably with the king and the council at Greenwich on 8 April, on the 10th he resumed his place at the council board. On 7 May Somerset attended his first council meeting, and on the 11th his access to the Privy Chamber was restored to him.[7] So by the middle of May he was back where he had been before the coup against him, except, of course, that he was no longer dominant. The Earl of Warwick had assumed the title of Lord President of the Council back in January, and had no intention of sharing that position with anyone.

It soon became apparent that there was no room for two such opinionated men in the same team, particularly when they disagreed over so many political issues. The Earl of Warwick had signed a peace treaty with France in March 1550, which resulted in the return of Boulogne to the French for a ransom of 400,000 crowns. Somerset had welcomed the money, but was opposed on principle to the surrender of Boulogne and to the amicable relations which ensued. When in power his policy had always been one of friendship with the Emperor, insofar as was possible, and of hostility to France. That was caused largely by his concern with Scotland, but that policy was now abandoned also. Scotland was included in the Treaty of Boulogne. English attempts to secure compliance with the Treaty of Greenwich were given up, and the English garrisons withdrawn. French influence predominated north of the border until 1560, and it is not surprising that Somerset was bitter about what he saw as a betrayal of his country's interests.[8] He maintained his allegiance to the moderate position adopted by Cranmer in the First Book of Common Prayer, and to a tolerant attitude towards Princess Mary in the exercise of her private Mass. Warwick adopted a much more rigorous evangelical attitude on both these issues, encouraging such radical preachers as John Hooper, and coming down severely on the princess for infringements of the privacy rule. He presided over the confiscation of Church goods, and showed himself intolerant of even the most moderate Catholic opposition. Above all, he supported the gentry position on all issues of social and economic reform, reversing the commonwealth tendencies which Somerset had shown in his dealings with the rebels of 1549, and which he had not hesitated to blame for the government's delayed response to those insurrections. So there were fundamental differences of policy and outlook between these two men which made it impossible for them to work together, however genuinely both may have desired to do so.

The best evidence for the reality of this desire is the marriage settlement entered into in April 1550 between John, Lord Lisle,

Warwick's eldest son, and Anne Seymour, Somerset's daughter.[9] This was a marriage which the Duchess of Suffolk had also wanted for her young son Henry, and it is testimony to Somerset's desire to mend fences with his former friend that he risked crossing the duchess in order to achieve it. The marriage took place in June, and the king was present:

> ... which done and a fair dinner made and dancing finished, the king and the ladies went into two chambers made of boughs, where first he saw six gentlemen of one side and six of another run the course of the field, twice over ...[10]

No expense was spared. However, as an attempt to find common ground between the earl and the duke, and establish a basis for mutual cooperation, it was an obvious failure. Although he could dominate the council when Warwick was absent, Somerset no longer found that that he could influence its decisions by persuasion. This was partly because his own credit was no longer what it had been, and partly because the council now contained many of Warwick's friends, such as the Marquis of Dorset. Moreover it was only too easy to represent moves of opposition by Somerset and his friends as directed against the security of the state. On 25 June 1550 Warwick sought out Richard Whalley, one of Somerset's less discreet servants, in order to convey a warning to the duke. He was, Warwick argued, showing much the same disposition that he had shown during the days of his protectorate, arguing obstinately for the release of Stephen Gardiner, 'which the whole council doth much mislike'. Nor was he as much in credit with the king as he believed, and was 'fondly persuaded' by his friends.[11] If only he would work through the council, he might have all that he could reasonably desire, but by going it alone he was risking ruining himself, as well as the causes for which he was striving. Interestingly this warning was conveyed through Whalley to Cecil, as Warwick realised that it would be, secure in the knowledge that Cecil would pass it on to Somerset, as indeed he did. Cecil was high in the confidence of both parties at this stage, and most of the correspondence relating to Somerset's position passed through him. There is, however, no evidence that the duke was trying to build a party for himself and his efforts on behalf of Gardiner and the Princess Mary were totally ineffectual. Somerset seems to have assumed that the remedy for his isolation lay in the reconvening of Parliament, and a fierce battle developed between the two peers over that. During Somerset's absence from the council during August, Warwick persuaded it that Parliament should not be summoned until January 1551, and while Warwick was away during October an earlier date was agreed upon. This was cancelled upon the earl's return, and Parliament was not in fact reconvened until January 1552, when the whole sad story of their rivalry was over.[12]

Meanwhile a test of their relative prestige had arisen over the demise of Somerset's mother, and the king's grandmother, Margery Seymour. Margery had been a widow since 1536, and had lived frugally and privately since then. There is no reference to her in the public records after the accession of her grandson, nor did the king notice her death in his chronicle. Somerset, however, brought the event to the attention of the council, to enquire whether a state funeral would be appropriate, considering her status. It would be customary, he argued, for the court to go into mourning for a stipulated period, and might provoke gossip if the custom was not followed.[13] The council, however, ruled against him on the grounds that the wearing of mourning 'profiteth not the dead and harmeth those of little faith'. They referred the matter to the king, who ruled that the duke's private grief should be confined to his household, and dispensed him from the wearing of public mourning, because such a demonstration was more a matter of pomp than edification.[14] Such a verdict undoubtedly sprang from Edward's Protestant convictions, but it still constituted a weakening of Somerset's position in the council, and an additional warning that he no longer enjoyed the fruits of power. During the autumn of 1550 the Imperial ambassador reported that the duke was for the first time deliberately trying to recruit supporters, and that he was encouraging rumours to the effect that the social and economic woes of the country were entirely the responsibility of the Earl of Warwick. These matters, he reported, would be brought before Parliament when it next met, with a view to persuading the members that the country was oppressed with unnecessary taxes, and that the council in its present form was led by selfish men who disregarded the common good.[15] It was probably for that reason that the Earl of Warwick strove successfully to defer the reconvening of Parliament.

By the winter of 1550/51 there are signs that the division in the council was spreading to the peerage at large. It was rumoured that the Duke of Somerset would go to the north in search of the support of the conservative peers there, and reported that the earls of Derby and Shrewsbury had quarrelled with Warwick. A list of peers drawn up sometime before March 1551 is thought to indicate which were considered to be reliable supporters of the earl, and a letter by the Earl of Shrewsbury to a friend in London, dated 17 February, is even more revealing. The recipient was almost certainly a member of the court, and in his letter the earl expressed his disquiet at being canvassed on his attitude towards Somerset and Warwick.[16] It was being suggested, he wrote, that by appearing equally friendly to both he was endeavouring to set them more at variance. Such a rumour was completely untrue, and his sole concern was to preserve unity and concord within the realm. Shrewsbury had heard reports of the discord between the two, but he doubted this. They were both too wise to fall out publicly, and in any case were bound by the marriage tie between them. He trusted that this was so, because any falling out at that level would do irreparable damage to the structure of authority in England. This was a careful letter, written by one watching his words, because Shrewsbury had never been an overt supporter of the Earl of Warwick, and was not so now, but he was aware of the construction which could be placed upon his words. Less cautious was Richard Whalley, who appears to have canvassed several Members of Parliament as to the desirability of restoring the Protectorate by statute. The Earl of Rutland reported this conversation to the council, which examined them both on 16 February, before committing Whalley to the Fleet.[17] It is obvious that the earl was being sounded out as to whether he was a supporter of Warwick or Somerset, but Whalley denied everything and was released early in April. Nevertheless, the spring of 1551 was troubled. Sir Ralph Vane, a partisan of Somerset, was arrested at the end of March, having picked a personal quarrel with Warwick, and several foreign observers thought that a political upheaval was imminent. On 24 April the king recorded in his chronicle that

> the lords sat at London and banqueted one another this day and
> [for] three days after to show agreement amongst them, whereas
> discord was bruited, and somewhat to look to the punishment of
> talebearers and apprehending of evil persons ...[18]

Rumours of dissention were clearly not confined to the diplomatic community, and the council felt it desirable to suppress them in this fairly high-profile manner. Thereafter a kind of calm descended on the council, and in June the king exchanged orders with Henry II of France, sending the Marquis of Northampton to bear the

Garter to Paris. In July the *Maréchal* de S. Andre returned the compliment, and on the 14th was met by the Duke of Somerset, who conducted him to Hampton Court.[19] There on the 16th he invested the king with the Order of St Michael, and was afterwards lavishly entertained. St Andre was a huge success as a courtier, and supped and hunted with Edward for several days, earning universal plaudits for his graciousness and skill. The king was obviously committed to Warwick's policy of friendship with France, and this was not good news for Somerset, who was opposed to such ideas. The latter was, however, unusually assiduous in his attendance at council meetings during July and August, and toward the end of August was entrusted with forces to dispel those assembled against the gentry in the region of Wokingham, executing several for their offences.[20] At the same time a fresh contretemps arose with Princess Mary over her Mass, and several of her servants were imprisoned to her great indignation. The duke's attitude to those events is not on record, but it is reasonable to suppose that he was not happy with them. Then during September Somerset was ill and away from the council, which gave the Earl of Warwick the opportunity to complete his plans for the final overthrow of one who had become in his eyes a terminal nuisance. Somerset's stock had meanwhile fallen very low, as councillors sensed a coming crisis. The evangelical group was offended by his persistent efforts on behalf of Stephen Gardiner, and his staunchest friend, Sir William Paget was upset by his refusal to accept good advice on his social and economic policies. Sir William Cecil, who probably sensed which way the wind was blowing, also withdrew his support, and even so robust a supporter as the Duchess of Suffolk was alienated.[21] Nor was the king affectionate towards his uncle. Having been upset by the tight rein on which the had been kept financially, he had then been distressed by being whisked off to Windsor on that chilly night in October 1549, an episode which seems to have killed off any lingering regard which he may have felt towards his kinsman. Moreover, following that episode his Privy Chamber had been carefully selected for him by the Earl of Warwick, and he is unlikely to have heard any complimentary words relating to the Duke of Somerset from those close about him. There is also evidence that he was much influenced by the earl, who was responsible for his political education, and who took great pains to ensure that he was kept informed about events. William Thomas, who helped him with his school exercises, and wrote position papers for him, was a dependent of Warwick's, and could be relied upon always to present views which were acceptable to him.[22] The only person who seems to have been quite unaware of the precariousness of his position was Somerset himself.

It seem likely that plans for proceeding against the duke were completed by the end of September, when letters were despatched to absent members of the council, requiring them to resort to the court with 'all convenient speed' for consultations about the king's affairs. On the same day a similar letter was sent to Somerset, requiring his presence also, in spite of the death from sweating sickness in his household which had kept him at home for the previous month.[23] The duke duly responded, then a few days later, on 7 October, Sir Thomas Palmer dropped his bombshell. He sought out the Earl of Warwick and revealed to him a conspiracy implicating the duke. The allegation was that on 23 April previous Somerset intended to ride north to raise the people, because he feared that his life was in danger, but had been deterred from such a course by Sir William Herbert and Lord Grey. Palmer also asserted that at a later date Somerset was privy to a conspiracy to summon Warwick and Northampton to a banquet at which they were to be murdered, while Sir Ralph Vane and others seized control of London and the Tower.[24] These wildly implausible accusations came from a man who was already a known adherent of the Earl of Warwick, and were never pressed, but they were sufficient to set in train the proceedings against the duke. On 10 October Jehan Scheyfve, the Imperial ambassador, reported that Warwick and his adherents were weaving a plot against Somerset, and that his arrest was imminent. The earl had secured himself by careful military preparations, and Paget, the duke's most loyal defender, was already in detention. Nevertheless the next stage in this drama was not the arrest of Somerset, but the promotion of the Earl of Warwick, who on 11 October was elevated to the title of Duke of Northumberland, a ceremony in which the Earl of Wiltshire was promoted to the marquisate of Winchester, Sir William Herbert was created Earl of Pembroke and William Cecil knighted.[25] At these ceremonies the former Protector played his accustomed role as if nothing were amiss. Being deprived of reliable sources of information, Somerset seems to have remained blissfully unaware of the trap which was being laid for him, until on the 14th he confessed to Cecil that he suspected some evil intention. He had always trusted Sir William, but the latter now gave him a brief and cold reply, which can only have increased his anxiety.[26] He then apparently challenged Sir Thomas Palmer, who denied all knowledge of the events of the previous week. The crunch came on 16 October when, having dined with the king, Somerset was arrested. Edward had already been briefed what to expect, and seems to have been totally convinced by the charges levied against his uncle, for whom he had scant regard. The people of London were harder to persuade, and the council's best propaganda efforts were reserved for attempting to do so, including a meeting with the city officials and the wardens of the livery companies on 22 October. At that meeting the council argued that Somerset had conspired to destroy the most substantial citizens, and required watch and ward to be kept day and night.[27] Nevertheless support for Somerset remained high, and the Imperial ambassador was of the opinion that the Duke of Northumberland, driven by ambition, had deliberately deceived the king as to Somerset's guilt.

Meanwhile Palmer had added to his testimony the charge that Sir Ralph Vane had been intending to take over the city by arousing the apprentices with the cry of 'Liberty, liberty', an accusation which was clearly designed to gain the sympathy of the city authorities, for whom apprentice power was a thing of ill omen.[28] During early November the interrogation of the prisoners in the Tower continued, the Earl of Arundel confessing that he had discussed the arrest of the Earl of Warwick several times with Somerset, but denied that any harm was intended to him. At the same time William Crane, who was a servant of the duke, alleged, probably under torture, that the venue for the assassination of Warwick and Northampton was to be Paget's house, but this was not supported by the testimony of any other witness.[29] The Earl of Arundel claimed that the *coup d'état* which was planned was to be ratified by Parliament, but this too was unsupported by other testimony. Altogether the case assembled by the Council against Somerset was feeble, and did not amount to treason. The assassination attempt was not pursued, and although Paget was imprisoned in the Tower on 8 November he was not charged with any such offence. Aware that awkward questions might well be asked, Northumberland was determined to dispose of his rival before Parliament reconvened in January, and set about preparing an indictment, appointing a special commission of judges for that purpose on 16 November.[30] The result was a tissue of fictions, including the allegation that on 20 April at Somerset House the duke had conspired to seize the king's person and to exercise the royal power himself. It was for this purpose that the Earl of Warwick was to be imprisoned and the citizens of London stirred to revolt. On 23 November the king recorded that the Marquis of Winchester had been appointed High Steward, and the court assembled at Westminster on 1 December, twenty-eight peers being gathered for that purpose. Somerset didn't just plead not guilty. He denounced Palmer as a personal enemy, and poured scorn on the notion that he could with the limited resources available to him have taken control of the City of London.[31] The peers obviously disagreed among themselves, and it is recorded that there was considerable discussion, in the course of which the Duke of Northumberland declared that no plot against himself should be construed as High Treason. Eventually, and on a divided vote, Somerset was found not guilty of treason, but guilty of felony for assembling men at his house and refusing to disband them.[32] The duke made no rejoinder to this verdict beyond a plea for his wife and children, servants and debts, and so departed with the axe turned away from him to signify that he was not guilty of treason. Misinterpreting this gesture to mean that he was 'quit of all', the citizens of London who had assembled outside the hall let out a great shout that could be plainly heard at Charing Cross. Somerset clearly had a great deal of support in the city, and what the peers had really determined was that he was a great deal too dangerous to be left alive. A few days later, on 7 December, and in a deliberate attempt to overawe the city, the councillors assembled with their retinues in a muster amounting to over 700 men-at-arms, together with the Gentlemen Pensioners, well mounted and armed. The young king was there to review them, as they passed 'twice about St James's field'. Only the Imperial ambassador was unimpressed by this display, commenting that the muster was confused and the troops unseasoned.[33] However, both the city and the Duke of Somerset got the message; the latter knew that he must die before Parliament reassembled.

In addition to his fear of Parliament, the Duke of Northumberland seems to have been apprehensive that Edward would intervene on behalf of his uncle, and therefore planned as many distractions as possible over the Christmas period. Sir Thomas Cawarden, the Master of the Revels, was instructed to appoint George Ferrers as Lord of Misrule, to be present in the royal household for the whole holiday period from 24 December to 6 January, and to be given all the assistance that he might require in the short time available.[34] With the support of the council, and of Northumberland, Ferrers did a good job. There were masques, dances and above all jousts. The king was enthralled, particularly by the tilting held on 3 January, when eighteen sons of peers and courtiers ran six courses each, all 'accomplished right well'. Three days later the same group staged a tourney, and pleased the king further. Edward kept Christmas at Greenwich, but there is more than a suspicion that these revels were intended to distract the citizens of London also. This was particularly true of the play of *Riches and Youth* and of the masque which followed it on 6 January. The latter featured a scene showing a mock procession of clergy and bishops for the purpose of deriding the celebration of the Mass, an exercise which deeply shocked the ambassadors of France, Venice and the Empire, who beheld it, but would have pleased those Londoners who had made their way to Greenwich, no doubt hoping to be edified.[35] This, as Edward noted sadly, was the end of Christmas, but not quite the end of the attempts to distract him because on the 17th another joust was organised to keep him entertained. Then on 21 January he returned to Westminster, well aware that his uncle was to be executed the following day, the instruction having been given on the 19th, with his full participation and consent. The Duke of Somerset was under no illusions; he did not expect mercy either from his nephew or the Duke of Northumberland, and had composed his mind by Bible reading and by private devotions. He was warned that he was to die while Edward was still on his way back from Greenwich, and the citizens of London were required at the same time to keep themselves and their servants within doors on the morning of the 22nd.[36] If this was intended to prevent a great crowd from assembling, then it failed utterly, and by seven o'clock in the morning several thousand had gathered on Tower Hill to witness the death of one who was to many of them a hero.

It was just before eight o'clock when Somerset was brought out of the Tower by the warden and the sheriff's officers, escorted by a contingent of the royal guard. He bore himself with great dignity, kneeling in prayer before delivering the customary oration to the people. In this he denied that he had ever offended the king either in word or deed, but died in obedience to the law. The Church, he thanked God, now conformed most closely to the primitive model which he urged his hearers to embrace as God's gift to England.[37] At this point there was a commotion in the crowd, caused apparently by the late arrival of some guards who had been assigned to the duty but had missed the time. Some thought that an attempt was being made to rescue Somerset, and others that a pardon had been brought. The spectators scattered, some falling into the Tower ditch. It was the duke who quietened the tumult, declaring that there would be no pardon, and that he was contented with his death. He then completed his oration, urging the crowd to be quiet lest they disturb his last moments, and knelt for the executioner's axe.[38] The spectators fell silent and many wept. On the 26th, much less dramatically, four of his principal associates were executed also. Sir Ralph Vane, Sir Thomas Arundell, Sir Miles Partridge and Sir Michael Stanhope; they were no more guilty of conspiracy than the duke had been, but their deaths aroused far less interest. Their property was distributed among the second-rank courtiers whose loyalty the Duke of Northumberland was anxious to buttress.[39] The Duke of Somerset was of course attainted in blood, his vast estates were forfeit to the Crown and were similarly redistributed over the next few years, leaving his widow her jointure to live upon and his son such limited lands as he had received in his own right. The king's reaction is most notoriously expressed in the brief entry in his chronicle – '[22 January 1552] the Duke of Somerset had his head cut off upon Tower Hill between eight and nine o'clock in the morning' – without a word of grief or regret.[40] The king appears from this to have been thoroughly convinced of his uncle's guilt, but an alternative tradition shows him in a much more sympathetic light. John Hayward, writing in the early seventeenth century, declared more fully,

> Upon the death of the Duke albeit the king gave no token of any ill distempered passion, as taking it not agreeable to majesty openly to declare himself, and albeit the lords had laboured with much variety of sports to dispel any dumpy thoughts which the remembrance of his uncle might raise, yet upon speech of him he would often sigh and let fall tears, sometimes holding opinion that his uncle had done nothing, or if he had it was very small and proceeded rather from his wife than from himself, and where then said he was the good nature of a nephew? Where was the clemency of a prince? Ah, how unfortunate have I been to those of my blood, my mother I slew at my birth, and since have made away two of her brothers and happily to make away for others against myself, was it ever known before that a king's uncle, a Lord Protector one whose fortunes had much advanced the honour of the realm, did lose his head for felony; for a felony neither clear in law and in fact weakly proved. Alas how falsely have I been abused? How weakly carried? How little I was master of my own judgement that both his death and the envy thereof must be laid upon me ...[41]

This expresses clearly the pious sentiments of a Reformation court, but where it actually comes from is not known. Perhaps it comes from an authentic tradition, or perhaps from mere conformity, but it certainly shows Edward in a much more sympathetic light than his chronicle entry, while explaining the latter's brevity.

The Duke of Somerset was a complex man, and very much a man of his times. He was ambitious and irascible, but he was also driven by a sense of duty. Duty to his young master, but also duty to the realm. He was very conscious of the royal responsibility to protect the poor, and of the tradition of doing that in previous reigns. It was that which made him receptive to the works of the commonwealth men, and set him on a collision course with the powerful gentry and nobility.[42] He was thus insufficiently aware that he was not the king, and that he depended upon the backing of the council to make his policies effective. It was this tendency to ride roughshod over his colleagues which brought about his initial downfall, rather than liberal ideas, which he did not have in any modern sense. He was a Protestant, but of a moderate variety, very much in tune with Cranmer's original Prayer Book of 1549 and thus not far from the evangelical reformers of the previous reign. How this would have related to Edward's increasing radicalism we cannot know, but it set him in opposition to the Earl of Warwick's religious policy after 1550. That he toyed with the idea of overthrowing Warwick and recovering power seems to be proved beyond doubt, but that he actually did anything about it is another matter. However between 1550 and 1551 he formed an alternative power focus to the earl in council, and Warwick could not risk the council becoming divided at such a sensitive time during a minority. He did his best to warn Somerset off, and in the end was justified in destroying him, although his method of doing so by bogus accusations and false charges of conspiracy was reprehensible. The duke was innocent as charged, but he was not altogether blameless, because he did seek to rebuild his power base, and refused to be warned of the dangers that he was running. This was not trivial, but whether it justified his execution is another matter. Given his arrogant temperament it is difficult to imagine him submitting to a terminal rustication, and the Duke of Northumberland (as he was by then) did not want to be bothered with him any longer. The king's role was clear, but limited. He must have approved of his uncle's removal, and signed his death warrant, but his private reaction may well have been more in accordance with Hayward's later tradition.[43] The Duke of Somerset was an easy man to respect but a difficult man to love, as even his duchess found from time to time.

8

THOMAS AND HENRY SEYMOUR

Thomas, the third surviving son of Sir John and Margery Seymour, was born at Wolf Hall in 1508 or 1509. It is not quite certain whether he was older or younger than his sibling Jane, but is usually assumed that he was the elder, it being the point of Henry's joke with Sir John that he only seemed to be capable of siring sons. Nothing is known of his childhood or upbringing, except what can be deduced from his later life. He was certainly literate in English, and probably in French, but had little or no Latin, which suggests a home-based education, similar to that which Edward had received. He was probably taught his letters by one of his father's chaplains, and his complete lack of interest in intellectual matters as an adult man, or in the world of ideas, indicates the limitations of his tutor's abilities. However, in spite of his junior status in the family, his father did not intend him for an academic career or for the priesthood, but rather for a life at court. At some point before 1530, probably about 1525 or 1526, he placed him in the service of the prominent courtier Sir Francis Bryan.[1] Bryan was also a kinsman, so this may have been a family arrangement. If so, it was a convenient one and Thomas, described as 'servant to Sir Francis Bryan', was rewarded in 1532 for bearing the king's letters to Bryan, then ambassador in France. There is no suggestion that he had actually accompanied Sir Francis on this mission, and his employment in this capacity probably indicates no more than that he was trusted at court. He may have had a minor attachment to the Privy Chamber, but this would have been unlikely for one identified as a courtier's servant. The king was very aware of the danger of divided loyalties. It was in the same year, in August 1532, that he received his first significant grant, that of Forester of Enfield Chase, which is a sufficient indication that his career did not depend upon that of his sister, who was still a lady-in-waiting to Queen Catherine at that point.[2] How long his dependence on Sir Francis Bryan lasted we do not know, but it must have been over by 2 October 1536, when Thomas was elevated to the rank of Gentleman of the Privy Chamber. This was undoubtedly connected to the fact that he was by then the king's brother-in-law, as were the grants which he received at the same time, notably the Receivership of the Lordship of Bromefield and Yale, and of the manors associated with that office.[3] Sir Francis was a man of influence, but it is unlikely that it extended to the Privy Chamber, and the most likely explanation of Thomas's appointment at this juncture is that he was on good terms with the new Chief Minister, Thomas Cromwell. His association with Cromwell later is well attested, and resulted in such grants as that of the stewardships of Chirk and Holt castles in Denbighshire in 1537, and of several manors and lordships in the Welsh Marches. He also received a number of manors from former monastic properties, and these too are more likely to have come via Cromwell's mediation rather than that of the queen.[4] Altogether he was to receive forty-eight manors in grants by the Crown, not as many as his brother, and not bringing him anywhere near Edward's landed income, but sufficient to satisfy him for the time being.

It seems to have been the birth of Prince Edward rather than Jane's marriage to the king which really transformed his position. He was one of the six gentlemen who held the canopy over the child at his christening on 15 October 1537, which was a mark of exceptional favour, and three days later he was knighted at the same ceremony which saw his brother created Earl of Hertford. There was no obvious reason for this dubbing, unless it relates to his sea service earlier in the year, and it can best be seen as a gesture of regard by the Lord Privy Seal. The queen was very sick by that time, and would not have been interested in such matters. In February 1537 Lord Lisle, the Deputy of Calais, was informed that Sir John Dudley (later the Duke of Northumberland) was going to the seas 'with the queen's brother and four of the king's ships' in a sweep against piracy.[5] Dudley was commissioned as Vice-Admiral, but there is no trace of a similar commission for Thomas, who was presumably one of the captains. His ship was the *Sweepstake*, and a fortnight later he turns up in that capacity, operating against Flemish pirates in the Channel. On 4 March, Sir Thomas Wingfield wrote to Edward's servant Richard Whalley:

> Tell my cousin Candish that Master Seymour, the Captain of the Sweepstake, thanks him for his cables, else had they died in foul weather ...[6]

This indicates a rescue operation of some kind, but we have no further details. For the next few weeks he joined with Dudley in sending back reports of their patrolling activities, but they seem to have enjoyed little success beyond forcing the pirates to transfer their activities from the Solent to the Straits of Dover. Four ships were just not enough to cover so much coastline. The whole fleet was mobilised in April, but that was a part of the general defence preparations, and it is not clear that it ever took to the seas.

Thomas's appearance as a captain at this juncture is something of a surprise, because being in charge of royal ship of 300 tons would have required a good deal of experience, and it is not at all clear where he got that from. Thomas must have been active on board the king's ships as a gentleman volunteer long before we get any notice of his being so, and how he doubled that with his activities at court remains something of a mystery. Equally mysterious is where he lived when not at court. Wolf Hall would have passed to his brother when his father died in 1536, and he does not seem to have lodged there. He probably rented a house in the London area, because it is unlikely that he kept any kind of establishment in his Welsh Marcher properties; they were too remote. It is possible that he maintained a house in one of the Berkshire or Essex properties which were granted to him in March 1538, but it cannot be shown that he did so.[7]

Although Thomas was by this time approaching thirty years of age, and as interested in the ladies as any man, he nevertheless remained unmarried. This unusual situation prompted the Duke of Norfolk to make a proposal on behalf of his daughter, the widowed Duchess of Richmond in 1537. Mary had been left a widow by the premature death of Henry's illegitimate son, the Duke of Richmond, in July 1536 at the age of seventeen, and Norfolk was undoubtedly trying to maintain the contact with the royal family that that marriage had brought about. Jane was still young, and might have had many years before her as queen. To be married to the king's brother-in-law would have brought many advantages, not only to Mary but also to her kindred, and that must be the reason why he concentrated on Jane's unmarried brother. Thomas Seymour was a personable man, and well endowed with the military virtues of courage and boldness, but that was hardly the point. His wealth was adequate for a Gentleman of the Privy Chamber, but no more, and that was not the point either.[8] Jane's premature death in October 1537 does not seem to have put off the duke, because although Thomas would no longer be the king's brother-in-law he would remain as uncle to the king's heir, and that would be almost equally advantageous. Unfortunately the lady herself was opposed to the whole idea, and although technically still a minor her wishes in so intimate a matter could not be ignored. Moreover her objections were fully endorsed by her brother the Earl of Surrey, who was acutely conscious of his lineage. To see his sister linked to so base a fellow as the fourth son of a Wiltshire squire was totally unacceptable to him, so between them the younger Howards killed off the negotiations, in spite of the fact that Seymour himself had been distinctly interested.[9] Surrey had a more imaginative role in mind for his sister. Why did she not take a leaf out of Anne Boleyn's book, and offer herself as the king's mistress? Once Jane was safely dead Henry would obviously need another woman, and might even marry her. However, such a proposal not only misread the king's intentions but also offended Mary's sense of propriety, so although it is not known what the duke thought of such a scheme, Mary's unwillingness effectively killed it off.[10]

Seymour was used in a sensitive diplomatic mission to Francis I in 1538, and apparently discharged his duties to Henry's satisfaction. His allowances were paid promptly, and more grants of former monastic property followed. In 1539 he was caught up in the general invasion scare, and raised 100 men for the king's service, although they seem never to have been deployed. He may have served with the fleet when that was mobilised, but the records are incomplete. The *Willoughby* was certainly placed on standby, but we do not know who commanded her on that occasion. In March 1540 he was one of the challengers in the tournaments which were then held, which was a mark of favour although Henry no longer took part, and he seems to have been quite untouched by the fall of his patron Thomas Cromwell in June. He had by then a recognised position of his own, both as a diplomat and as a soldier, but he was not a member of the council and therefore avoided any entanglement in the events of those days. On 30 April 1543 he was named along with Nicholas Wotton to be resident ambassador in the Low Countries, whence he sent dutiful reports until he was recalled in July to be marshall of the army which the king was intending to deploy in France.[11] In the event the king was preoccupied with Scottish affairs during that summer, and his royal army never assembled. Thomas did not serve on the Borders, but his post as Marshall seems to have been continued to the Boulogne campaign of 1544, in which he certainly served. Meanwhile marriage had entered his calculations again, only this time on his initiative rather than another's. The lady concerned was Catherine, Lady Latimer, better known by her maiden name of Catherine Parr. She had been born in about 1512, and was the eldest child of Sir Thomas Parr of Kendal in Westmorland and of Maude Green, whom he had married in about 1510.[12] Thomas was a courtier companion of the young king, and had been knighted at his coronation. He was thus somewhat similar in his antecedents to Sir Thomas Boleyn and Sir John Seymour, and might have enjoyed a similar career had he not died in 1517. Rather unusually Maud never remarried, and the circumstance of Catherine's upbringing are obscure. In 1529, when she was about seventeen she was married on her mother's initiative to Edward Borough, the son of Thomas, Lord Borough, a man of good prospects. Unfortunately Edward enjoyed the worst of health, and he died in 1532, leaving his twenty-year-old widow not only childless, but very possibly still a virgin.[13] By that time Maude was also dead, but the family rallied round and in 1533 Catherine married the forty-year-old John Neville, Lord Latimer of Snape. Neville had been married twice before and had grown children. She was an excellent stepmother and ran his great Yorkshire household with skill and determination, but was unavoidably mixed up in the Pilgrimage of Grace in 1536 while her husband was away at court. Lord Latimer was not subject to any process, but his health seems to have been broken by the experience, and he took to spending long periods of time at his London residence in Charterhouse Yard.[14] Good doctors were easier to come by in London than in Yorkshire. This meant that for the second time in her young life Catherine found herself married to an invalid. Living in London had its compensations, however, and she became discreetly involved in the life of the court, becoming friendly with Princess Mary and beginning to learn Latin. Her evangelical interests also brought her into contact with the Seymour brothers, who by 1542 were tending in the same direction, or at least Edward was. However, it was with the swashbuckling Thomas that she became most deeply involved, and with Lord Latimer's health in terminal decline early in 1543, they began to think of marriage once she was at liberty. Several years later she wrote to him,

> ... as truly as God is God, my mind was fully bent, the other time I was at liberty, to marry you before any man I know. Howbeit God withstood my will therein most vehemently for a time, and through his grace and goodness made that possible which seemed to me most impossible; that made me utterly renounce mine own will, and to follow his will most willingly ...[15]

Perhaps Thomas was in love with her, but he was certainly on the lookout for a rich widow. However, the will of God was represented in this context by Henry VIII, who became emotionally involved with her during her visits to the court. What first attracted him to this thirty-one-year-old we do not know. It was not a sophisticated intellect, nor the ready wit which had first drawn him to Anne Boleyn. Nor was it her great physical beauty, because Henry was no longer looking for such. His body was a corpulent wreck and he was looking for a companion rather than a bedfellow. It did not start with the familiar games of courtly love, because owing to the recent draconian legislation no woman would have dared to respond positively to such an advance, and that the king knew perfectly well.[16] His first recorded advance took the form of a gift, dated 16 February 1543, two weeks before Lord Latimer's death, which she seems to have accepted without demur. At what point Henry made his intentions clear is not known, but it was probably before mid-June when her increased presence at court was noted by shrewd observers. Seymour effaced himself, and the couple were duly wed in the queen's closet at Hampton Court on 12 July. This was something of a triumph for the evangelical party on the council, and the only person offended by it appears to have been Anne of Cleves, who imagined that the fall of Catherine Howard would lead to her own recall. In venting her indignation to Chapuys she complained that Lady Latimer was less beautiful than herself, not realising that such a consideration was no longer relevant.[17] Catherine Parr was recognised by all who knew her as lively, friendly and gracious, and that was the main point. As queen she was a benign presence rather than a power, and brought the king back into contact with his daughters by running a domestic rather than a regal household. She did not attempt to challenge Henry even indirectly, and escaped the plot against her by religious conservatives by her complete submissiveness.[18] She also had to cope with his tantrums as his leg became increasingly painful, and was in every respect the ideal companion for the king in his declining years. The fact that this landed her in a third virtually sexless marriage was apparently a price which she was willing to pay.

Whether the king was aware of Sir Thomas's interest in his bride we do not know, but Thomas continued to receive grants from the Crown, and on 18 April 1544 was appointed Master of the Ordnance for life. This last was a striking gesture of confidence on Henry's part, and indicates that as a soldier Thomas was not far behind his brother.[19] As well as serving at Boulogne, as Master of the Ordnance he was expected to supply all the munitions used by the garrison and by the troops at Calais as is clear from his correspondence with the council there. On 10 November he was reproved by the Privy Council for disobeying his instructions, and of returning to Portsmouth without doing any of the things that he was instructed to, which indicates a naval command. This would be consistent with his letters of similar date describing the deployment of the fleet, and assessing the number of men required for particular operations. An attack on Étaples seems to have been contemplated, but was not eventually attempted because of Seymour's reluctance to engage with the resources available to him – hence the correspondence and the reprimand.[20] Perhaps he was right; the king, at any rate, does not seem to have been disappointed with his service, and in March 1545 commissioned him as Vice Admiral under Viscount Lisle when the fleet was deployed to meet the threat from France. In February he had been granted a licence to retain twenty-four men in his livery, apart from his usual servants, and this was similarly a gesture of confidence, although it probably had more to do with his functioning as Master of the Ordnance rather than as a naval commander.[21] In the parliament of November 1545 he was returned as a knight of the shire for Wiltshire, and served on various commissions, including that of the peace for the city of Salisbury and of array for east Kent. In September he was excused an expedition to the Narrow Seas on account of illness, but the indisposition does not seem to have been serious and he was back functioning as normal by the following month. He was not involved in the peace negotiations which occupied the early weeks of 1546, his time being mainly spent about his duties as Master of the Ordnance and on naval administration including the payment of seamen and the raising of men for sea service. Towards the end of that year he was sworn of the council, and was named as an assistant executor of the king's will, both these promotions probably owing more to his membership of his brother's evangelical party than to his own service, which already been adequately rewarded.[22]

Henry died on 28 January 1547, and Sir Thomas Seymour did not find himself as close to the centre of power as he may have anticipated. The council of which he was a member had died with the king, and as an assistant executor he was not automatically a part of the power sharing which then took place. When the honours were handed out, and his brother became Duke of Somerset and Lord Protector, he found himself raised to the peerage as Lord Seymour of Sudeley, but was not given the office which he coveted, that of Governor of the King's Person.[23] Whether he had been jealous of his brother before is not on record, but he certainly was now, especially as his peerage was accompanied by the grant of lands worth only £500 a year, as opposed to the £1,300 which was received by Edward. As he pointed out, the last time a minority government had been set up, in 1421, the young king had had more than one uncle and the protectorship of the realm had been awarded to one and the governorship of his person to another. In this case, he complained, both offices had been conferred upon the Duke of Somerset. Edward had no intention of giving way over such an important issue, but he did persuade John Dudley, now Earl of Warwick, to surrender his office of Lord Admiral into Seymour's hands, and he thus became *ex officio* a member of the new king's Privy Council.[24] This was an appropriate reward for his naval service in the latter part of Henry VIII's reign, but it did not satisfy Seymour, whose jealousy and dislike of his brother now began to fester, with disastrous consequences as we shall see.

Surprisingly for one so personable, he was still unmarried, and his first thought was to turn this situation to account. He made friends with John Fowler, one of the Grooms of the Privy Chamber, and with this thought in mind enquired of Fowler whether the king ever spoke of him, to which the reply was that he did so, in general terms. He then prompted Fowler to ask the boy whether he would have any objections to him marrying, and if not, whom he should choose. Edward did not take these questions seriously, and suggested first Anne of Cleves, 'and then he said no, but he should marry his sister Mary to turn her opinions'.[25] The next day Seymour spoke again to Fowler, and laughed at the reported words, but he then followed that with a more pertinent question. Would the king be content if he should marry the queen dowager, and if so would he write a letter in support of his suit? Edward was very fond of his stepmother, and complied with Seymour's request, eliciting a response from Catherine, the contents of which are not known but were presumably favourable. The Lord Admiral then began to feed Fowler modest sums of money for the king's use, because Edward complained that the Lord Protector kept him so short of cash that he did not have the wherewithal to reward his own servants.[26] By these means he sought to win the boy's confidence, and successfully solicited his favour when he married Catherine at some point in April or May 1547. This was a union which was bitterly opposed by both the Protector and the council, when they found out about it. They argued, rather unrealistically, that it had happened so fast that if the queen fell pregnant it might be doubted whether the child was Seymour's or Henry's, 'whereby a marvellous danger might have ensued to the quiet of the realm'. However, there was nothing to be done about it, especially as the king had given his personal endorsement, and Somerset worked out his anger by claiming that most of Catherine's jewellery actually belonged to the Crown.[27] This the queen and Lord Seymour vehemently denied. It had been given to her by Henry and was her own personal property. This dispute was never resolved, and soured relations between the brothers for the next two years, because although Catherine died in September 1548 her personal possessions passed to her husband, and he had no intention of surrendering so valuable a treasure. Meanwhile the queen's jointure lands were added to Seymour's more modest possessions, and she moved into Sudeley with a considerable train of servants, transforming his domestic arrangements.

> His house was termed a second court, of right,
> Because there flocked still nobility,
> He spared no cost his lady to delight
> Or to maintain her princely royalty.[28]

Although it is only fair to add that she was paying for most of this magnificence herself!

As might be expected, Catherine soon ran into quarrels with the Duchess of Somerset, both claiming precedence on state occasions, the queen dowager by virtue of her superior status and the duchess by being the partner of the current head of government. At some point later in 1547 or in 1548 Catherine actually complained that she was no longer able to present requests or petitions to the Protector, because of the malice of his duchess arising out of this dispute. Early in 1548 Catherine fell pregnant, a feat which she had not performed in any of her previous three marriages, and which indicates that in spite of his prickly and acrimonious nature Seymour was a loving husband. However, while she was unavailable to him for that reason, he made an advance to Princess Elizabeth, who was living in his household at the time by virtue of having resided with Catherine during the latter's days as queen.[29] At first this took the fairly innocuous form of horseplay. Seymour would enter the princess's room before she was up in the morning and make as though to get into bed with her; on another occasion he cut the dress which she was wearing into ribbons. This kind of play does not seem to have disturbed Catherine at all, indeed she is alleged to have held Elizabeth while the cutting was in progress. However, a few days later she caught the couple in a compromising embrace, and that was a different matter altogether. How she expressed her indignation to Seymour is not known, but Elizabeth was sent away in disgrace to live in the household of Sir Anthony Denny. Lady Denny was the sister of Kate Ashley, Elizabeth's principal gentlewoman, so the arrangement was presumably a convenient one.[30] Catherine gave birth to a daughter shortly after, and in early September she died of puerperal fever, that lethal post-natal affliction which cost so many lives during the sixteenth century. So the one restraint upon Seymour's irresponsible conduct was removed, and with her went her dower and household, leaving him a poorer but not necessarily a wiser man. Just a week before Catherine's death, the Protector had written to his brother, advising him to be more gentle in his relations with others. Somerset had received many complaints which he could not afford to ignore. 'We would wish rather,' he wrote, 'to hear that all the king's subjects were of you gently and liberally entreated with honour, than that any one should be said to be of you either injured or extremely handled.' 'Such,' he went on, 'is the hard affection which we do bear towards you.'[31] This rebuke, needless to say, increased Seymour's bitterness towards his brother, and caused an increase in his indiscreet behaviour rather than the reverse. The Marquis of Dorset had understandably withdrawn his daughter from Seymour's household after his wife's death, but the latter tempted him into reversing his decision with a gift of £2,000 and a vague undertaking to arrange a marriage with the king. More seriously, at the same time, Seymour began to build a party in Parliament with the specific aim of annulling his brother's patent of appointment by statute, which was the only way in which it could be done.[32] In the latter part of 1548 the Protector was unpopular with many of the peers on account of his high-handed style of government, so this was not as unrealistic as it might appear. He also established an understanding with Sir William Sharrington, the Under Treasurer of the Bristol Mint, to supply him with money, and began to mobilise men on his various estates, turning his home at Sudeley into a veritable arsenal of weapons. Just what his purpose was in these warlike preparations we do not know, but the overthrow of the Protector by force is a distinct possibility, and they certainly constituted a conspiracy against the king's peace. That may have been treason, but his third venture certainly was, because not long after Catherine's death he again approached Princess Elizabeth, speaking this time of marriage.[33] To what extent the princess encouraged these advances is not clear, but her chief gentlewoman, Kate Ashley, who seems to have been quite bowled over by the Lord Admiral, certainly did. To conspire to marry with one so close to the throne without the consent of the council was unquestionably treasonable, and it cost Kate Ashley her job and spell in the Tower. Elizabeth herself, when she was interrogated by the council, denied any intention of marrying with Lord Seymour because she knew that the council would never permit it, but her honour was nevertheless sullied. It may have been an emotional experience which influenced her whole attitude to men and to sex for the rest of her life.[34]

In the closing weeks of 1548, Seymour began to speak with a wild recklessness resembling that of the later Earl of Essex. He spoke to numerous peers about his plans for Parliament, expressing always a violent hatred of his brother, which inspired more than one of them to testify to these conversations before the council. This would undoubtedly have led to the Admiral's detention in due course, but events were precipitated by the arrest of Sharrington on unrelated matters early in January 1549. Sharrington was accused of debasing the currency, and of buying up and then minting large quantities of church plate, but the most significant discovery was made during a search at his home, Lacock Abbey, on 6 January 1549. This was a document recording the understanding between Sharrington and Seymour that the proceeds of the Bristol Mint would be placed at the latter's disposal for his military purposes.[35] This caused the Lord Admiral to be summoned to a private interview with his brother, an invitation which he declined. The matter was then laid before the whole council at a meeting on 17 January, which voted unanimously to lodge him in the Tower. Seymour was accused of plotting to overthrow the Protector and council, of seeking by means of bribes to gain control over the person of the king, and of planning to marry with the Princess Elizabeth. These accusations were drawn up in the form of thirty-three articles at a meeting on the 22nd, and were presented to the Lord Admiral the following day, when he declined to make any answer, reserving his defence for an open court.[36] John Fowler was also arrested, and it was upon his testimony that the charges of bribery in the Privy Chamber were largely based. The king also signed a statement of the facts as he remembered them which was equally damning. During the first session of parliament, Seymour had urged him to write a letter on behalf of the queen, which he had declined to do, and then at a later date had urged him to take the government into his own hands 'within this two years at least' in order to free himself from the constraints under which the Lord Protector had placed him. 'Ye are but a very beggarly king now; ye have not to play nor to give to your servants,' he had told him in the context of supplying him with pocket money.[37] When Somerset had been in Scotland in September 1547 he had expressed grave doubts as to his safe return, and when he returned in triumph

Seymour had withdrawn to Sudeley, warning the king against any who should speak evil of him.

The council laid these depositions before the Lord Protector, together with Seymour's refusal to respond to them on 24 January, when it was agreed to place the whole case before the king, which was done later the same day. Each member of the council declared his own opinion, and Somerset concluded by observing how sad a day this was for him, but that he was bound to respect his duty to the king before any ties of blood. Edward responded that he perceived that the charges against his uncle extended to treason, and willed therefore that the council should proceed to justice, as they had requested.[38] They decided against a trial in the Marshall's court, allegedly out of consideration for Somerset's feelings, and a bill of attainder was drawn up and presented to the House of Lords on 25 February, containing all the thirty-three articles of accusation already mentioned. The judges declared that the articles amounted to manifest treason, and the bill passed its third reading on 27 February, being sent to the Commons the same day. The bill had its first reading in the Lower House on 28 February, and its second on 1 March, when a committee was appointed to ask the Lords to present the evidence, as they had received it. On 4 March the Master of the Rolls declared that it was not the king's pleasure that Seymour himself should appear before the Commons, but that other peers were at liberty to do so. Some did, and after a full debate in a 'marvellously full' house the measure passed by an overwhelming majority.[39] There then followed a pause, as the council debated whether to exact the full penalty of treason as they were entitled to do, and possibly while Somerset decided whether he was really prepared to execute his deplorable brother. On 10 March the matter was again laid before the king, who thanked them for their concern over his security, and willed them to proceed by the law without further troubling either himself or the Lord Protector.[40] In spite of this clear lead, the final decision was not made at once and it was not until the 15th that the death warrant was eventually signed. A few days later, on the 19th, Lord Sudeley was executed and the king made a note of it in his journal. It was later alleged that Somerset's reputation never recovered from this act of fratricide, but the evidence at the time contains no hint of this. The council was unanimously behind him, and if any of the peers were resentful they kept quiet about it. It is also difficult to see what else he could have done, because Seymour was undoubtedly trying to subvert the lawfully established order of the realm, and to gain control over the king's person. Even without the attempt to marry Elizabeth, the charges against him amounted to treason, and he could not have been allowed to continue. Would Seymour have escaped with his life if he had had the opportunity for a private interview with the Lord Protector, as was later alleged? In 1554, when she was in the Tower following the Wyatt rebellion, and seeking an interview with her sister, Elizabeth remembered that Somerset had told her

> that if his brother had been suffered to speak with him, he had never suffered, but the persuasions were made to him so great that he was brought to believe that he could not live safely if the Admiral lived, and that had made him give consent to his death.[41]

This may be authentic, but given the similarity of the princess's position we cannot be sure, and in any case Somerset had been merely attempting to excuse a course of action which may well have preyed on his conscience. That is not the same thing at all as believing that he had made a mistake, and of that there is no sign, either at the time or subsequently. Nor was he accused of such an offence in the circumstance of his own fall two and half years later. At the time he was supported, not only by his fellow councillors but also by the popular court preacher Hugh Latimer, who in a number of sermons described Seymour as a Godless man, and well deserving of his fate. If these sermons were intended to pacify the Protector's conscience, then they certainly appear to have succeeded.[42]

The offender who did escape with his life was Sir William Sharrington. He confessed that from May to July 1547 he had pocketed a large personal profit from buying up church plate which he then coined into testons, which were only about one-third silver, in contravention of the council's orders.[43] He had also clipped the coinage and used the clippings as his own bullion, falsifying the records in order to conceal these malpractices. He guessed that he had made about £4,000 from these actions, but he had never supplied the Lord Admiral with any money, in spite of his undertaking to do so. He also seems to have had only the vaguest idea of Seymour's true purposes, and as his second confession pointed out the real reason for his frauds was the expense of maintaining and refurbishing Lacock. Sharrington reckoned that he was owed about £3,800, while he himself was in debt to the tune of £9,300, of which about £3,000 was owed to the king, and a similar amount to Seymour. In other words, he was in no position to resist the Lord Admiral's advances.[44] A bill of attainder was laid against him, passing the Lords on 19 February and the Commons on 6 March, ahead of that against Seymour. However at that point the similarity ends, because Sharrington was pardoned and restored in blood by the end of the year. He had effectively turned state's evidence against the Lord Admiral, and this was his reward. He was able to buy back his beloved Lacock, and served as sheriff of Wiltshire in 1552, which was no mean accomplishment for a fraudster on his scale. He must have blessed Lord Seymour for getting him off that particular hook.

The office of Lord Admiral was left vacant until 28 October

1549, when John Dudley, Earl of Warwick was reappointed to that office in the shake-up following the fall of the Lord Protector.[45]

Henry Seymour is the missing man in this family history. He must have been born in about 1504 or 1505, and it seems that his father intended a court career for him also, because he first appears as a boy in a household list of 1516, where he is described as an extraordinary esquire of the chamber.[46] This does not mean that he was in regular, or even frequent attendance, but that he had his foot in the door. This position he was not prepared to exploit, and his next recorded appearance was as a servitor at Anne Boleyn's coronation banquet on 1 June 1533. By this time he seems to have married, although the identity of his bride is not known. Although settled at Marriotts in Hertfordshire, he had acquired lands in other places, presumably by purchase as there are no records of grants to him. Some of these he sold to Thomas Cromwell in September 1535 for £819, and there are other signs that he was active in the land market. When Sir Francis Weston died in May 1536, Henry Seymour was prominent among those to whom he owed money, and this was probably for lands purchased as there is no trace of a loan.[47] Henry also maintained a low-key presence at court, Henry Phillips writing late in 1535 that he was intending to meet him there about some necessary business. Queen Jane also bestowed some valuable chains upon him, which argues his presence, a fact which emerged when an inventory was taken of her jewels after her death in October 1537.[48] During her lifetime he functioned as Receiver of Berkhamsted and Kings Langley, and money was due to him on that account when the queen's affairs were wound up. These lands remained in the hands of the Crown after Jane's demise, and Henry retained his office there. Although he is described as 'of the household' in 1538, there is no suggestion that he was in regular attendance, and he never obtained any court office or promotion. He was named as a residual legatee in the statute of 1539 which settled the Earl of Hertford's affairs, but was clearly not close to his brother. In May 1544 he was granted the office of Bailiff of Hamstead Marshall in Berkshire and a clutch of stewardships in Somerset, but was not conspicuously well rewarded for his services, which consisted mainly of membership of local commissions.[49] Rather surprisingly, when the navy was listed on 30 October 1544 Henry Seymour appears as captain of the *Lyon of Hamburgh*, a ship of 500 tons specifically taken up for the occasion. If this is the same Henry Seymour it indicates that he was following his two brothers into sea service, but this is the only mention of him in this connection, so we cannot be sure. If it was the same man, that might explain the knighthood which he received in the hand-out of honours which preceded Edward's coronation in 1547, although his local service would by then have fully justified such recognition.[50] On 5 October 1549 the king, or more accurately the Lord Protector, wrote to Sir Henry instructing him to mobilise men for the king's service against a most dangerous conspiracy, and to bring them to Hampton Court. He appears to have ignored the instruction, and thereby saved himself a spell in the Tower.[51] He was not involved in the Duke of Somerset's death in 1552, having by then distanced himself from the duke and reverted to his local service. So little was Sir Henry identified with the Edwardian regime that he kept his position on the commission of the peace for Hampshire under Mary, appearing in its renewal in May 1555. This was continued also under Elizabeth until he eventually died at Marriotts as the last survivor of the Seymour siblings in 1578. He appears not to have left any children and the line was continued by Somerset's eldest son, also Edward, who was created Earl of Hertford in 1559. Altogether Henry was typical of someone who stayed away from the centre.

9

KING EDWARD VI

Edward VI was a Seymour, although he took after his father far more than his mother, Jane. His interest in warlike deeds and his enthusiasm for jousting and tournaments, which emerge through the journal he later kept, were characteristic of Henry at a similar age. His concern with diplomacy was very much on the same lines, solemnly noting the growing hostility between the Emperor and the King of France and the vicissitudes of battle when the war recommenced. He also allowed himself the indulgence of recording the manoeuvres of the Turks, and particularly the adventures of Dragut Reis in the Mediterranean. The way in which he applied himself to his studies and his early mastery of Latin also reflect his father's priorities. Only in his cheerfulness and in the amiability of his disposition, to which all early observers testify, can the legacy of his mother be detected. It might have been different if Jane had lived to play a part in supervising his upbringing, but probably not given her lack of interest in things intellectual, and her known submissiveness to the king's wishes. Rockers for his cradle and other nursery servants had been appointed to wait on the prince before he was born, but it was not until March 1538, when he was already six months old, that a formal household was set up for him, and he seems to have spent the early months of his life at Havering, a house in Essex which had been part of his mother's jointure.[1] Meanwhile improvements were made to those lodgings at Hampton Court which had been designated for his use, including the addition of a washroom and a kitchen, to enable his establishment to be as separate as possible from the main court. Looking ahead he was also provided with a set of public rooms, including a 'Chamber of Presence', in which his accomplishments would shortly be displayed for diplomatic inspection. Sir William Sidney, the grandfather of the well-known Elizabethan courtier Philip Sidney, was appointed Edward's first Chamberlain, Richard Cox as his Almoner, and Lady Bryan, the wife of Sir John, to oversee the nursery.[2] The last was well qualified, having discharged the same function for Elizabeth in 1533, and even for Mary as far back as 1516. Although bringing up a boy might have presented some challenges, there was not much about rearing royal infants in general that Lady Bryan did not know. This was just as well because Henry drew up the instructions for Edward's household himself. The introduction to the text highlights his anxiety over the health and safety of his son, for whom nothing in the world must be 'so noble, just and perfect' as his domestic arrangements. The regulations themselves are meticulous, ranging from the tasting of any food which the prince was to consume to the washing and airing of the clothes which he was to wear. The household servants were bound to their duties by solemn oaths, and were strictly confined to avoid the risk of any infection from the outside world penetrating the fastness which the baby's quarters were to become.[3] A detailed checklist of every servant on duty, outlining their age and estate, was to be presented to Henry whenever he called for it, and no one under the degree of a knight was to be allowed into the prince's presence. Above all, no one, of whatsoever degree, was to touch the child, unless expressly ordered by the king to do so. A general dispensation was given to the nursery staff to ignore this last order. Under this strict regiment Edward's health, like his spirits, continued to be good, and he behaved himself admirably, allowing privileged courtiers the honour of kissing his hand, which he thoughtfully displayed for that purpose. Only the ambassadors from Saxony and Hesse found him less than cooperative in this respect, burying his face in his nurse's shoulder at the approach of these bearded strangers. In spite of her 'cheering, dandying and flattering' by both his nurse and Lady Bryan, he 'ever cried and turned away his face' until the envoys were compelled to beat an ignominious retreat. The Earl of Essex, who witnessed this fiasco, attributed it to the fact that the Germans were Lutherans, and suggested that it demonstrated the child's godly credentials![4]

Then, in October 1541, this placid routine was interrupted, when Edward contracted what was known as a quartan ague, which was probably a form of malaria. In the days of primitive medicine this could be a dangerous ailment for a child, and Henry was desperately anxious. He sent for the best doctors in the realm and for about ten days the child's life was thought to be in danger. One of the doctors, contradicting most contemporary testimony, told the French ambassador, Marillac, that the danger was real because Edward was basically unhealthy, being both flaccid and overweight.[5] Nevertheless, after about a fortnight he recovered, throwing off the infection with considerable resilience. The same doctor informed the ambassador that he would not predict a long life for Edward, on the same evidence as before, in spite of the fact that he had got rid of his ague in a fraction of the time that it had taken his half-sister, Mary.

Until the age of six Edward had lived among the women, as he later put it, but in 1543 his household was reconstructed, and men took over most of his care. The exception was Sybil Penn, who was appointed his 'Dry Nurse', the time for a 'Wet Nurse' being passed. This change was symbolised by the promotion of his Almoner, Richard Cox, to be his tutor. Cox was a graduate of King's College, Cambridge, and had been one of the founding fellows of Wolsey's new establishment, Cardinal College in Oxford, and had then moved on to become headmaster of Eton. From 1533 he had been a chaplain to Archbishop Cranmer before being appointed the prince's almoner in 1538. He was thus well qualified for his new responsibilities, and it may well have been he who suggested the establishment of a group of Edward's contemporaries to share his lessons, being aware of the difficulties of teaching one boy on his own. This group contained girls as well as boys and consisted, among others, of Henry Brandon, the son of the Duke of Suffolk, Jane Dormer and Barnaby Fitzpatrick, who later became Edward's especial friend.[6] Nevertheless the difficulties persisted, and in 1544 John Cheke, the Regius Professor of Greek at Cambridge, was recruited to assist him. Roger Ascham, Elizabeth's tutor, was also drafted in to help with the boy's handwriting 'by Mr Cheke's means'. It is not surprising that under this formidable team Edward learned fast, and by December 1544 Cox thought that he was ready to read Cato and Aesop in the original Latin, supplemented by suitable extracts from the Vulgate Bible. In fact the prince's education followed closely upon the model established originally for the training of Mary, and afterwards followed for Elizabeth and Henry's illegitimate son, Henry Fitzroy, in concentrating heavily upon the Classics, the Bible and Erasmus.[7] In these studies Edward soon began to outdistance his companions and earned the warmest praise from his teachers. However, Cox became Dean of Christ Church in 1546 and Vice Chancellor of Oxford in the following year, which restricted the amount of time that he was able to spend with his royal pupil, and made his role thereafter more that of a director of studies, leaving the regular tutoring in the competent hands of John Cheke. In spite of the mildness of his disposition, Edward could at times be difficult, and Cox was forced to use stratagems in order to overcome this. Realising his interest in things military, he invited him on one occasion to besiege and capture the fortresses of ignorance, with beneficial effects for his Latin grammar. At another time he was instructed to conquer 'Captain Will', a military way of describing his difficulties of temperament, and an instruction which was reinforced by a judicious beating, which Cox was empowered but reluctant to administer.[8] There seems to be no truth in the later story that Barnaby Fitzpatrick was Edward's 'whipping boy', receiving the punishments which should have been inflicted upon the prince himself. In addition to the Classics and the Bible, Edward also appears to have been instructed in geography. In his father's residences he was constantly surrounded by maps and globes, representing Henry's interests, but in 1549 he himself ordered the hanging in the Privy Chamber of a new woodcut world map, designed by Sebastian Cabot and showing the Northwest Passage. As late as 1551 Cheke designed for him an astronomical quadrant and bought a copy of Robert Record's *Pathway to Knowledge*, both of which gifts indicate his continuing interest in the subject. Edward was also taught music, probably by Philip Van Wilder, who was a member of his Privy Chamber and 'Master of his Highness singing children', who were attached to the Chapel Royal. He certainly played the lute and probably also the virginals, because he dispensed some of the money which his uncle Thomas Seymour supplied for him in rewarding John Aysshley for teaching him the latter instrument.[9]

Apart from being on display in his Privy Chamber, Edward also played a modest part in the public life of the court. In June 1546, when Claude d'Annebault, Admiral of France, came to ratify the Treaty of Camp, Henry decided that his son should welcome him. The boy was consumed with anxiety, but it was to his stepmother rather than to the king that he turned for comfort and advice. Queen Catherine reassured him, and urged him to rehearse his Latin speech carefully beforehand. In the event he need not have worried. Riding at the head of a reception committee of 2,000 horsemen, he greeted the Admiral on his landing with an embrace in the French fashion, including a kiss on either cheek, and his speech of welcome won general approval for its modesty and relevance. He had passed his first test, but he did not even begin to learn French until the December of that year, when his tutor was Jacques Belmain.[10] Consequently when he received the French ambassador at the beginning of his reign, in February 1547, it was in Latin that they conversed, the young king's recent beginning to learning French being offered as the reason. It is a tribute to the nine-year-old's proficiency in the Latin language that he was able to hold a conversation at all. Henry's decision to bring his young son out in this fashion was a reflection of another aspect of his upbringing. No one was to doubt that he was destined to become king, and a great king at that. This was expressed both in the deference which was insisted upon in all dealings with him and in the portraits which were authorised at the time. At New Year in 1539 Hans Holbein presented the king with such a picture, to which Richard Morrison added a Latin verse panegyric, urging Edward to excel his father, should such a thing be possible.[11] A solemn infant stares out of the canvas, bearing in his right hand a sceptre in the guise of a rattle. Similarly the anonymous portrait of Henry VIII and his family, painted shortly after, shows the king with his arm around his young son, while his queen, not the contemporary queen Catherine but Jane Seymour, kneels submissively nearby. The dynastic message is clear. The one thing which is not clear is the nature of the religious education which the young prince was given. Cox, Cheke and Belmain all emerged later as strong Protestants, but there is no evidence that they held such doctrines while Henry VIII was alive. They were, as far as anyone knew, Erasmian reformers in the same mould as the king; staunch upholders of the Royal Supremacy, but otherwise orthodox in their convictions.[12] However, the fact that they were probably promoted on the recommendation of Queen Catherine makes one suspect that they passed on some quasi-Protestant ideas to the young prince. Ideas which bore fruit in the very beginnings of his reign, when he began to speak of the Protector's 'godly proceedings' and to quote the scriptures in support of the actions of the government which was acting in his name. The only clue is provided by a letter which he wrote to his half sister, Mary, towards the end of 1546 in which he admonished her for her love of dancing and other frivolities 'not becoming to a Christian princess', which suggests that he already held a puritanical, not to say priggish, view of the world. However if he held any unorthodox views of the sacrament or of justification, it is fairly safe to assume that his father did not know of them. Perhaps, as Mary believed, he was in any case too young for such sophisticated theological notions.[13] His journal gives little indication, the king's observations being confined to formal notes such as 'Smith of Oxford recanted at Pauls certain opinions of the Mass' and 'There was also a parliament called (in November 1547) wherein all chantries were granted to the king', entries which give nothing away in terms of his actual beliefs. Later on he involved himself in the council's campaign against Mary's Mass, and early in 1551 demonstrated to her that he understood the issues only too well, a revelation which shocked his sister into a period of illness. Thereafter he made no attempt to stand in the way of the council's efforts, defending his position in numerous interviews with the Imperial ambassador.

One of the best-known representations of Edward VI is that published in 1563 in John Foxe's *Acts and Monuments of the English Martyrs*, wherein the king sits attentively listening to a sermon preached by Hugh Latimer in the privy garden at Whitehall. There is no doubt that he did attend such sermons, but the idea that they should be held as typical of his lifestyle must be rejected. In the first place such occasions are mentioned only by the reformers themselves, who were anxious to present the young king as a 'godlly imp'; a second Josiah, who was himself responsible for the destruction of images, which began in 1549. In fact such a policy was promoted by Protestant bishops such as Thomas Cranmer and Nicholas Ridley and carried out first by Protector Somerset and then by John Dudley, Earl of Warwick, who took over the leadership of the council in October 1549. Edward did no more than acquiesce in this destruction, and although there is some evidence that he looked on it with favour, the real testimony to his radical convictions lies elsewhere. When he was called upon to express an opinion, as in the case of Princess Mary and her Mass, he consistently sided with the reformers, although in that case it was mainly a matter of upholding the law, which was an aspect of the Royal Supremacy. One of the best examples of his attitude is his intervention in the position of John Hooper, the radical preacher named to the see of Gloucester in July 1551. Hooper objected to the wearing of vestments for his consecration, an objection with which the king clearly sympathised, and he intervened personally in an effort to get the requirement lifted. He did not succeed, but Hooper eventually agreed to be consecrated wearing vestments, so his effort was not wasted.[14] The best evidence for his Protestant views lies in the fact that the Earl of Warwick, who took over the leadership of the council after the Duke of Somerset's dismissal, continued and intensified the reforming religious programme after October 1549, when he could so easily have followed a conservative course. He knew that the young king held advanced reforming opinions, and he aimed to be the chief councillor to the adult Edward when he took over the reins of government on achieving his majority in 1555. The king's journal, which records every aspect of the public life of the realm, makes few references to religious matters, except in a formal manner, and scarcely mentions sermons, which would be an odd omission if he was really preoccupied with the divines that he had listened to.

Being only nine years old when he came to the throne, the king's participation in government was initially confined to the formal and ceremonial. It is carefully recorded that the king gave his consent to every aspect of the formation of the Protectorate in February 1547, including the establishment of his Privy Chamber.[15] This last, which was under the control of the Protector's brother-in-law, Sir Michael Stanhope, consisted mainly of Somerset's friends. Managing access to the king was more a matter of security than it was of politics at this stage, and almost immediately there was a problem. The Protector's brother, Thomas, Lord Seymour of Sudeley, thought that he should have been made Governor of the King's Person, and began to act as though he was. He obtained impressions of the keys, and made friends with John Fowler, who was one of the Gentlemen Ushers. The former he used to make unheralded visits, and the latter to give presents of small sums of money to the king, establishing a secret line of communication with the boy, whose aid he solicited in various projects of his own. He even observed that the security surrounding Edward was inadequate, a point which he demonstrated in 1548 when in the course of one clandestine visit he shot the king's dog, which was treating him as an intruder, and thus roused the whole establishment.[16] Although they were aware of these activities, neither Somerset nor Stanhope did anything to stop them, and they continued to keep Edward short of money, which was Seymour's main line of approach. It is perhaps hardly surprising in the circumstances that Edward felt small affection for his uncle the Protector, and seems to have been easily convinced of his guilt at the time of his fall in October 1549.

As we have seen, Edward kept a journal wherein he made a note of all such affairs as interested him. These consisted in the first place of all matters military, and after a description of the coronation and a brief reference to Lord Seymour's marriage to the queen dowager 'with which marriage the Lord Protestor was much offended', he proceeds straight to the Scottish campaign of September 1547. He describes how Somerset 'mustered all his company' at Berwick to the number of 13,000 foot and 5,000 horsemen and proceeded straight to Musselburgh, where the Scots awaited them, to the number of 36,000. There then follows a brief but detailed description of the Battle of Pinkie Cleugh, culminating in the statement that 10,000 Scots were slain, including 1,000 noblemen.[17] Where the king got his information from is not apparent, but it may well have been from Somerset himself, who had an obvious interest in exaggerating the Scottish casualties. Following this exuberant outburst is the bald statement, 'There was also a parliament called, wherein all chantries were granted to the king and an extreme law made for vagabonds, and divers other things.'[18] Almost immediately thereafter the journal proceeds to the siege of Haddington in 1548, which is again given generous treatment. This is fairly typical of the king's memory in what was clearly a schoolroom exercise, in which there is extensive treatment of battles, sieges and feats of arms, but only the most perfunctory narrative of events like the fall of the Duke of Somerset in October 1549, or even more of his arrest, trial, and eventual execution in January 1552. The latter is entangled with the events surrounding the visit of Mary of Guise, the dowager Queen of Scots at about the same time, and ends with the notorious statement that 'the Duke of Somerset has his head cut off upon Tower Hill between eight and nine o'clock in the morning'. It is fairly clear that Edward did not think his journal an appropriate place for any display of emotion, and his real reaction to these events may have been rather different, but the only evidence to that effect is much later.[19] Apart from military matters, the journal is most revealing about the entertainments of the court, which the king obviously enjoyed and in some of which he took part. The festivities of New Year 1552, which saw the reintroduction of the Lord of Misrule in the person of George Ferrers, were particularly impressive. These were designed to distract the king from any 'dumpy thoughts' about his uncle the Duke of Somerset, then under sentence of death, and to divert the citizens of London, in both of which aims they seem to have been completely successful.

Like his father, Edward had an excellent ear for music, and maintained a large establishment. In the first two years of his reign he paid wages to a wide variety of instrumentalists, including a bagpipe player and a performer upon the rebec, a stringed instrument resembling a lute. These players were members of the King's Music, and had been taken over from Henry, but to them he added those who had been members of his household as prince, and continued to add to their numbers down to 1552. In addition there was the whole establishment of the Chapel Royal, which also performed for the king when summoned to do so, as is recorded in his journal. The main purpose of this ensemble was functional. It was called upon for all sorts of ceremonial occasions from the coronation to the daily service of meals. Aristocrats usually maintained bands of instrumentalists, and the mission from France which brought the king the Order of St Michael in 1551 was similarly accompanied, a fact which the king duly noted in the distribution of gifts at the end of the mission.[20] The religious changes of the reign also called the musicians of the Chapel Royal into action. Thomas Tallis and John Sheppard grappled successfully with the requirements of the new English liturgies, while Christopher Tye, Thomas Causton and William Hunnis also produced settings and anthems. Other gentlemen who were not connected with the Chapel Royal also made their contribution in this connection. Thomas Sternhold, a gentleman of the Privy Chamber, set the metrical psalms to music and John Marbeck, the organist of St George's Chapel at Windsor, produced the *Book of Common Prayer Annotated* in 1550. Marbeck explained that a childhood devoted to the study of singing had left him almost illiterate, but that his burning desire to study the scriptures had inspired him to overcome that handicap. He was almost unique in thus displaying his Protestant convictions, a position which was to land him in trouble in the following reign.[21] There is good evidence that Edward actively enjoyed the music with which he was surrounded, and the words of Thomas Sternhold, written in 1549, deserve to be taken seriously:

> seeing further that your tender and godly zeal doth more delight in the holy songs of virtue than in any fained rhymes of vanity, I am encouraged to travail further in the said book of psalms ... so you will also delight to command them to be sung to you of others ...[22]

Throughout his reign Edward delighted in taking part in masques and disguisings, the details of which are available in the Revels accounts, revealing also that specially made small costumes had to be devised for him. In doing so the king was following his father, who also participated with enthusiasm, and in 1551 he not only performed but also directed, the plays and pastimes being frequently altered to 'serve his majesties pleasure'. This pious boy obviously enjoyed the frivolities of the court life, and did not allow his godliness to overcome him. He also enjoyed sartorial finery, and in that also he followed his father. He habitually dressed in garments of red, white and violet. His buttons and the tags on the laces which fastened his doublet were of gold, and he possessed a number of caps of black and white garnished with pearls, rubies and diamonds. At the time of his death, his chest contained also a black velvet 'muffler' furred with sables and 'having thereat a chain of gold enamelled green, garnished with certain pearls', which was obviously one of his favourite adornments.[23] So although Edward's court was centred on a child, there was nothing childish about his appearance, or his surroundings, which consisted largely of the rich trappings Henry had left behind. Despite his reputation for piety, Edward's court, like that of his father, was both cosmopolitan and worldly. His meals were served to the sound of trumpets in vessels of gold and silver, set with precious and semi-precious stones, and in a chamber lined with rich tapestries depicting classical and biblical scenes. Altogether the young king inherited from Henry over 2,000 such pieces of tapestry, more than 150 paintings, vast quantities of plate and scores of books. To this collection he did not have either the need or the resources to add very much. Only in the purchase of jewellery does he seem to have spent at all lavishly. In May 1551, for example, he purchased from Jacob Fugger the great Burgundian jewel known as the Three Brothers, at a cost of 100,000 crowns, a sum so large that it had to be paid in instalments. He also bought a 'fair ring of gold' set with a diamond and coloured enamels from Erasmus Skette, a merchant of Antwerp, and clearly enjoyed wearing such things. One French observer at Hampton Court in 1551 commented that Edward's garments were so covered with jewels that he glittered in the light of the candles.[24]

Meanwhile his education continued, but with one significant change. When the Earl of Warwick took overall responsibility for the government in 1550, he introduced an element of physical training into his curriculum. The boy was taught to ride, and to run at the ring, was encouraged to hunt, and to take part in shooting competitions with the yeomen of his guard. These were clearly exercises which the king greatly enjoyed and they play an increasing part in his journal. On one occasion he recorded that his side had lost at a wager of shooting, but 'won at rovers', which was a type of free-range archery, aimed at moving targets.[25] Warwick also rearranged his Privy Chamber in the wake of Somerset's fall in October 1549. Out went Sir Michael Stanhope and other of the duke's cronies, and in came six Lords of the Council including the Marquis of Northampton, the Earl of Arundel and Warwick himself, who were to attend on him two at a time. Four knights were also designated for the same duty, one of whom was Warwick's brother, Sir Andrew Dudley. Although these appointments were all made, as Edward makes clear 'by my consent', there is no doubt that they were intended to increase the earl's control over access to the king's presence, in which they seem to have been entirely successful. Henry Neville and Henry Sidney, who were added to the Privy Chamber in April 1550, were also nominees of Warwick and served the same purpose. Sir Robert Dudley, Warwick's own son, and Barnaby Fitzpatrick, Edward's special friend, were sworn on the same terms in April 1551.[26] These last two had been members of Edward's band of fellow students and their transfer signals the end of that arrangement. At the end of October, having attained the age of fourteen, the king's formal education was brought to an end, and what might be termed his political training began. Under the guidance of William Thomas, the Clerk of the Privy Council and a creature of Warwick's, the king began to attend specially convened council committees, and to express his views. There is no evidence that at this stage such views had any influence on the decision-making process, but they did give Edward an enhanced sense of participation.

The king also wrote a number of essays or position papers, on the reform of abuses and the establishment of a mart or exchange in London to rival that in Antwerp. These show a sophisticated understanding of the issues involved, and the latter in particular demonstrates a knowledge of the coinage and its value quite remarkable in one so young.[27] In September 1551 he noted in his journal,

> Deliberation touching the coin. Memor that there were divers standards – 9 ounces fine, a few; 8 ounces fine as ill as four, because although that was fine yet a shilling was reckoned for two shillings; 6 ounces very many; 4 ounces many also; 3 ounces £130,000 now of late. Whereupon agreed that the teston being called to sixpence, 4 with the help of 6 should make ten fine, 8 fine with help of nine, being fewer than those of eight, should make ten ounces fine; the two ounces of alloy should quit the charges of minting ...[28]

Although obscurely worded, this appears to show a detailed understanding of the workings of the mint. The council's instructions, issued to Sir Edmund Peckham on 25 September, confirm that the matter had been referred personally to the king, and that only then were directions issued respecting the standard and impression of the new coinage. In this respect at least Edward's opinions seem to have been taken seriously. Thomas presumably read these papers and returned them to the boy, among whose papers in the Cotton and Landowne MSS in the British Museum they still remain. By the summer of 1552 Edward was attending formal council meetings, organised by the Earl of Warwick, and wrote further position papers on how that body conducted its business, which again show an acute understanding of the realities of power, although it is unlikely that they had any influence they warned the councillors that Edward would be in due course a 'hands-on' king, as his father had been. Commentators at the time noted how devoted he was to the Earl of Warwick, to whose influence he rightly attributed this enhancement of his position. The French ambassador declared that he regarded the earl as a father figure, whose will was not to be crossed. It is obvious that Warwick was looking ahead to that time in 1555 when Edward would attain the age of eighteen, and would be freed from the constraints of his minority. In spite of dubious health, which periodically kept him out of action, the duke had every intention of becoming the chief councillor of the adult king.[29] By early in 1553 this influence had become very marked, and led to many misunderstandings as to what happened thereafter.

By the Treaty of Boulogne, signed in March 1550, Edward had been betrothed to Elizabeth Valois, the young daughter of Henry II of France and Catherine de Medici. Although he was quite keen on the idea, and sent her his portrait, the marriage had not yet taken place on account of the youth of both parties. Edward again entrusted his thoughts on this matter to his journal, in which he seems to have been more concerned with the size of her dowry than the charms of the young lady herself. Given her youth, it was probable that those charms had yet to manifest themselves. Consequently there was a question mark over the succession unless or until Edward had heirs of his body, and early in 1553 someone – it may have been William Thomas or it may have been Northumberland himself – suggested that he should write a position paper on what would happen if he were to die without direct heirs. Edward therefore wrote an essay on that subject, at about the same time that he wrote 'Certain Articles devised ... for the quicker, better and more orderly despatch of causes by his Majesty's Privy Council'. Like the 'Certain Articles', this essay was a practical distillation of Edward's own ideas, based partly on prejudice and partly on his limited experience of affairs.[30] There was already on the statute book an Act of 1544, decreeing that in the event of him dying without heirs of his body 'lawfully begotten', the crown was to pass to his half-sister Mary, followed by Elizabeth if circumstances so dictated. The only condition attached to this was that Mary should not marry without the consent of the council. The illegitimacy of both girls was blandly overlooked. Edward, however, set this Act aside. As far as he was concerned, the bastardy of both Mary and Elizabeth ruled them out of the succession, the statute being ultra vires in that respect. He was concerned, as his father had been, to identify a male heir, but whereas in 1544 he himself had stood in that capacity, in 1553 there was not another man or boy in sight.[31] He therefore started his 'Device' with any male child who should be born to the Duchess of Suffolk, Frances, the daughter of Henry's younger sister Mary Rose. The more senior line, derived from Henry's elder sister, Margaret, was ignored, partly because that was also represented by a female, the young Queen of Scots, and partly because she was born outside the realm, having been delivered at Linlithgow Palace in Scotland in December 1542. It was several years since Frances had conceived, and the chance was a slight one, but any boy born to the Duchess of Suffolk would undoubtedly have had a claim. Following Frances were her three daughters, Jane, Catherine and Mary, and any boy born to any of them came next in Edward's list. Unfortunately they were still adolescents, and were not even married at the time when he was writing, so he was clearly not thinking short-term.[32] Unfortunately the king was ill, with what was probably pulmonary tuberculosis, which had resulted from a severe cold caught over the Christmas season. He had not thrown off this infection with his customary resilience, and on 1 March was compelled to open Parliament with a ceremony held in his chambers at Whitehall instead of going to Westminster as was customary. On the 17th he was described as being confined to his room, and as looking very weak and thin. He did not go to Greenwich for Easter, as had been intended because, according to the Imperial ambassador, he was still troubled with catarrh and a cough. However he did begin to take the air in the park at Westminster whenever the weather was good, although this exercise and his diet were carefully monitored by his physicians. On 11 April he was well enough to move to Greenwich, which he did by river to the thunderous salutes of the Tower's guns, but was able to appear only once in the grounds, a few days after his arrival. Scheyfve, who clearly had reliable information from the Privy Chamber, declared shortly after that the king was becoming daily weaker, and was voiding phlegm which was sometimes green and sometimes pink 'like the colour of blood'. The doctors, the ambassador added, were perplexed by the nature of his illness, and a week or so later some of them were of the opinion that his life was in danger.[33] He was declining from day to day, Scheyfve observed, and unless there was a dramatic change, he could not last much longer. Nevertheless, undiagnosed pulmonary tuberculosis is a cruel disease in that it goes through many remissions, and on 7 May the Duke of Northumberland himself wrote that Edward was much amended, and expected soon to be able to take the air again. Things did not progress that well, however, and on 12 May Scheyfve wrote that

> the physicians are now all agreed that the king is suffering from a suppurating tumour on the lung ... He is beginning to break out in ulcers and is vexed with a harsh and continuous cough ... he has a slow fever upon him that never leaves him ...[34]

On the 17th he was able to receive the French ambassadors, but they found him weak and troubled with a cough. By the end of the month he was again reported to be wasting away, and unable to rest except by the application of medicines, both internal and external.

It must have been at about this point that the succession was raised as a serious issue. Edward might recover, but then he might not, and if he were to die, then his Device became highly relevant, expressing as it did his considered thoughts on the subject. As it stood, it was no use, being focussed on boys as yet unborn, and not likely to be born within the next twelve months. Jane Grey was married to Lord Guildford Dudley on 21 May, a union blessed by the king but not likely to be fruitful immediately, and Catherine and Mary were alike unwed. Clearly, if Edward were to die within the next twelve months, as seemed increasingly likely, then the Device would have to be altered. As it stood it envisaged the monarchy being placed in virtual abeyance, with Frances as regent until she or one of her daughters should bear a son. It has been assumed that the Duke of Northumberland did the altering, but it is now believed that Edward made the necessary changes himself, having been persuaded of the need to do so. The result was simple but dramatic. In place of the crown descending to 'the heirs male of the Lady Jane', it was now to go to 'the Lady Jane and her heirs male', thus inserting Jane into the order of the succession.[35] If a woman was to wear the crown, then better Jane than Mary, whose known devotion to the Old Religion would threaten the whole reformed establishment which Edward had set up. The king knew Jane and approved of her Protestantism. There is also some evidence that he liked her as a person, and of course her marriage to his son meant that the Duke of Northumberland would support her claim. This alteration also had the effect of cutting Frances out altogether, which had no logic to commend it, although it can be assumed that the king did not fancy the Duke of Suffolk as king consort. On 12 June, by which time Edward was in extremis, with a burning fever and unable to keep anything in his stomach, the judges were summoned to a meeting of the Privy Council to discuss the king's Device. They asked for a few days of consultation and on the 15th came back with the answer that the succession was too high a matter for them to meddle with, carrying with it the threat of treason whatever their reply. Whereupon the Duke of Northumberland flew into a rage, denouncing them as traitors for refusing to obey the king's commands.[36] On the same day they were summoned before Edward, who, in spite of his weakened condition, was able 'with an angry countenance' to command them to draw up a will in accordance with his instructions. According to a later account he then went on to explain the religious reasons for his rejection of Mary, and the fact that Elizabeth was the daughter of the adulterous Anne Boleyn, both being illegitimate. He then went on to praise Jane and Guildford, who were of the right religion and undoubted legitimacy. Faced with this tirade from the dying boy, the judges submitted, and carried those members of the council who had doubts, such as Archbishop Cranmer, with them. Between 15 and 21 June Letters Patent were prepared embodying the substance of the Device, and signed by most of the council, the Law Officers of the Crown and the leading citizens of London. Subsequently a letter was drawn up, and attested by most of the same people, guaranteeing their support for the succession as King Edward had willed it, but it is not clear that the Letters Patent ever passed the Great Seal.[37] Their validity could consequently be challenged.

Northumberland sought to strengthen his position with a lavish distribution of lands at the end of June, and also by negotiating for French help. On 26 June he took the unusual step of visiting Noailles, the French ambassador, at his home and spending many hours in consultation with him, a circumstance which the Imperialists naturally found sinister, being convinced that he was conspiring to hand England over to the French. He apparently told Noailles that he had taken adequate precautions against any possible counter-claim from Mary and was looking for diplomatic rather than military assistance. Scheyfve meanwhile had been called home, and his replacement Simon Renard had been given strict instructions not to interfere with the political situation in England. In spite of his natural instinct to support Mary, he was simply to do business with whichever side emerged successfully from the power struggle.[38] Meanwhile Northumberland had failed to secure possession of Mary, who on 4 July, warned that the end was imminent, had fled from Hunsdon to her estates in East Anglia, where she was gathering supporters. Throughout these days Edward's decline continued. On 19 June prayers for his recovery were published, and on the 27th he appeared briefly at a window, to dispel rumours that he was already dead, but his appearance was so thin and wasted that few were cheered. Finally, on 6 July between eight and nine in the evening, he died in the presence of doctors Owen and Wendy and of certain trusted members of his Privy Chamber. According to a later French source, it was Thomas Goodrich, the Protestant Bishop of Ely, who heard his last confession, and he expired with the words, 'Lord have mercy upon me and take my spirit.' His death was kept secret for several days, and it was not until 10 July that Jane was proclaimed in London, to the embarrassed silence of the citizens. Mary, meanwhile, who had good information, had already proclaimed herself queen in Norfolk, to general acclamation.[39] She moved from Kenninghall to Framlingham, which was more defensible for the campaign which she expected to have to fight, and Northumberland set out from London with the household troops to confront her. However his men soon began to desert him, in the face of rumours that Mary had assembled a great power, and the council in London changed their minds. To the speechless amazement of the Imperial ambassadors, on 19 July Mary was proclaimed in London to the joy of the spectators, and Jane found that the Tower of London, recently her palace, was now her prison, where she was confined by the lords of the council, even her father having deserted her cause. Meanwhile Mary was making her leisurely way from

Framlingham, gathering supporters as she came, and arrived in
London on 3 August. Apart from freeing the Duke of Norfolk
and other prisoners from the Tower, one of her first tasks was to
see to the interment of her predecessor. Because of the confusion
caused by the disputed succession, this did not take place until 8
August. The queen was inclined to bury her brother with the full
traditional rites of the old religion, but was persuaded that this
would be inappropriate as he had died a heretic, and she allowed
the ceremony to be conducted with the reformed rite, celebrated
by Archbishop Cranmer.[40] It was modelled closely on that of
Henry VIII, except that the place of burial was Westminster Abbey
rather than Windsor. The procession was led by the children and
singing clerks of the Chapel Royal, accompanied by twelve of
Henry VIII's bedesmen. There then followed two heralds and the
banner of a dragon, signifying the deceased's descent from Owen
Tudor, and a throng of the late king's servants clad in mourning
black. Then came a second standard, this time of a Lancastrian
greyhound, many officials and heralds and a third standard, that
of the lion, which Henry had adopted for his own use. Norroy,
King of Arms carried the king's helmet and crest, Clarencieux
his shield, garter and sword, which was richly ornamented, and
Garter his coat armour. There was no suggestion anywhere that
Edward had not even attained his majority. The Kings of Arms
were followed by a chariot, drawn by nine great horses trapped
to the ground with black velvet, and ridden by nine henchmen
also clad in black. This chariot appears to have been empty, and
its purpose is obscure, but it was followed by the funeral vehicle
itself, covered in cloth of gold and drawn by seven horses. This
conveyed the body, and was surmounted as was customary by
an effigy of the king wearing his crown and garter, and bearing a
sceptre in his hand; the work of Nicholas Bellin of Modena, who
had created a number of sculptures for the living king. Round the

coffin were four standards, the Garter and the red rose, designed to establish the late king's status, and those of Jane Seymour and her mother to display the other side of his ancestry.[41] A canopy of blue velvet was carried over the coffin by select gentlemen of the Privy Chamber, who rode in the funeral chariot. After the body came the chief mourner, the Marquis of Winchester, on a horse trapped in black velvet; the Master of the Horse, whose mount was trapped in cloth of gold; and Edward's champion in full armour. Both his armour and the horse which he rode were subsequently donated to the Church. Winding up the funeral procession came nine more henchmen, mounted and hooded in black. At Westminster a great hearse draped in black cloth had been prepared, of eight panes or panels of cloth and thirteen principals, or upright pillars designed to bear tapers. It was remembered that the hearse of Henry VII had had only nine principals, so in spite of the fact that the rites were to be of the reformed faith, nothing was spared to make the spectacle as grand as possible.

Meanwhile Mary's conscience was active. Having been persuaded to allow the official funeral to be conducted in the Protestant fashion, and in English, the night before she instructed that the traditional service for the dead should be held in the chapel of St Peter ad Vincula at the Tower of London. Stephen Gardiner, the Bishop of Winchester, newly released from prison, officiated in Latin, and the queen was present.[42] It is not quite clear who preached at the official funeral, but several sources mention George Day, the Bishop of Chichester, and this would be appropriate because Day, having been deprived in 1551, had been restored at the beginning of the new reign and was presumably acceptable to both sides. Edward's body was laid in a white marble vault beneath the altar made by Pietro Torrigiano for the tomb of Henry VII, but no memorial was erected to him. It was not until 1573 that any serious plans were made for a tomb. Then William

Cure of Amsterdam designed a monument in marble and bronze, to be erected, curiously enough, not at Westminster but beside his father's tomb at Windsor. The association with Henry VIII was obviously felt to be the most striking thing about Edward VI. Cure's proposal was never carried out, and even the site of the vault where his remains were deposited remained unknown until 1685 when workmen prospecting a suitable burial place for Charles II came upon it accidentally.[43]

Protestants mourned the death of Edward, their godly imp, and believed that it was a judgement on England for having been insufficiently grateful for his actions, a feeling greatly magnified by the burnings carried out by his Catholic successor. However, when his sister Elizabeth restored the reformed faith at the beginning of her reign, she was little inclined to celebrate his life. He had been too radical for her cautious approach, and even John Foxe's celebration did not move her from that attitude. It was not until John Hayward wrote *The Life and Reign of Edward VI* in the early seventeenth century that a proper appreciation of his life was committed to paper, and that owes little to his mother's legacy. Edward is always regarded, rightly enough, as very much his father's son, but he seems to have inherited his gentle disposition and his genuine piety from his mother. Had he been Anne Boleyn's son, he would have been a very different kind of person, as his sister Elizabeth was to demonstrate.

10

THE SECOND EDWARD SEYMOUR AND HIS GRANDSON, WILLIAM

Edward's father, the future Duke of Somerset, had married twice. His first marriage was to Katherine Fillol, the daughter and coheir of Sir William Fillol of Horton, Dorset. Sir William died in May 1527, and his will, which is dated the 14th, makes no reference to Edward Seymour. He seems to have envisaged Katherine retiring to a nunnery.[1] Nevertheless, before the year was out she had married Edward, and probably in 1528 she bore him a son, who was christened John. In spite of this, it was not a happy union and Seymour seems to have doubted the paternity of the child, as he did also with his second son, Edward, who was born in 1529. By 1531 Sir Edward Seymour had repudiated his wife on the grounds of adultery, and she seems to have died in about 1535. John was to die in the Tower in 1552, shortly after his father's execution, but Edward was knighted at the Battle of Pinkie Cleugh in 1547, and was to enjoy a long and undistinguished career, dying eventually in 1593.[2] The Earl of Hertford (as he had then become) accepted responsibility for the bringing up of both boys, but they were excluded from his inheritance by statute in 1539, although not on the grounds of illegitimacy, which could not be proved, but rather on the insistence of his second wife, Anne Stanhope. She was the daughter of Sir Edward Stanhope and of Elizabeth Bourchier, whose ancestry went back on her mother's side to Edward III, a fact which she never allowed him to forget. Anne was a proud and tetchy woman, who was later to be blamed for much of the trouble which befell her husband.[3] He married her before the end of 1535, probably as soon as the news of Katherine's death was confirmed, because there was never any suggestion that the union was bigamous. She appears to have become pregnant towards the end of 1536 or early in 1537, and gave birth on the same day as Queen Jane, 12 October 1537. The child was female, and had as godparents the queen, Princess Mary and Thomas Cromwell. There is no record of her baptism, or of anything else relating to her, and it must be presumed that she died in early childhood. Anne tried again, and on 25 May 1539 was delivered of a second child, this time a son, who lived and thrived. Again we know very little about his early childhood, beyond the fact that his godparents were the dukes of Norfolk and Suffolk, which, as with his firstborn, is a sure indication of the favour which the Earl of Hertford was enjoying at court. He was placed at first under the tuition of Thomas Norton, but soon began to share the lessons of the young Prince Edward, who was two years his senior.[4] At what point this began is unclear, but it appears to have lasted as long as the king was under formal tuition. On 19 November 1552, Norton wrote to Calvin that the late duke's son and heir was then thirteen years old, and that seem to have marked the end of his days in the schoolroom. Already, on 11 April 1550 at the age of eleven, he had been sent as one of the English hostages for the honouring of the Treaty of Boulogne with France. This group of youngsters, all of whom were about the king's own age, were generously entertained, and returned home after about three weeks. Apart from this we know very little of his life during Edward's reign, except that he attended the wedding of John Dudley, Viscount Lisle with Anne Seymour, the Duke of Somerset's daughter, on 3 June 1550, because Edward in his journal recorded that the Earl of Hertford was one of twelve gentlemen who 'ran the course of the field', presumably a form of jousting, before the masquers took over the entertainment.[5] We also know that some of the lands which he had lost by his father's attainder were returned to him by Letters Patent before the end of Edward's reign, although this would have been a largely cosmetic exercise on account of his minority.

Edward Seymour was styled Earl of Hertford from his father's elevation to the dukedom of Somerset in February 1547 until his attainder in January 1552, when he reverted to his original name. After the duke's execution his property was forfeit to the Crown, and Edward's mother and siblings appear to have subsisted upon her dower lands, which were not touched by the forfeiture. He, however, became a ward of the Crown, and his wardship was granted first to the Marquis of Winchester and then to the Duke of Northumberland. He seems to have spent most of his time under the care of Sir John Thynne, an arrangement probably made by the duke, which may well have continued after he was restored in blood in the first parliament of Mary's reign.[6] We know nothing of how he was occupied during this reign, except that he was not at court, and was not troubled as far as we know for his religious beliefs. In other words he kept a low profile, which would not have been difficult. With the accession of Elizabeth he returned to the limelight, because the new queen's relations with his father had always been good, in spite of the trouble caused to both of them by the behaviour of Lord Thomas. Within a few weeks of her coming to the throne, on 13 January 1559 he was created first as Baron Beauchamp and then as Earl of Hertford, with an annual fee of £20 drawn on the customs of Southampton.[7] His wardship had of course reverted to the Crown on the attainder of the Duke of Northumberland in 1553, but the arrangement with Sir John Thynne seems to have continued, until on 7 May 1559 he was licensed to enter all of his father's lands which remained in the hands of the Crown. This appears to have involved some creative arithmetic, because he was granted issues 'from the time that he attained the age of twenty-one years', which according to the best information we have should not have occurred until 29 May 1560.[8] Such mistakes are understandable in the days before birth certificates, and his mother, who must have known the true date, was not minded to enlighten the Master of the Wards, who was Sir William Cecil, also the queen's powerful Secretary. The new Earl of Hertford was by this time a man about the court, and at some time late in 1560 he met and fell in love with Catherine Grey, the younger sister of the ill-fated Jane. Catherine had a claim to the throne in her own right, as Jane had had, derived from her mother, Frances (*née* Brandon), and could be described as the 'Protestant claimant' to the succession should Elizabeth miscarry. As such she had a lot of support, the more obvious heir, Mary Queen of Scots, being barred by her Catholic faith and by the fact that she was also Queen Consort of France. One so close to the throne required the queen's permission to marry, and this Catherine neglected to obtain, secretly marrying the Earl of Hertford at some time in November or December 1560. This was concealed from Elizabeth until the summer of 1561, when her advancing pregnancy could no longer be ignored. The queen was furious, and refused to recognise the legitimacy of her action, consigning her to the Tower, where later that same year Catherine gave birth to her first child.[9]

Meanwhile, when they were not at court the newly-weds apparently lived with the Duchess of Somerset, who must have been aware of the subterfuge. On 19 April 1561 she wrote to Sir William Cecil, without giving anything away, applauding the latter's decision to send the young earl abroad as a possible remedy for his 'wilfullness', hoping only that he would be accompanied by some who were to the queen's liking. Sir William had in fact resolved to send his difficult eldest son, Thomas, then aged nineteen, to Paris to give him a little polish and to improve his knowledge of languages. His first intention had been to commend the young man to the care of Gaspard de Coligny, the Huguenot leader. However he quickly changed his mind, and on 8 May wrote to Sir Nicholas Throckmorton, the ambassador in France, explaining his intention to send Thomas to Paris:

> I will only rest upon your advice ... if he might without corruption of life have been in that court three months I think that he should thereby learn more, both in tongue and in knowledge than otherwise in double space ...[10]

The boy was physically strong, but his personality was weak, and Sir William trusted Throckmorton to keep him on the straight and narrow path of virtue that his father had so often mapped out for him. He accepted the ambassador's offer to find him chambers as close as possible to the court, and on 29 May 1561 young Thomas set forth, under the fatherly eye of Thomas Windebank, a reliable dependent of Cecil's and accompanied apparently by the Earl of Hertford, who would have been his senior by about two years. In spite of Windebank's best efforts, and the heavy parental instructions which he bore with him, Thomas soon went off the rails, and the influence of the Earl of Hertford may be suspected.[11] He began gambling and soon outran his allowance, forcing Windebank to borrow on his behalf and on his father's credit. In July he was presented at the French court, where he was kindly received by Mary Queen of Scots, and apart from his gambling appears to have been behaving himself reasonably well. The Earl of

Hertford, however, returned to England in August. This may have been on Windebank's advice, or it may have been connected with the queen's discovery of his marriage, because on 5 September he joined his wife in the Tower of London.[12] The couple were clearly not kept apart, because before the end of 1562 Catherine was pregnant again, and on 10 February 1563 gave birth to a second son, who was named Thomas. Meanwhile Edward Seymour had been arraigned before the Court of Star Chamber and fined the massive sum of £15,000. Of this the queen was pleased to remit £10,000, and to reach an understanding with her victim that he would pay off the balance at the rate of £500 every six months. Then in August 1563 there was an outbreak of the plague which threatened the occupants of the Tower, and the couple were moved out into the custody of the Duchess of Somerset and her second husband, Francis Newdigate. This relative leniency he may well have owed to the intercession of Lord Robert Dudley, Elizabeth's personal favourite, with whom he maintained an amicable correspondence during the summer of 1564, because on 26 May they were transferred to the care of Sir John Mason, who was a member of Dudley's affinity.[13] In April 1564 Hertford also wrote to Lord Robert's brother Ambrose, Earl of Warwick, and received assurances of his support as well. It is by no means clear how they lived under this kind of restraint, or where they resided, but the earl clearly continued to receive the profits of his estates, which is how he was able to meet the fine payments which had been arranged. Presumably he also had to pay his host for his 'entertainment' and for his own and his wife's personal servants, but the expenses of such an arrangement would have been nothing like those involved in running his own establishment.

How Catherine survived under such pressure is even more mysterious, but she seems to have borne her husband no more children, and she died on 27 January 1568.[14] Thereafter, the chief cause of the queen's resentment being no more, the earl was kept under increasingly lax surveillance at various country houses until the restrictions were finally lifted in 1571. He must have passed at least a part of this time in study, because he was admitted an MA of Cambridge University on 30 April in that year, and enrolled as a member of Gray's Inn shortly afterwards. He was thirty-two years old, and having worked out his disfavour was ready to take his part in the government of the country. Nevertheless this did not happen immediately, and the reason may well have lain in a lawsuit which touched the title to most of his lands, and about which he wrote to Cecil (now Lord Burghley) on 10 June 1571. Burghley referred it to Sir Walter Mildmay, who wrote to him on 26 November to say that he had taken order in the case. We do not know the nature of the issue but the fact that it was taken up by the Lord Treasurer, and dealt with by the Chancellor, suggests an Exchequer matter, probably connected with the lands which his father had forfeited and which had been returned to him in May 1559.[15] It was not until 1578 that he eventually took his place on the commission of the peace for Wiltshire, which seems to have marked the end of his long period of disfavour. In the following year he was also named as a muster commissioner for the same county, a favour which he may well have owed to the Earl of Leicester (as Lord Robert Dudley had then become), who was strong in the military counsels of the Crown. On 23 June 1582 he received an 'exemplification' of the grant of his father's lands in 1559. This referred back to the statute of 1539, which had settled the inheritance on him, and may well have been intended as a legal protection against any suit from his elder half-brother.[16] It may also have been intended to protect his right to alienate such property, as over the previous months he had been granted two such licences, having sold manors in Wiltshire to Edward Stanhope and Richard Wheeler. It may also have been connected with his second marriage, which he contracted quietly before 1582, to Frances, the daughter of William, Lord Howard of Effingham, by whom he had no children. She was sufficiently intimate with the queen to be addressed as 'Good Franke' in a letter of November 1595, and she died on 14 May 1598. Meanwhile, the earl had corresponded frequently first with Walsingham then with Lord Burghley about his legal affairs and about his duties as justice of the peace. In January 1579 he had been sufficiently in favour to be granted the wardship and marriage of his nephew John, the son and heir of his father's brother, Sir Henry Seymour, who had not been at court and seems to have confined himself to his local responsibilities.[17]

On 3 January 1596 the queen wrote in a letter to Lord Buckhurst that the Earl of Hertford had been committed as a prisoner to the Tower 'under just cause of displeasure', but that, being penitent and acknowledging his fault, he was to be released into the custody of the Archbishop of Canterbury. What this cause of displeasure may have been is unclear, but it may have been connected with a tract written at about this time concerning the 'State of England', which dealt inevitably with the forbidden question of the succession. In this the author dealt with the rival claims of the King of Spain, the King of Scots, Arabella Stuart, the Earl of Hertford and the Earl of Huntingdon.[18] It may be that Hertford had not distanced himself sufficiently clearly from this work, or was even suspected of having promoted it. How long he remained in the care of Whitgift is not known, but by 22 April of the following year he had apparently been fined £5,000, which suggests a Star Chamber matter rather than the succession as the cause of his incarceration. Of this fine the queen remitted £2,500 and he entered into an undertaking to pay the balance at the rate of £500 within sixty days, and £500 every half-year.[19] However, he seems not to have kept to this because three years later the arrangement was repeated, only this time £500 was to be paid within six days, and the rest discharged in equal instalments at Michaelmas and Easter then following. Since Hertford was in amicable correspondence with Robert Cecil by November 1599 it must be concluded that his disfavour did not extend that far and that the queen was remarkably indulgent over the payment of his fine, because he was certainly not short of funds. Hertford was not a supporter of the Earl of Essex, and seems not to have corresponded with him at all during his days of favour, which suggests that he did not take his position at court very seriously. In fact on 25 February 1601 he was one of those peers who was summoned to witness Essex's execution, and if this was intended as a warning then the reason is not clear. In October 1601 Hertford was sent on a diplomatic mission to France. This was a congratulatory trip to the queen rather than one of serious business, and Hertford discharged it well, but it did not lead on to more regular diplomatic employment. Instead a more obvious mark of favour followed, when on 27 April 1602 he was commissioned as Lord Lieutenant of Somerset and Wiltshire, including the towns of Bristol, Bath, Wells and Salisbury, with authority to muster the trained bands, suppress dissidents and to appoint such Deputy Lieutenants as he thought fit.[20] This was a position to which he was reappointed by James, and which he continued to hold for the rest of his life.

Meanwhile, on 17 May 1598 John Chamberlain had informed his correspondent, Dudley Carleton, in Paris, of the death of the Countess of Hertford. Edward married again, in spite of being almost sixty years old, in December 1600, his third wife being Frances, the daughter of Thomas Viscount Howard of Bindon through whom he established a link with the Howards. They had no children, but that may be attributed to his advancing years.[21] His son by his first wife, Edward, in spite of his illegitimacy was always known by the courtesy title of Lord Beauchamp. He had passed the early days of his life at Hanworth in Middlesex under the care first of his mother, and after her death that of his grandmother the dowager Duchess of Somerset. His relations with his father always appear to have been somewhat fraught, although it must have been on the earl's initiative that he matriculated at Magdalen College, Oxford, on 22 December 1576, and although he left without taking a degree that was normal for the sons of the aristocracy. How he occupied himself after his studies were completed is something of a mystery, because he does not seem to have enrolled at an Inn of Court, which would have been the next logical step. He may have used his grandmother's contacts to hover on the fringes of the court, although there is no record of his having done so. At some point he met Honora, the daughter of Sir Richard Rogers of Baynton, Dorset, whom he secretly married in 1581, much to his father's annoyance, and seems to have spent the next three years trying in vain to get permission to live with her.[22] Perhaps his grandmother was equally opposed to their union. On his way to London in 1585, Lord Beauchamp was virtually kidnapped by his father at Reading, and the pair of them made a joint appeal to Elizabeth to sort out the difficulties between them. This must have been successful up to a point because by 1586 Beauchamp was certainly living with Honora, who presented him with his first son, Edward, early in 1587. The queen did not, however, resolve the question of his legitimacy because to do so would have involved recognising the earl's first marriage, which she consistently refused to do, in spite of the fact that Catherine Grey had been dead for almost twenty years. However, no proceedings were taken against Beauchamp in 1585, and the unsatisfactory de facto situation was allowed to continue, much to the earl's annoyance. Honora, meanwhile, had conceived again with great promptness, and Edward was followed by William before the end of 1587. A third son, Francis, was born to the couple in 1590. King James turned out to be more sympathetic to Seymour's dilemma than Queen Elizabeth had been, and in 1608 issued an edict which allowed Lord Beauchamp to succeed to his father's titles, without regard to his legitimacy.[23] This turned out to be an academic matter, however, as Beauchamp died before his father, at Wick in Wiltshire on 13 July 1612. He was buried at Bedwyn Magna, and was later transferred to a tomb in Salisbury Cathedral.

Meanwhile, the Earl of Hertford continued to enjoy the king's favour. On 15 March 1609, he received a warrant for 'certain allowances' connected with the discharge of a debt to the Crown of £15,180 which he had apparently incurred when he had been allowed to inherit certain lands which had belonged to his grandfather, Charles Brandon, Duke of Suffolk.[24] In September 1612 he was granted the manor of Kingsbury in Somerset, but most of his correspondence, first with the Earl of Salisbury and then with the council, relates to his duties as Lord Lieutenant of Somerset and Wiltshire, and with the failure of those counties to muster adequately. However, in March 1616 he was one of those ordered to prepare twenty-five men to serve in Ireland, which apparently he did satisfactorily because on the 13th a warrant was issued for the payment of coat-and-conduct money for these men to his nominated representative. His main concern between 1611 and 1616 was the behaviour of his grandson, William. Having been born in 1587, William matriculated at Magdalen College, Oxford, in 1605, and gained his degree in 1607. How he occupied his time is not apparent, but he does not seem to have stayed in Oxford. He seems to have hovered on the fringes of the court, and early in 1611 he met and secretly married the king's kinswoman Arabella Stuart.[25] This was an echo of his grandfather's adventure of fifty years before, but when James found out, he did not disallow the marriage as Elizabeth had done but moved swiftly to keep the couple apart. William was sent to the Tower, and Arabella consigned to the keeping of Archbishop Abbot at Lambeth. It was probably in connection with this misdemeanour that the Earl of Hertford was sent for on 5 June 1611. Surprisingly both the miscreants had contrived to escape on the night of 3/4 June, and his connivance was clearly suspected. He was not guilty, and may not even have known about his grandson's escapade. The person responsible appears to have been the Countess of Shrewsbury, who quickly replaced William in the Tower.[26] Arabella was retaken at sea soon after as she endeavoured to get to Calais, but William got clean away to Paris. What he lived on is not known, but presumably the city was not short of expatriates who would have been prepared to offer him hospitality. Arabella joined the countess in the Tower.

The Earl of Hertford was only too anxious to redeem his grandson's blunder, and on 26 June sent to the Earl of Salisbury, for the council's approval, the draft of a letter which he had written to the 'disobedient and unfortunate' William.[27] What that letter contained we do not know, but it was presumably a plea to him to return and face the consequences of his actions. William clearly responded because the earl was soon making anxious enquiries as to whether his response had been satisfactory. The answer is not known, but William did not return, at least not for some considerable time. Meanwhile Arabella continued to languish in the Tower, being released into house arrest only weeks before her death in the spring of 1615. Whether this untimely death was in any way connected with her treatment in prison is unknown, but probably not, as she was a valuable person. She had had no opportunity to cohabit with her husband, and there were no children of the union, so the nature of their relationship remains problematic. However, Arabella's death opened the way for the rehabilitation of William Seymour, who had become Lord Beauchamp on the death of his father in 1612. One of the more remarkable features of this whole episode is the absence of Lord Beauchamp's intervention in the troubles of his son. It was the Earl of Hertford whom the council held responsible for William's actions, and he who intervened in an attempt to redeem him. Perhaps Lord Beauchamp's health was in serious decline as early as the summer of 1611, but he certainly played no part. William returned apparently in January 1616, and was one of those nominated as a Knight of the Bath at the creation of Charles as Prince of Wales the following November, which confirms his rehabilitation.[28] He had returned to the court earlier that year on the intercession of his grandfather, and in April 1618 contracted a second and more fortunate marriage, to Frances Devereux, the sister of Robert Devereux, 3rd Earl of Essex, who was nineteen at the time. He was elected in December 1620 to serve in the House of Commons for the borough of Marlborough, but sat only in the first session, because he succeeded his eighty-two-year-old grandfather as Earl of Hertford in April 1621. For the next few years he virtually disappears from the records. In 1624, although partly restored to favour by the Prince of Wales in 1625, he was not present at the parliament, either because he was not summoned or more likely was warned to absent himself. In May 1625 he appealed to the Duke of Buckingham for his help in a lawsuit which was hanging over from his grandfather's days. This apparently was not granted, because by 1628 he was opposing the duke, and was noted as being one of his enemies. In the 1620s his friendship was given rather to his brother-in-law the Earl of Essex, who is known to have visited his Wiltshire homes on a number of occasions.[29] The death of the Duke of Buckingham in September 1628 did not, however, mark any immediate return to the court for the Earl of Hertford. Rather he hovered on its fringes, featuring in the correspondence of the period mainly in connection with property disputes, of which he seems to have had several. In

1631 he sent his apologies when summoned to the trial of Lord Audley, to the annoyance of the king who had wanted twenty-five peers to be present, and was compelled to summon three others to make up the numbers. Nevertheless, he accompanied the court to Oxford in September 1636 for the installation of Archbishop Laud as Chancellor, when he is noted as being lodged in Merton College along with his brother-in-law. He held no office, either central or local, until he was appointed Lord Lieutenant of Somerset in 1639, the Earl of Pembroke, who had held that position, being occupied with the king's campaign against the Scots.[30]

William's attitude towards Charles's personal government appears to have been ambiguous. In August 1640 he was one of the twelve peers who signed the petition to the king to reconvene Parliament, but once the Long Parliament was assembled did his very best to find a rapprochement between the two sides which were visibly forming. He accepted an office in the service of the Prince of Wales, but on 7 May absented himself from the crucial vote on Stafford's attainder. Meanwhile he had presented a petition from Somerset in December 1640 in support of episcopacy and the Prayer Book, and on 3 January 1641 had been elevated to the title of marquis.[31] On 19 February he was appointed a Privy Councillor, and shortly after refused the Lieutenancy of Somerset when it was offered to him under the terms of the Militia Ordinance. By this time he was unequivocally on the king's side, and in April joined Charles at York, ignoring all invitations to return to Parliament. He was a regular presence in Royalist councils throughout the civil war, a position which was not as out of keeping with his earlier constitutional opposition as might appear. He had, for instance, been a warm supporter of the Petition of Right, and throughout the war sought to uphold constitutional propriety and the rule of law, a rule which to his mind was represented by the king, Parliament having forfeited its advantage in that respect by taking up arms. On 2 August 1642 Hertford accepted the positions of Muster Commissioner for Somerset, and of Lieutenant Governor of the South West and South Wales, and succeeded in raising 2,000 men for the king, with whom he joined Charles at Oxford in January 1643.[32] Shortly afterwards he linked up with Prince Maurice in Somerset, and took Taunton, Bridgewater and Dunster Castle. Joining forces with Sir Ralph Hopton at Chard on 4 June, their combined forces defeated Sir William Waller at Langport on 5 July. However, growing disputes between Hertford and princes Maurice and Rupert led to his being recalled to Oxford. This should not be seen as indicating any diminution of the king's confidence, however, as he was appointed Chancellor of Oxford University on 31 October 1643 and Groom of the Stool, or Chief Gentleman of the Privy Chamber, in January 1644. This position did not carry the intimacy which it had originally done, and he did not accompany the king when the latter set out on campaign in May 1645. Instead he was left behind in Oxford, as a member of the commission appointed to govern the town in the king's absence.[33] The king was poorly informed and failed to take the opportunity of negotiations which the worried moderates of both sides were offering in the January of 1645. Hertford was one of Charles's assessors in that abortive attempt, but prevarication cost the king his chance and by April rumours of the queen's activities on his behalf in France closed the ranks against him. On 3 April the House of Lords at last accepted the Self Denying Ordinance, and those parliamentary commanders like the Marquis of Newcastle and the Earl of Essex, who had not known quite what to do with victory when they obtained it, were replaced with men such as Fairfax and Cromwell, who were dedicated to winning the war.

Once the New Model Army had taken the field, the issue was not long in doubt. After some indecisive campaigning the king's main field army was brought to battle on 14 June at Naseby, near Market Harborough, and virtually destroyed. On 10 July a similar defeat was inflicted on Lord George Goring at Langport, near Bridgewater in Somerset, and Montrose's royalist rising in the highlands of Scotland was defeated at Philiphaugh in September.[34] The king's cause no longer had the resources to recover from such setbacks, and by the end of the year only mopping-up operations remained. Sir Jacob Astley led the last fragment of a royalist army to defeat in March 1646, after which he uttered the prophetic words, 'You have now done your work and may go play, unless you will fall out among yourselves.' Parliament and the New Model Army would shortly do just that because play did not come naturally to the likes of Cromwell and Fairfax.[35] A final attempt was made to salvage something from the ruins at Woodstock in June 1646, in which the Marquis of Hertford was involved, and he signed the articles of surrender at Oxford in October. He was deprived of the chancellorship of the university by the parliamentary visitors in 1647, and seems to have retired to live on his estates. In the autumn of 1647 his composition was fixed at £12,603, but this was reduced in the January following to £8,345. There is no sign that this large sum was ever paid. In October 1647 Hertford was one of the small group of peers whom Charles summoned to Hampton Court to advise him, with what effect is not known, and in the autumn of 1648 was one of the king's commissioners for the trials at Newport. In January 1649 he made an unsuccessful petition for the king's life, and on 8 February was one of the few peers permitted to attend his funeral.[36] Hertford was a man with considerable estates in Somerset and Wiltshire, but he did not serve under the Commonwealth, and the Council of State kept him under constant surveillance for a number of years. In July 1650 he was placed under house arrest at Netley, and in the following year instructed to move to another of his houses in the vicinity. Securities were taken from him for his good behaviour, and that he would not get involved with any actions of the disaffected. His son Lord Beauchamp, however, became a commander in the Western Association in May 1650, and spent the months of April to September 1651 in the Tower in consequence, although he is not known to have been involved in any active opposition to the government. Nevertheless his health seems to have been undermined by the experience, and he died to the great distress of his family in April 1654.[37] Hertford had been in touch with John Penruddock, but was not involved in his abortive rising in 1655, indeed he was reported at the time to be 'not much inclined' to such ventures, a verdict which says much for his wisdom as well as his advancing years. He turned seventy in 1657. The marquis was inclined to the quiet life, and for that reason did not object to paying the £315 decimation tax for which he was assessed in May 1656. Indeed he appears to have dined amicably with Oliver Cromwell in 1657 in an unsuccessful attempt to persuade him to recognise Charles II as his heir. By that time his debts amounted to over £19,000, and his wife had taken over the management of his estates, making agreements with creditors and other emergency arrangements. He is not known to have been involved in any of the intrigues which led to the restoration of Charles II, but he was nevertheless one of those who welcomed him on his return at Dover on 26 May 1660. He was promptly restored to the Chancellorship of Oxford University, and on 13 September the first session of the Convention Parliament obligingly elevated him to the dukedom of Somerset.[38] He did not, however, live long enough to enjoy his good fortune, dying on 24 October in the same year. He was buried alongside his son at Bedwyn Magna in Wiltshire.

Epilogue

SUBSEQUENT GENERATIONS

Henry Seymour, Lord Beauchamp left an only son and heir, William, who succeeded his grandfather as Duke of Somerset on the latter's death in 1660. In 1648 Henry had married Mary, the sister of Arthur Capell, Lord Capell, later Earl of Essex, and died on 14 March 1654, at the age of twenty-seven.[1] William was born on 17 April 1652, and was consequently eight years old when he succeeded to the dukedom, far too young to undertake any of the duties normally associated with that rank. In spite of being styled Lord Beauchamp from his father's death, he seems to have inherited an unhealthy gene, because he died, unmarried and without achieving his majority, at the age of nineteen on 12 December 1671. He was succeeded by his uncle, John Seymour, the second son of the second duke, who had been born in 1640. John had apparently anticipated a career in the law. He was elected MP for Marlborough in 1661, and entered Gray's Inn on 28 October 1666, becoming a bencher on 9 January 1667, a step which indicates the seriousness of his intentions.[2] He became Recorder of Lichfield and Lord Lieutenant of Somerset in 1672. In 1661 John had married Sarah, the widow of George Gostwick and daughter of Sir Edward Ashton, the President of the College of Physicians. However, it was not a happy union, and he had been separated from his wife for some years by the time that he died on the 29 April 1675 at the age of thirty-five. John had never shown the slightest interest in the life of the court, and was by training and instinct a provincial lawyer. The title sat uneasily on him, and he is not known to have played any active part in the House of Lords. Because of his estrangement from his wife, he left no children, and was succeeded by his cousin Francis. His widow was, however, accorded the status and precedence of a duchess in 1681.[3]

Francis was the son and heir of Charles Seymour, Baron Seymour of Trowbridge, the third son of the second duke. He was born on 17 January 1658, and educated apparently at Eton College, which he entered in 1670. He succeeded to his father's barony on the latter's death on 25 August 1665 and to the dukedom ten years later. As duke he seem to have undertaken a Grand Tour, which was becoming increasingly fashionable by then. Something went seriously wrong because at Asti, in the state of Genoa, he was shot out of an open window and killed by Horatio Botti, a Genoese nobleman who claimed that Seymour had insulted his wife.[4] Just what offence he is supposed to have committed remains unclear, but it brought his tour to an untimely end, and led to a third vacancy in the dukedom of Somerset within ten years. He died unmarried and twenty years old. He was succeeded in the title by his younger brother Charles, who had been born in 1662 and was sixteen at the time. Charles was born on 13 August at Penshute, Wiltshire, his mother being the elder Charles's second wife Elizabeth, the daughter of William Alington, 1st Baron Alington of Kinnard in Ireland. Little is known of his early life. He is said to have been educated at Harrow School and Trinity College, Cambridge, but left no mark on the record of either institution. He suffered an attack of smallpox in the spring of 1679, but was well enough by October of that year to set out on his own Grand Tour, an adventure in which he was accompanied by his tutor Alexander de Regislade. Perhaps for that reason he managed to avoid the fate of Francis, and returned in May 1681. Nothing is known of where his tour took him, although it probably started at one of the academic institutions in the Netherlands, either Utrecht or Leiden, both of which were much favoured by British aristocrats at that time, and study being the alleged reason for the tour in the first place.[5] From there their journey probably took them through Germany into Italy, where a study of the great works of antiquity would be undertaken, and back through the Low Countries.

In May 1682, aged twenty, Charles married the twice-widowed Elizabeth Thynne, who was the greatest heiress in England. This marriage put him in possession of a vast estate, which twenty years later was valued at between £20,000 and £30,000 a year. It also put him in line for a number of other honours and responsibilities. In November 1682 he became Lord Lieutenant of the East Riding of Yorkshire, which was a rare distinction for one so young, and in July 1683 of his 'home' county of Somerset. On 10 January 1684 he was nominated to the Order of the Garter, and installed at the Garter feast on 23 April.[6] He also found himself called upon to discharge number of ceremonial functions at court. At the funeral of Charles II in 1685, he was the second mourner, a position which he was also to occupy at the funerals of William III in 1702 and Prince George of Denmark, the spouse of Princess Anne. He carried the orb at the coronations of Queen Anne, George I and George II, and in December 1703 was sent in the queen's name to greet the new King of Spain, Archduke Charles of Austria. At first he was in favour with James II, who named him as Gentleman of the Bedchamber in May 1685, and as Colonel of the Queen's Regiment of Dragoons in August of the same year. As Lord Lieutenant of Somerset he played an active part in the suppression of the Duke of Monmouth's rebellion, deploying the county levies in support of the royal cause. However, owing to his pride of ancestry he was to prove a difficult colleague both for his fellow lieutenants and for the senior military commanders in that operation, a circumstance which earned him the opprobrious title of the 'proud duke', by which he was known thereafter. He fell out with James II in 1687 when the king required him as a Gentleman of the Bedchamber in attendance to introduce the newly arrived papal nuncio to the court. Somerset refused on the grounds that any dealing with the papacy was treason by law, and rejected the pardon which James then offered him.[7] On being confronted with the statement that the king was in any case above the law, he is alleged to have replied that that was all very well, but he himself was not so emancipated. Not surprisingly this act of defiance cost him all preferments both in the court and in the country, and led him to abandon James and join forces with the Prince of Orange when the latter landed in the autumn of 1688.

In spite of this commitment, he remained very much his own man, voting in Parliament against the concept that James's flight amounted to abdication. He was in favour of a regency, and against the offer of the crown to William and Mary in January and February 1689, sticking strictly to his view of constitutional law.[8] It is probable that he felt quite safe in indulging himself in this fashion, knowing that he would be on the losing side. At the same time he voted for reversing the previous judgement in the case of Titus Oates, a man whom he clearly thought had been wronged. For most of the reign he was classed as a Tory, and refused to join the Whig-dominated Association in 1689. Somerset became connected with the political opposition in 1692, when he resisted pressure from the king and the queen and accepted Princess Anne's appeal for the loan of Syon House after she and her husband, Prince George of Demark, had been expelled from the court. He joined the Association in 1696, but again demonstrated his independence by voting in the Lords against the attainder of Sir John Fenwick, and supporting the impeachment of the Whig ministers.[9] A little earlier he is listed as opposing the Place Bill in January 1693, but that was before he had joined the Association. In spite of these political vagaries, and the fact that he held no position at court, the king seems to have been personally well disposed towards him. He stayed with him at Marlborough on his return from his Irish campaign in September 1690, dined with him at Petworth on his way to Portsmouth in February 1693, and at Northumberland House in May 1699. William also stayed with him on his return from Portsmouth in May 1700. The fact that Princess Anne was now reconciled to the king may have had an effect on their relationship, because Somerset was named as a Lord Justice and Privy Councillor on 28 June 1701. He became Lord President of the Council and a commissioner of the Board of Trade on 20 January 1702, less than two months before William's death.[10] His qualification for the latter position is obscure, except that at the age of forty and as a man of vast wealth he would have been well versed in the ways of the city. He may even have been a shareholder in the recently established Bank of England.

Within a few weeks of her accession, and as a reward for his earlier friendship, Queen Anne gave him a position at court, creating him Master of the Horse on 20 July, a position for which he was well suited. At the same time his duchess became a Lady of the Bedchamber, a post which guaranteed access to the sovereign at all times. The Mastership of the Horse was at this time a cabinet ranking office, and Somerset seems to have discharged his duties conscientiously. However he undoubtedly used his position, and his extensive electoral patronage, in an attempt to increase his political importance. At the beginning of the reign, and in a predominantly Tory cabinet, he was one of the few advocates of a more aggressive strategy in the War of the Spanish Succession, and was consequently a supporter of John Churchill, Duke of Marlborough, who was constantly pressing for such a policy.[11] However, his pride and indiscretion made his support problematic, and led to accusations that he had leaked secret information from cabinet meetings. In April 1704, his partisan role as a committee chairman in an investigation into the Scottish Plot led Daniel Finch, the Earl of Nottingham and Secretary of State, to demand his dismissal. The queen, however, thought differently and instead purged her cabinet of Nottingham and a number of his fellow Tories. With his unique access to the Ladies of the Bedchamber, Somerset had become an ill man to cross. While he was in office he was a reasonably assiduous attender at the House of Lords, serving regularly on committees, and as a representative in conferences with the House of Commons. His voting record during Anne's reign was consistently Whig, starting with his opposition to the occasional conformity bills of 1703. Sometimes Somerset was used by the queen to convey her wishes about particular issues, most notably early in 1710, when he helped her to frustrate a parliamentary attack upon her favourite Abigail Masham, who had supplanted Sarah, Duchess of Marlborough in the queen's affections.[12] This was, of course, the time of the Anglo-Scottish Union, and in 1706 he was named as a Commissioner for the Union, which is another indication of the high regard in which he was held at court. From about 1707 or 1708 Somerset began to use this influence with the queen, and his huge electoral patronage, to put pressure on Marlborough and Godolphin for the granting of numerous political favours, most notably military positions for his son Algernon, the Earl of Hertford, but also including numerous other clients. Some of these, notably James Stanhope and Thomas Meredith, were men of real ability, but that did not affect the resentment which the duke's attitude had aroused. The ministers began to find the task of placating Somerset increasingly tedious, while he, spurred on by success, increased the number and frequency of his demands.

In the winter of 1707/08, Robert Harley, the Secretary, was scheming to supplant Godolphin as Lord Treasurer, and attempted to woo Somerset and the other great Whig courtier, John Holles, Duke of Newcastle. The crunch came at a cabinet meeting on 8 February 1708, a meeting which was boycotted by both Godolphin and Marlborough. When Harley, as the chief minister present, attempted to carry on as usual, it was Somerset who got up and pointed out the impossibility of conducting business in the absence of both the Queen's Treasurer and her Commander-in-Chief.[13] In taking this action he was supported by the dukes of Devonshire and Newcastle, and by the earls of Pembroke and Cowper, a solid front which convinced Anne that a ministry formally headed by Robert Harley would not be appropriate. Harley's time was yet to come. He resigned as Secretary shortly after this rebuff, on 13 February 1708, but became Earl of Oxford and Lord Treasurer early in 1711.[14] Meanwhile, by December 1708 Somerset had fallen out with the Whigs, feeling increasingly isolated in a ministry dominated by the Earl of Poulett, as First Lord of the Treasury. By the summer of 1709 he and his duchess were increasingly going behind Marlborough's back in their dealings with the queen, and may have been making common cause with Robert Harley. The first sign of a break with the Churchill circle came over the trial of Dr Sacheverell in March 1710, in which Somerset played an ambiguous part. He absented himself from the vote upon the doctor's guilt, but then voted for a light sentence. By June 1710 he was intriguing with Harley and with the Duke of Shrewsbury to bring down the ministry, his object being apparently to install a more moderate Whig team, led by himself.[15] By mid-August it was clear that the queen intended to dissolve the Whig-dominated House of Commons and that a Tory ministry was in the offing. Parliament was dissolved on 21 September, and fresh elections called on the 27th, so the intention is obvious. Meanwhile, Somerset had fallen out again with Harley, and in spite of being named as the keeper of the new park at Hampton Court in October 1710, had withdrawn from the court. He became reconciled to the Whigs, used his electoral influence on their behalf in the elections of October/November, and began to undermine the Harley ministry. An attempt to resume his seat in the cabinet was defeated on 12 August 1711 when Henry St John, the Secretary of State, refused to sit with him, and the cabinet as a whole forced his withdrawal.[16] In December 1711 Somerset played an important role in the Lords in convincing them that the queen supported their position of 'no peace without Spain' when he was 'loud in the House' against the peace. In fact Anne backed the treaty, and her regard for the duke consequently diminished. Towards the end of December it disappeared entirely when he attempted to deceive her over his opposition to the proposal that the Duke of Hamilton be allowed to take his seat in the House of Lords under his title in the British peerage as Duke of Brandon. On 19 January 1712 he was removed from his position as Master of the Horse, and there then followed several days of difficult negotiations as the queen and a small circle of court Whigs strove to gain his permission for the duchess to retain her post as Groom of the Stool.[17] This was eventually achieved, presumably on the grounds that a second-hand contact with the person of the sovereign was better than no contact at all. During the last year of the reign, Somerset was a consistent Whig voter in Parliament, opposing both the French commercial treaty of June 1713 and the Schism Bill in the spring of 1714.

During the queen's final illness, and after she had already given the Treasurer's staff to the impeccably Hanoverian Duke of Shrewsbury, on 30 July Somerset and John Campbell, the 2nd Duke of Argyll, turned up at a cabinet meeting to argue for the German succession. How effective their advocacy may have been is uncertain, but the decision certainly went that way. Not surprisingly, on the accession of George I Somerset was restored to his office as Master of the Horse, and his direct contact with the court thereby restored also. However, this was not to last because his son-in-law Sir William Wyndham was suspected of involvement in the Jacobite movement in 1715. The duke offered to give sureties for him, but this was rejected and the cabinet voted to place Wyndham in custody. In high indignation, Somerset resigned his office and broke off connections with the court.[18] Thereafter he played only a minor role in public affairs. He is recorded as voting for the acquittal of Robert Harley, by that time Earl of Oxford, in 1717 and in 1740–1 as giving his proxy in support of various motions aimed at the removal of Robert Walpole. He was by that time in uncertain health, and in the habit of absenting himself from the House of Lords. In November 1722 his wife of more than forty years died, but the absence of ostensible mourning on the duke's part makes it appear that their relationship had broken down some years earlier. In spite of his sixty years he began at once an energetic pursuit of his late wife's old nemesis, Sarah, the Dowager Duchess of Marlborough. This did not result in a marriage, but it did cause Sarah to modify her attitude towards Somerset, whom she had previously regarded as insufferably proud, and this change is reflected in her memoirs, *The Conduct of the Dowager Duchess of Marlborough*, which were written soon after.[19] Nothing daunted, the duke tried elsewhere and on 4 February 1726 married Charlotte, the third daughter of his old antagonist Daniel Finch, the Earl of Nottingham, a lady then in her twenties. Presumably she knew what she was taking on, because by that time Somerset was looking for a companion and occasional nurse rather than a bedfellow, and indeed she spent much of her time over the next twenty years ministering to his various ailments. He died eventually at Petworth on 2 December 1748 in his eighty-seventh year, and was buried on 26 December in Salisbury Cathedral. His second wife survived him by almost a quarter of a century, dying on 21 January 1773 and being buried at Chiswick.[20]

The sixth duke was, as we have seen, a man of vast pride, or so his contemporaries thought. According to Philip Yorke, 1st Earl of Hardwicke, he was so 'humoursome, proud and capricious that he was rather a ministry spoiler than a ministry maker', while William Legge, 1st Earl of Dartmouth described him as 'a man of vast pride [who] having had a very low education, showed it in a very indecent manner'. If Charles Seymour had ever been at Cambridge, it had clearly escaped the attention of the Earl of Dartmouth. William, Earl Cowper was even more derogatory, calling him 'a mean-spirited knave' who at the same time pretended the greatest courage and steadiness.[21] His courage was not in doubt, however. He had stood up to James II over the latter's promotion of Catholicism, and to William III in defence of Princess Anne. He also defied Anne's own wishes in his opposition to Harley in 1708, and George I in defence of his son-in-law in 1715. These actions undoubtedly contributed to his loss of office, and to the general reduction of his influence in the court. It was this reduction which was so offensive to his pride, and caused his total withdrawal after 1715, a withdrawal which he shared with his first duchess in the years before her death. Various anecdotes are told of his pride, which are almost impossible to confirm. He is alleged to have communicated with his servants only through hand gestures, and to have ordered them to clear the road in advance of the passage of his coach, in case he should be stared upon by the common multitude. It is also claimed that he rebuked his second wife for playfully striking him with her fan on the grounds that his first wife, who was a Percy by birth, would never have dared to take so great a liberty.[22] Apparently he needed one of his daughters to stand sentry while he took his afternoon nap, and when Charlotte ventured to sit down, he vowed to cut her out of his will. However, if he ever carried out that intention he had clearly thought better of it before he actually died, as Charlotte takes her expected place in the will as actually proved. He was an able and effective Master of the Horse and an avid sportsman whose horses won a number of important trophies at Newmarket and elsewhere during the reign of Queen Anne. Nor was he without taste and an appreciation of scholarship. He was Chancellor of Cambridge University from March 1689 to his death, and was awarded an Honorary DCL by the University of Oxford during the royal progress to Bath in the late summer of 1702. More significantly he was a patron of artists, who embellished Petworth and suggested the idea of the Kit Kat Club to Sir Godfrey Kneller.[23] Altogether, pride or no pride, he was a significant presence at many of the important political actions of these years from the death of Charles II to the accession of George I.

Charles was succeeded as the 7th Duke of Somerset, by his second but eldest surviving son, Algernon. Algernon was born on 11 November 1684 at Petworth and was baptised on the 26th of the same month. For most of his life he was known as the Earl of Hertford, but very little is known of his upbringing, beyond the fact that he undertook the Grand Tour in 1703 accompanied by John Colebatch of Trinity College, Cambridge. Whether this means that he was a student at the college we do not know; the records are silent on the subject. While he was away he was elected MP for Marlborough, on his father's interest, a seat which he continued to occupy until 1708. He returned from his Grand Tour in 1706, having narrowly escaped the attentions of pirates in the English Channel, and presumably took his seat in the House of Commons.[24]

Before the end of that year he had been appointed Lord Lieutenant of Sussex, a position which he continued to occupy until his death. From 1708 to 1722 he transferred his parliamentary allegiance to the county of Northumberland, but he cannot have been very assiduous in his attendance as from 1708 to 1713 he was serving as an officer in the Duke of Marlborough's campaigns in Flanders. He was present at the Battle of Oudenarde in 1708, and was an ADC to the Duke at Malplaquet in 1709, which suggests military training. At the same time he was appointed Colonel of the 18th Regiment of Foot, and commanded them in the campaigns of 1710, 1711 and 1712.[25] While still on active service, on 8 December 1710 he was appointed Governor of Tynemouth Castle, a post that he was to hold until his death, and which he presumably discharged by deputy, as there is no record of his having resided in the north-east of England. Nor was he ignored at court, although his promotion there did not occur until his military involvement was over. In September 1714 he was appointed a Lord of the Bedchamber to the Prince of Wales, a position of some sensitivity given the bad relations which appertained between the monarch and the prince, a circumstance which may have led to his resignation in December 1717. More in keeping with his command of regiments, however, was his appointment as Colonel of the 2nd Troop of Horseguards, a position which he occupied from February 1715 until 1740, when advancing years caught up with him. Meanwhile he was not neglecting his duties in Parliament. In 1711 he voted for 'no peace without Spain', and against the expulsion of Richard Steele in 1714. On 24 June in the latter year he made his most significant contribution to parliamentary discussion when he introduced a proposal for a bounty of £100,000 to be awarded for the apprehension of James Stuart, the 'old Pretender', should he venture to set foot in Britain.[26] The fact that his motion failed was no reflection on its origins. In 1723 he was summoned to the House of Lords as Lord Percy, it being erroneously supposed that that barony had been vested in his mother, who had died in 1722. He took his seat on 23 November, and the error was never corrected, nor realised at the time. In spite of his military background he was obviously a man of some culture, because he was elected a Fellow of the Society of Antiquaries on 16 January 1724, and served as president of that society from 1724 until 1749.[27]

As a member of the House of Commons he generally supported the ministry, moving the impeachment of William Gordon, Viscount Kenmure in 1716, and voting for the Peerage Bill in 1719. In the Lords he continued his support for Robert Walpole, and continued his career as a professional soldier, being promoted Brigadier General in 1727, Major General in 1735, Lieutenant General in 1739 and General in 1747. He was governor of Minorca during the English occupation of the island from September 1737 to March 1742, a function which he seems to have discharged with some distinction, because as soon as Minorca was relinquished he was transferred to the less demanding but still strategic governorship of Guernsey. He occupied that position from March 1742 until his death eight years later, visiting the island from time to time but never (as far as is known) living there. He was estranged from his father for most of his adult life, and did not share the sixth duke's pride of ancestry. He was well regarded by his contemporaries, both as a soldier and as a patron, and was described by Walpole as being 'as good a man as lives', a description which he would certainly not have applied to his father.[28] Algernon married, soon after 1 March 1715, the sixteen-year-old Frances, the daughter and co-heir of Henry Thynne, the son of Thomas Thynne, 1st Viscount Weymouth. Their only son George, known as Viscount Beauchamp, was born on 11 September 1725, but did not survive his Grand Tour, dying of smallpox on his nineteenth birthday at Bologna in the Papal States. Nothing else is known of the circumstances, but his body was repatriated and buried in Westminster Abbey on 6 July 1745. On 2–3 October 1749 the 7th Duke was also created Baron Warkworth and Earl of Northumberland and Baron Cockermouth and Earl of Egremont, these titles being apparently intended for different branches of the family. Algernon was survived by his daughter Elizabeth when he died at Percy Lodge near Iver in Buckinghamshire on 7 February 1750, and her husband Sir Hugh Smithson inherited the Northumberland title. Since he died without an heir male, the Somerset title went to a fifth cousin, and the direct line of descent may be said to have come to an end. The title, however, remained in the family and the present duke, John Michael Edward Seymour, is the nineteenth holder of the Somerset style. He was educated at Eton, and succeeded his father, Percy Seymour in 1984. Appointed a deputy lieutenant for Wiltshire in 1993, and for Devon in 2003, he lost his automatic right to sit in the House of Lords following the Act of 1999. However, he returned as an elected hereditary peer following a by-election in December 2014, and presently sits as a cross-bencher. On 20 May 1978 he married Judith-Rose Hull, the daughter of John Folliet Hull, and their eldest son Sebastian was born on 3 February 1982. The present seat of the Duke of Somerset is Bradley House, at Maiden Bradley with Yarnfield in Wiltshire.

NOTES

Introduction: The Importance of the Seymour Family

1. This was well expressed before the end of the fifteenth century by Sir John Fortescue who wrote 'hence I praise highly the magnificence and grandeur of the king's household, for within it is the supreme academy for the nobles of the realm, and a school of vigour, probity and manners by which the realm is honoured and will flourish ...', *De Laudibus legum Angliae.* p. 111.
2. Loades, *The Tudor Court* (1986), p. 65. PRO LC5/182.
3. *Ibid.*, pp. 168–9.
4. They were so described in the Act of Apparel of that year. 7 Henry VIII, c.6.
5. Greg Walker, 'The expulsion of the minions in 1519 reconsidered', *Historical Journal*, 32, 1989.
6. Judith Richards, 'Love and a female monarch. The Case of Elizabeth Tudor', *Journal of British Studies*, 28, 1999; P. Wright, 'A change of direction; the ramifications of a female household, 1558–1603', in D. Starkey, *The English Court* (1987), pp. 147–72.
7. Loades, *Tudor Court*, p. 95.
8. S. Anglo, 'The Foundation of the Tudor Dynasty', *Guildhall Miscellany*, 2, 1960; S. B. Chrimes, *Henry VII* (1972), pp. 305–7.
9. *Letters and Papers*, X, no. 601.
10. Ives, *The Life and Death of Anne Boleyn* (2004), p. 325.
11. Bodleian Library, Ashmole MS 861, f. 332; *The Life of Cardinal Wolsey, by George Cavendish*, ed. S. W. Singer (1827), p. 451.
12. Loades, *The Boleyns*, p. 163.
13. Thomas was born in about 1478, and John in 1474. *Letters and*

Papers, I, no. 20. The entry is for Sir John Seymour of Wolf Hall, Wilts., and Margery his wife, daughter of Sir Henry Wentworth.

14. *Oxford Dictionary of National Biography*; J. Foster Watson, *Vives and the Renascence Education of Women* (1912).
15. Loades, *Jane Seymour* (2013), p. 33.
16. *Letters and Papers*, X, no. 282; *Calendar of State Papers, Spanish, 1536–38*, ed. G. A. Bergenroth *et al.* (1862–1954), pp. 39–40.
17. *Letters and Papers*, X, no. 1047.
18. For a full discussion of Anne's political involvement see Ives, *Life and Death*, passim.

1 The Origins

1. H. St Maur, *Annals of the Seymour Family* (1902), p. 2.
2. *Ibid.*, p. 3, quoting *L'Histoire de Sable*, p. 254.
3. Loades, *Jane Seymour* (2013), p. 14.
4. O. Morgan and J. Wakeman, *Notes on Penhow Castle* (1867).
5. A. Jacob, *Complete Peerage* (1766). On the differences in the arms of the two families, see J. R. Planche in the *British Archaeological Journal* for 1856, p. 325.
6. *Calendar of the Close Rolls*, 1259–1261, pp. 234, 277, 330.
7. *Ibid.*, 1269–1272, p. 22; *Ibid.*, 1272–1279, p. 284.
8. *Ibid.*, 1313–1318, pp. 115–116.
9. *Ibid.*, 1318–1323, p. 173.
10. H. St Maur, *Annals*.
11. Loades, *Jane Seymour*, p. 16.
12. *Ibid.*
13. *Oxford Dictionary of National Biography*. It was with reference to this marriage that Edward Seymour's later title of Lord Beauchamp was chosen.
14. *Victoria County History of Wiltshire*, 16, p. 17. He was known as 'of Wolf Hall' by 1402.
15. *Calendar of the Fine Rolls*, 1430–1437, pp. 16, 78.
16. A sheriff was entitled to claim routine expenses, but entertainment came out of his own pocket, which made the office beyond the reach of the average gentleman.
17. *Cal. Close Rolls*, 1461–1468, p. 396.
18. *Calendar of the Patent Rolls*, 1452–1461, pp. 170, 347, 401, 405, 435, 536.

19. *Cal. Close Rolls*, 1429–1435, p. 78.
20. St Maur, *Annals*, p. 16.
21. *Cal. Pat.*, 1476–1485, p. 537.
22. *Cal. Pat.*, 1485–1494, p. 61. The failure to sue for livery at the proper time may account for his appearance on the Pardon Roll.
23. Loades, *Jane Seymour*, p. 20; *Letters and Papers of the Reign of Henry VIII*, I, no. 20. The entry relates to Sir John Seymour of Wolf Hall and his wife Margery.
24. Loades, *Jane Seymour*, p. 20.

2 Sir John and Robert

1. *Calendar of the Close Rolls*, 1483–1494, p. 452. *Letters and Papers*, I, i, no. 20. Describing him as Sir John Seymour of Wolf Hall, Wilts., and Margery his wife, daughter of Sir Henry Wentworth.
2. Loades, *Jane Seymour*, p. 20.
3. *Cal. Close Rolls*, 1494–1509, pp. 53, 564.
4. *Ibid.*, p. 43.
5. The duke was a powerful figure in the region, in spite of Henry VII's efforts to curb his activities. It would be hard to imagine such promotions taking place without his consent.
6. *L & P*, I, i, no. 438.
7. *Ibid.*, no. 707.
8. J. J. Scarisbrick, *Henry VIII*, pp. 28–9.
9. A. Spont, *Letters and Papers relating to the War with France, 1512–1513*, pp. x–xi.
10. *Ibid.*, pp. 27–33.
11. *Ibid.*, pp. 48–9. The majority of the French fleet retreated into Brest harbour without engaging.
12. Loades, *Henry VIII* (2011), p. 77.
13. *L & P*, I, ii, no. 2053
14. *Ibid.*, no. 2575.
15. Glenn Richardson, *The Field of Cloth of Gold* (2013), p. 213.
16. L & P, III, i, no. 2288.
17. S. J. Gunn, 'The Duke of Suffolk's march on Paris, 1523', *English Historical Review*, 101, 1986.
18. *L & P*, III, i, no. 2166.
19. *Ibid.*, IV, i, no. 214.
20. Loades, *Jane Seymour*, p. 22; *L & P*, I, no. 3409.

21. Loades, *Thomas Cromwell* (2013), p. 118. In 1518, when the French ambassadors arrived to ratify the peace agreement, Sir John had been described as a 'Gentleman of the Palace', a designation not otherwise known but signifying a close attachment to the court.
22. *Ibid.*
23. George Cavendish ed. R. S. Sylvester, *The Life and Death of Cardinal Wolsey* (1962), p. 97.
24. G. R. Elton, *The Tudor Constitution* (1982), pp. 350–53.
25. Scarisbrick, *Henry VIII*, p. 307.
26. *L & P*, X, no. 1257.
27. *Ibid.*, II, no. 1513.
28. *Ibid.*, IV, i, no. 2839.
29. *Ibid.*, Appendix, no. 247.
30. *Ibid.*, IV, i, no. 6418
31. *Ibid.*, V, no. 761.
32. On Cromwell's care in this connection, see Loades, *Thomas Cromwell*.
33. He had been enjoined to surrender his command on pain of 500 marks. *L & P*, IX, no. 195.
34. Robert Seymour to the Earl of Hertford, 3 March 1539. *L & P*, XIV, no. 428.
35. From the Book of Augmentations, *ibid.*, XV, no. 1032.

3 Jane and Henry

1. Thomas was born in about 1509, and it is quite uncertain whether he was older or younger than Jane. She was described as being 'more than twenty five years old' in 1536, so the chances are that he was the elder. *Oxford Dictionary of National Biography*.
2. There is an indication that he was finding life difficult in a letter of 1523, in which he was reported as requesting more time to find the money for the loan contribution for which he was assessed. *L & P*, III, no. 3491.
3. The Countess of Sussex has been suggested. Loades, *Jane Seymour*, p. 31.
4. E. Salter, 'Courts and courtly love', in D. Daiches and A. Thorlby, eds, *The Medieval World* (1973).
5. E. W. Ives, *The Life and Death of Anne Boleyn* (2004), pp. 144–5.
6. *Letters and Papers*, V, no. 1548.

7. Scarisbrick, *Henry VIII*, p. 309.
8. Ives, *Life and Death*, p. 165.
9. Her transfer at this point is a matter of deduction. Her name does not appear on any list of Anne's establishment until January 1534. Loades, *Jane Seymour*, p. 33.
10. *L & P*, VI, nos 948, 1004.
11. *Ibid.*, XII, no. 483.
12. Loades, *The Boleyns* (2011), p. 108.
13. Lady Shelton, writing to Cromwell about Mary's communication with the Carews, described her letters as having been carried 'by her servant Randall Dodd'. *L & P*, VII, no. 1172. There is reason to suppose that he was her normal messenger.
14. Loades, *Mary Tudor* (1989), p. 82.
15. *Ibid.*
16. Ives, *Life and Death*, p. 193.
17. *L & P*, VII, no. 1193.
18. *Ibid.*, nos 1257, 1279, 1297, 1554.
19. *Calendar of State Papers, Spanish, 1534–5*, pp. 292–3; Ives, *Life and Death*, p. 192.
20. *Ibid.*, pp. 80–92.
21. *Cal. Span., 1531–1533*, pp. 592–8. The original sentence had never been promulgated.
22. *Ibid., 1534–1535*, p. 12.
23. Loades, *Jane Seymour*, p. 39.
24. *Cal. Span., 1534–1535*, p. 529.
25. This matter was hushed up, but it caused Henry to talk about his wife's pregnancy for the first time. *L & P*, VI, no. 1164, as he tried to damp down speculation about Mary's future.
26. Garrett Mattingly, *Catherine of Aragon* (1963), pp. 308–9.
27. Ives, *Life and Death*, p. 295.
28. *L & P*, X, nos 200, 427.
29. Retha Warnicke, 'The fall of Anne Boleyn: a reassessment', *History*, 70, 1985; *ibid., The Rise and Fall of Anne Boleyn* (1989).
30. Henry Clifford, *The Life of Jane Dormer, Duchess of Feria* (1887).
31. *L & P*, X, no. 351.
32. Loades, *Jane Seymour*, p. 44.
33. *L & P*, X, no. 601.
34. This depended upon the evidence of the Marchioness of Exeter. Ives, *Life and Death*, p. 304.
35. TNA SP6/1, f. 8.

36. Loades, *Henry VIII*, p. 264.
37. *Wolsey*, ed. Singer, pp. 451, 456.
38. Loades, *The Boleyns*, pp. 151–75.
39. Ives, *Life and Death*, pp. 354–6.
40. Chapuys to Granvelle, 18 May 1536. *L & P*, X, no. 901.
41. Ives, *Life and Death*, pp. 354–6. The cause papers for this case do not survive.
42. Loades, *Jane Seymour*, p. 48.
43. *L & P*, X, no. 1047.
44. Chapuys to Charles V, 6 June 1536; *ibid.*, no. 1069.
45. *ODNB*.

4 The Heir Provided

1. Chapuys to Charles V, 12 August 1536. *L & P*, XI, no. 285.
2. Loades, *Mary Tudor*, pp. 98–9.
3. *Ibid.*, p. 99.
4. *L & P*, X, no. 1022.
5. *Ibid.*, no. 1136.
6. Chapuys to Charles V, 1 July 1536. *L & P*, XI, no. 7.
7. Princess Mary to the Queen, 21 June 1536. *L & P*, X, no. 1204.
8. Mary to Cromwell, probably 30 June 1536, *ibid.*, no. 1186; Loades, *Mary Tudor*, p. 105.
9. Scarisbrick, *Henry VIII*, p. 335.
10. 28 Henry VIII, c. 7. J. R. Tanner, *Tudor Constitutional Documents* (1930), p. 389 *et seq.*
11. *L & P*, XI, no. 580.
12. The Lincoln Articles, R. W. Hoyle, *The Pilgrimage of Grace* (2001), pp. 455–6.
13. *L & P*, XI, no. 860.
14. *Ibid.*, nos 746, 843. *The State Papers of Henry VIII* (1830–52), I, pp. 463 *et seq.*
15. The Pontefract Articles, Hoyle, *Pilgrimage of Grace*, pp. 460–63.
16. 27 Henry VIII, c. 28. G. R. Elton, *The Tudor Constitution* (1982), p. 383.
17. The Ten Articles of 1536, made a few moves towards compromise with the new ideas. G. Burnet, *History of the Reformation of the Church of England*, ed. N. Pocock (1865), IV, p. 278 *et seq.*
18. *L. & P*, XI, no. 475. Martin Luther to Nicholas Harman.

19. Hoyle, *Pilgrimage of Grace*, pp. 339–64.
20. *Ibid.*, p. 358.
21. Scarisbrick, *Henry VIII*, p. 345.
22. John Edwards, *Archbishop Pole* (2014), pp. 63–73.
23. *L & P*, XII (i), no. 1207, items 16 to 21, is a record of the court's proceedings; Loades, *Mary Tudor*, p. 108.
24. Bishop of Tarbes to Francis I, 4 July 1537, discussing the breakdown of the Anglo-Portuguese discussions. *L & P*, XII, no. 212.
25. *L & P*, XI, no. 1250. Bishop of Faenza to Messire Amborgio, 4 December 1536.
26. Report of Tomas Anderson, priest (to Cromwell?) from Murton, Rutland, 18 January 1537. *L & P*, XII, no. 126.
27. *L & P*, XI, no. 1397.
28. *L & P*, XII, no. 1164. John Hussee to Lord Lisle, 9 May 1537.
29. Norfolk to Cromwell, 3 June 1537. *L & P*, XII (ii), no. 22.
30. Loades, *Jane Seymour*, p. 70.
31. Hoyle, *Pilgrimage of Grace*, pp. 390–91.
32. *L & P*, XII, nos 448, 492.
33. *Ibid.*, nos 846, 863, 1064.
34. Hoyle, *Pilgrimage of Grace*, p. 410. For a full account of Norfolk's time in the north see M. H and R. Dodds, *The Pilgrimage of Grace* (1915), II, chapter 21.
35. Loades, *Jane Seymour*, p. 71.
36. *L & P*, XII (ii), no. 242.
37. John Hussee to Lady Lisle, 21 July 1537. *Ibid.*, no. 298.
38. *Ibid.*, no. 77.
39. *Ibid.*, no. 228. Loades, *Jane Seymour*, p. 72.
40. *Ibid.*, no. 271.
41. *Ibid.*, no. 626.
42. Sir Thomas Palmer to Lord Lisle, 16 September, and John Hussee to Lady Lisle, 17 September. *L & P*, XII, (ii), nos 704, 711. A yeoman usher was the lowest rank of chamber servant.
43. *L & P*, XII (ii), no. 808.
44. C. Wriothesley, *A Chronicle of England*, ed. W. D. Hamilton, I (Camden Society, 1875), p. 64.
45. BL Add. MS 6113, f. 81; *L & P*, XII, (ii), no. 911.
46. Wriothesley, *Chronicle*, pp. 66–7.
47. College of Arms, MS 6, ff. 23–26; J. Loach, *Edward VI* (1999), pp. 5–6.
48. Loades, *Princes of Wales* (2008), pp. 81–105.

49. Loades, *Jane Seymour*, p. 78.
50. Loach, *Edward VI*, p. 7. With acknowledgement to Trevor Hughes.
51. *L & P*, XII, (ii), no. 971. Norfolk to Cromwell, 24 October 1537.
52. *Ibid.*, no. 988.
53. Loades, *The Tudor Queens of England* (2009), p. 132.
54. Cromwell to Lord William Howard and Stephen Gardiner, ambassadors in France. *L & P*, XII, (ii), no. 1004.
55. *Ibid.*, no. 1012.
56. Loades, *Jane Seymour*, p. 82.
57. *Ibid.*, p. 80.
58. 'A book of the Queen's jewels'. *L & P*, XII, (ii), no. 973.
59. *Ibid.*, no. 974. The sums owed are not recorded.

5 Edward Seymour

1. See the family tree included in H. St Maur, *Annals*. The exact dates of the births of these siblings is not known, but Thomas appears to have been older than Jane.
2. *Letters and Papers*, I, no. 3357.
3. Loades, *The Tudor Court* (1986), pp. 118–26.
4. *L & P*, II, no. 3474.
5. S. J. Gunn, 'The Duke of Suffolk's march on Paris, 1523', *English Historical Review*, 101, 1986.
6. *L & P*, IV, no. 1512. 'The establishment of Henry Fitzroy as Duke of Richmond'.
7. *Ibid.*, no. 3216; Peter Gwynn, *The King's Cardinal* (1990).
8. Richmond to Henry VIII, 21 July 1528. *L & P*, IV, no. 4536.
9. Manus to Wolsey, 22 July 1528. *Ibid.*, no. 4547.
10. *Ibid.*, no. 6516. A valor of Wolsey's possessions.
11. *L & P*, V, no. 395.
12. *Ibid.*, no. 817. M. L. Bush, 'The Lisle/Seymour land disputes; a study of power and influence in the 1530s', *Historical Journal*, 9, 1966.
13. Loades, *Jane Seymour*, p. 37; Bush, 'The Lisle/Seymour land disputes'.
14. *L & P*, VII, no. 159. Sir Edward Seymour to Lord Lisle, 7 February 1534.
15. *L & P*, V, no. 1205; *ibid.*, VI, 32; Loades, *Jane Seymour*, p. 28.
16. *ODNB*.
17. *L & P*, VII, no. 1338.
18. M. St Clare Byrne, *The Lisle Letters* (1981), no. 108, etc.

19. Loades, *Henry VIII*, p. 264.
20. Loades, *Jane Seymour*, pp. 42–3.
21. Scarisbrick, *Henry VIII*, p. 349. The charge of incest was particularly feeble, and was ably defended. It rested mainly on the amount of time which the couple had spent together.
22. *L & P*, X, no. 1001.
23. *Ibid.*, no. 871.
24. Statutes, 4 June 1536. *Ibid.*, no. 1087 (nos 8 & 9); *ibid.*, no. 1266.
25. *L & P*, XI, no. 280.
26. *L & P*, XII, no. 806.
27. Sir Richard Bulkeley to Lord Beauchamp, 8 May 1537. *L & P*, XII, no. 1154.
28. *L & P*, XII, (ii), no. 269; *ibid.*, no. 629.
29. *Ibid.*, no. 617, Grants in August 1537.
30. G. E. Cokayne, *The Complete Peerage*, ed. V. Gibbs *et al.* (1910–59); *L & P*, XII, (ii), no. 939.
31. *Ibid.*, no. 804; Loades, *Jane Seymour*, p. 91.
32. *L & P*, XIII, (ii), no. 732; *ODNB*.
33. *L & P*, XIII, no. 175. 30 January 1538.
34. *L & P*, XII, (ii), no. 345.
35. Hazel Pierce, *Margaret Pole, Countess of Salisbury, 1473–1541* (2003).
36. Scarisbrick, *Henry VIII*, pp. 362–6.
37. *L & P*, XIV, no. 717.
38. *Ibid.*, no. 947.
39. Retha Warnicke, *The Marrying of Anne of Cleves* (2000).
40. 22 November 1539. *L & P*, XIV, (ii), no. 572.
41. Loades, *Thomas Cromwell* (2013).
42. *L & P*, XVI, no. 465. Instructions dated 18 January 1541.
43. *Ibid.*, no. 594.
44. *Ibid.*, no. 637.
45. *Ibid.*, no. 947. Grants in June 1541.
46. Loades, *Catherine Howard* (2012), pp. 157–69.
47. Loades, *Jane Seymour*, p. 137.
48. Scarisbrick, *Henry VIII*, p. 436; *L & P*, XVIII, no. 44.
49. Loades, *John Dudley, Duke of Northumberland* (1996), pp. 59–61.
50. England's greater population and economic muscle would have given it the advantage in any such union, a fact of which the Scots were only too keenly aware. Loades, *Jane Seymour*, p. 137; Scarisbrick, *Henry VIII*, pp. 438–9.

51. Scarisbrick, *Henry VIII*, pp. 443–4.

52. *L & P*, XIX, no. 172.

53. C. S. Knighton and D. Loades, 'Lord Lisle and the invasion of Scotland, 1544', in S. Rose, ed., *The Naval Miscellany*, Vol. VII (2008), pp. 61–2.

54. *Ibid.*, pp. 91–2.

55. *Ibid.*, pp. 94–5.

56. Scarisbrick, *Henry VIII*, p. 448. Loades, *Jane Seymour*, p. 138.

57. These are for the most part to be discovered in TNA SP1, the State Papers domestic of the reign of Henry VIII, and are calendared in the *Letters and Papers*.

58. Margaret Rule, *The Mary Rose* (1982), pp. 24–5; D. Loades, 'The Mary Rose and the fighting ships', in P. Marsden, ed., *Mary Rose, Your Noblest Shippe* (2009), pp. 1–12.

59. *L & P*, XX, no. 906.

60. *L & P*, XX, (ii), no. 501.

61. John Bale, *Select Works* (Parker Society, 1849); Loades, *Henry VIII*, p. 326.

62. Scarisbrick, *Henry VIII*, p. 480, citing Foxe; Sarah E. Wall, 'Editing Anne Askew's Examination, John Bale, John Foxe and Early Modern Textual Practices', in C. Highley and J. N. King, eds., *John Foxe and his World* (2002), pp. 249–62.

63. J. Foxe, *Acts and Monuments*, ed. 1583.

64. Scarisbrick, *Henry VIII*, pp. 488–9.

6 The Lord Protector

1. John Foxe, *Acts and Monuments*, ed. 1583. His reproof to Sir Anthony Browne.

2. J. Strype, *Ecclesiastical Memorials* (1822), II, i, p. 17.

3. W. K. Jordan. *Edward VI; the Young King* (1968), p. 51.

4. W. K. Jordan, *The Chronicle and Political Papers of King Edward VI* (1966), p. 4.

5. *Ibid.*

6. E. W. Ives, 'Henry VIII's will; a forensic conundrum', *Historical Journal*, 35, 1992.

7. J. G. Nichols, 'The second patent appointing Edward Duke of Somerset Protector', *Archaeologia*, 30, 1844.

8. *Cal. Span.*, IX, pp. 19–20.

9. A. Kreider, *English Chantries; the road to dissolution* (1979), pp. 106–8. J. Loach, *Protector Somerset* (2001), p. 5.

10. W. R. D. Jones, *William Turner; Tudor Naturalist, Physician and Divine* (1988), pp. 19–26; D. S. Bailey, *Thomas Becon and the Reformation in England* (1952), p. 54.

11. H. Robinson (ed.), *Original Letters Relative to the English Reformation* (Parker Society, 1946–7), pp. 68–9, 410.

12. *Acts of the Privy Council*, II, p. 16.

13. Jordan, *The Young King*, p. 64.

14. J. Stowe, *The Annales of England* (1592), p. 594.

15. *Acts of the Privy Council*, II, pp. 34–5.

16. Leigh was described as an esquire of the body at the funeral of Henry VIII. TNA LC2/2; Loach, *Edward VI*, p. 31.

17. J. G. Nichols (ed.), *The Literary Remains of King Edward VI* (1857), I, p. 95.

18. S. Anglo, *Spectacle, Pageantry and Early Tudor Policy* (2nd ed., 1997), pp. 283–94.

19. Jordan, *Chronicle*, p. 5; Wickham Legg, *English Coronation Records* (1901) p. 31.

20. Loach, *Edward VI*, p. 37. For the text of Cranmer's sermon, see J. E. Cox (ed.), *Miscellaneous Writings and Letters of Thomas Cranmer* (Parker Society, 1846), p. 126 *et seq.*

21. Jordan, *The Young King*, p. 89.

22. Jordan, *Chronicle*, p. 5.

23. Strype, *Ecclesiastical Memorials*, II, ii, pp. 329–330.

24. *APC*, II, pp. 63–4.

25. *Ibid.*, pp. 56–7.

26. J. A. Muller, *Stephen Gardiner and the Tudor Reaction* (1970), pp. 145–6.

27. *Ibid.*, pp. 154–60.

28. *Cal. Span.*, 1544–45, p. 12.

29. The text of Paget's memorandum is BL Cotton Titus B ii, 47, ff. 79–81.

30. M. L. Bush, *The Government Policy of Protector Somerset* (1975), pp. 28–9.

31. W. Patten, *The expedition into Scotland* (1547), in A. F. Pollard, ed., *Tudor Tracts* (1903), p. 128.

32. *Ibid.*, p. 137.

33. For a full discussion of Somerset's garrison policy, see Bush, *Government Policy*, pp. 13–23.

34. Jordan, *The Young King*, p. 264; *Cal. Span.* IX, p. 225.

35. Bush, *Government Policy*, p. 22.

36. J. Harrison, *An Exhortation to the Scottes* (1547), no pagination.

37. Jordan, *The Young King*, p. 283.

38. *State Papers, Scotland*, I, p. 62. TNA SP50/II/12.

39. Statute 1 Edward VI, cap. 12. *Statutes of the Realm*, IV, p. 18; G. R. Elton, *The Tudor Constitution* (1982), p. 65.

40. I Edward VI cap. 14. *Statutes of the Realm*, IV, pp. 24–33; Elton, *Tudor Constitution*, pp. 391–4.

41. Frances Rose-Troup, *The Western Rebellion of 1549* (1913), pp. 110–122.

42. *ODNB;* Deposition of John Fowler. C. S. Knighton (ed.), *Calendar of State Papers, Domestic, Edward VI* (1992), no. 185. TNA SP10/6/10.

43. TNA SP10/5/1. *Cal. Dom.* no. 150.

44. Jordan, *The Young King*, pp. 373–4.

45. *Cal. Dom.*, nos 177–78; *Cal. Span.*, IX, pp. 332–3.

46. *APC*, II, pp. 247, 256.

47. *Ibid.*, pp. 257–8. 24 February 1549.

48. *Ibid.*, p. 262. 10 March 1549.

49. 'One can only conclude that Seymour was more than a little mad, and wonder whether he could not have been safely stowed away in the Tower for the remainder of the reign'. Jordan, *The Young King*, p. 381.

50. *Cal. Dom.*, no. 217.

51. F. Rose-Troup, *The Western Rebellion*, p. 234. *Edward VI, Chronicle*, p. 13.

52. *Edward VI, Chronicle*, p. 12.

53. Jordan, *The Young King*, pp. 416–26.

54. Rose-Troup, *The Western Rebellion*, pp. 135–6.

55. *Ibid.*, appendix K.

56. *Cal. Dom.* no. 287.

57. Jordan, *The Young King*, pp. 471–2.

58. Rose-Troup, pp. 538–9.

59. S. T. Bindoff, *Kett's Rebellion, 1549* (1949), p. 15; Joseph Clayton, *Robert Kett and the Norfolk Rising* (1912), pp. 19–46.

60. J. Blomefield, *An Essay towards the Topographical History of the County of Norfolk* (1745), III, p. 225.

61. Clayton, *Robert Kett*, pp. 83–4.

62. Blomefield, *Norfolk*, III, pp. 241–4.

63. Raphael Holinshed, *The Chronicles of England, Scotland and Ireland* (1808), III, pp. 977–8.
64. Jordan, *The Young King*, p. 491.
65. BL Harleian MS 6989, f. 141.
66. A. F. Pollard, *England Under Protector Somerset* (1900).
67. P. L. Hughes and J. F. Larkin, *Tudor Royal Proclamations*, I (1964), no. 350.
68. *Ibid.*, no. 351.
69. *Cal. Dom., Edward VI*, no. 390; Jordan, *Edward VI's Chronicle*, pp. 17–18.
70. TNA SP10/9/23.

7 The End of the Duke of Somerset

1. *Calendar of State Papers, Spanish*, IX, pp. 462–3. Van der Delft to the Emperor, 17 October 1549.
2. BL Cotton Titus B ii, 49, f. 104.
3. D. Hoak, *The King's Council in the reign of Edward VI*, p. 255; H. James, 'The Aftermath of the 1549 coup, and the Earl of Warwick's intentions', *Historical Research*, 62, 1989, pp. 91–7.
4. BL Add. MS 48126, fol. 16; Hoak, *The King's Council*, p. 255.
5. W. K. Jordan, *Edward VI, The Threshold of Power* (1970), pp. 33–4.
6. Stow, *Annales*, p. 604; Jordan, *Threshold*, p. 71.
7. *APC*, II, p. 427, 10 April 1550; *Ibid.*, III, pp. 19, 29, 27 April 1550.
8. Bush, *Government Policy*, pp. 33–9.
9. Jordan, *Edward VI's Chronicle*, p. 32.
10. *Ibid.*
11. TNA, SP10/10/9. *Cal. Dom., Edward VI*, no. 442. Richard Whalley to William Cecil, 26 June 1550.
12. *APC*, III, pp. 104, 107, 141.
13. Jordan, *Threshold*, p. 77.
14. Nichols, *Remains*, I, pp. cxlviii–cxlix.
15. *Cal. Span.*, X, p. 186. 4 November 1550.
16. BL Cotton MS Titus B ii, 38, f. 73.
17. Jordan, *Edward VI's Chronicle*, p. 52–3. *APC*, III, p. 215.
18. Jordan, *Edward VI's Chronicle*, p. 60.
19. *Ibid.*, p. 72. The whole entertainment of S. Andree is set out in detail in the king's chronicle, which is a fair reflection of the impression which he made at court.

20. *Ibid.*, p. 78. Somerset had been appointed Lord Lieutenant of Berkshire and Buckinghamshire on his return to the council in May 1550. The incidents referred to are otherwise unknown.

21. Jordan, *Threshold*, p. 84.

22. BL Cotton MS, Vespasian D, xviii, ff. 2–45. The six discourses actually prepared by Thomas for the king's benefit.

23. *APC*, III, p. 374. Somerset was listed as attending council meetings on 4, 5, 6, 11, 12, 13 and 16 October.

24. Jordan, *Edward VI's Chronicle*, pp. 86–88.

25. *Ibid.*, p. 86.

26. *Ibid.*, p. 88.

27. C. Wriothesley, *A Chronicle of England*, ed. W. D. Hamilton (Camden Society, 1875, 1877), II, p. 57; *The Diary of Henry Machyn*, ed. J. G. Nichols (Camden Society, 1848), pp. 10–11.

28. Jordan, *Edward VI's Chronicle*, p. 89.

29. *Ibid.*, p. 92. The king dates these revelations to the 26 October.

30. Jordan, *Threshold*, p. 93.

31. *Fourth Report of the Deputy Keeper of the Public Records* (1843), Appendix II, pp. 228–9. Baga de Secretis, pouch xix.

32. This was felony under the Act of 3 and 4 Edward VI, cap. 5. For a full account of the trial, albeit from a hostile point of view, see the king's *Chronicle*, pp. 98–100.

33. *Cal. Span.*, X, p. 408.

34. A. J. Kempe, ed., *The Loseley Manuscripts* (1836), pp. 23–5.

35. *Cal. Span.*, X, p. 444. Report of the 18 January 1552.

36. Stow, *Annales*, p. 607. John Stow was an eye witness of the events of the 22 January.

37. The account of Somerset's speech is taken from John Foxe, *Acts and Monuments* (ed. 1583) via Jordan, *Threshold*, p. 101.

38. Stow, *Annales*, p. 607.

39. Strype, *Ecclesiastical Memorials*, II, i, pp. 541–2; Nichols, *Remains*, II, p. 431.

40. Jordan, *Edward VI's Chronicle*, p. 107.

41. BL Harleian MS 2194, ff. 20r-20v. Hayward, *Life and Raigne of Edward VI*, ed. B. L. Beer (1993), p. 147.

42. Loach, *Edward VI*, pp. 61–3. G. R. Elton, 'Reform and the Commonwealthmen of Edward VI's Reign' in P. Clark, A. G. R. Smith and N. Tyacke, *The English Commonwealth 1547–1640* (1979), pp. 23–38.

43. Loach, *Edward VI*, pp. 103–5.

8 Thomas and Henry Seymour

1. Loades, *Jane Seymour*, p. 93.
2. *ODNB*.
3. *Letters and Papers*, XI, no. 943. Grants in October 1536.
4. Queen Jane did not normally concern herself with issues of patronage, and got Cromwell to promote anyone she particularly favoured. Loades, *Thomas Cromwell* (2013).
5. John Hussee to Lord Lisle, February 1537. *L & P*, XII, i, no. 457.
6. *Ibid.,* no. 566.
7. *Ibid.*, XIII, no. 646.
8. John Maclean, *The Life of Sir Thomas Seymour, Knight* (1869), p. 3.
9. *Ibid.*, pp. 5–6.
10. Loades, *Jane Seymour*, p. 95.
11. *Letters and Papers*, XIII.
12. Susan James, *Catherine Parr; Henry VIII's Last Love* (2008), pp. 53–6.
13. *Ibid.* The boroughs were an old Lincolnshire family. It is very likely that on account of Edward's poor health the marriage remained unconsummated.
14. Loades, *The Six Wives of Henry VIII* (2009), pp. 132–3.
15. *Letters and Papers*, XX, i, no. 266.
16. The king's third succession act of 1543, 35 Henry VIII, cap. 1, had laid down the draconian penalties of treason for anyone seeking to deceive the king about the virginity of any future bride that he might take.
17. *Letters and Papers*, XX, i, no. 65.
18. John Foxe, *Acts and Monuments* (1583), pp, 1242–9.
19. *L & P*, XIX, no. 442.
20. *Ibid.*, no. 588.
21. *Ibid.*, XX, i, no. 242.
22. Loades, *Jane Seymour*, pp. 159–60.
23. W. K. Jordan, *The Young King*, pp. 63–5.
24. Loades, *John Dudley, Duke of Northumberland*, p. 91.
25. Deposition of John Fowler, January 1549. TNA SP10/6. No. 10. *Cal. SP, Dom., Edward VI*, no. 185.
26. *Ibid.*
27. Jordan, *The Young King*, pp. 72–7.
28. Emma Dent, *The Annals of Winchcombe and Sudeley* (1877), p. 163.
29. *Historical Manuscripts Commission*, Salisbury MSS, I, nos 61, 62, 64.

30. Jordan, *Edward VI; The Young King*, p. 372.
31. TNA SP10/5/1. The Duke of Somerset to Lord Seymour, 1 September 1548. *Cal. Dom., Edward VI*, no. 150.
32. Depositions by the Marquis of Northampton, the Earl of Southampton and Lord Russell. TNA SP10/6, 14–16. *Cal. Dom. Edward VI*, nos 189–91.
33. Depositions by Katherine Ashley. TNA SP10/6/19–20; *ibid.*, nos 195–6.
34. For an examination of this aspect of Elizabeth's life, see Carole Levin's *The Heart and Stomach of a King. Elizabeth I and the Politics of Sex and Power* (1994).
35. Jordan, *The Young King*, pp. 373–4.
36. *APC*, II, pp. 247, 256.
37. Deposition of John Fowler. TNA SP10/6/10. *Cal. Dom., Edward VI*, no. 185.
38. *APC*, II, pp. 257–8.
39. *Ibid.*, p. 260.
40. *Ibid.*, p. 262.
41. Loach, *Edward VI*, p. 57.
42. G. E. Gorrie, *The Sermons of Hugh Latimer* (Parker Society, 1844), p. 164.
43. The Deposition of Sir William Sharrington. TNA SP10/6/13; *Cal. Dom., Edward VI*, no. 188.
44. *Ibid.*
45. E. B. Fryde *et al.*, eds, *The Handbook of British Chronology* (1986), p. 142.
46. *Letters and Papers*, II, ii, no. 2735.
47. *Ibid.*, IV, no. 869.
48. *Ibid.*, XII, no. 973.
49. Loades, *Jane Seymour*, p. 92.
50. Jordan, *The Young King*, pp. 35–6.
51. TNA SP10/9/3. *Cal. Dom., Edward VI*, no. 370.

9 King Edward VI

1. M St Clare, Byrne, ed., *The Lisle Letters*, V, 79 (no. 1130).
2. J. Loach, *Edward VI*, p. 9.
3. BL Cotton MS Vitellius C. x. fol. 65.
4. J. A. Muller, *The Letters of Stephen Gardiner* (1933) pp. 161–2.

5. J. Kaulek, *Correspondence Politique de MM de Castillon et de Marillac* (1885), pp. 350–54.

6. C. Skidmore, *Edward VI; the lost king of England* (2007) p. 164, etc.

7. On the education of Henry's illegitimate son, see B. A. Murphy, *Bastard Prince* (2001), pp. 41–68.

8. TNA SP1/195, ff. 261–2.

9. BL Harley MS 249, f. 31v; Loach, *Edward VI*, p. 15.

10. C. Wriothesley, *A Chronicle of England*, ed. W. D. Hamilton (Camden Society, 1875), I, 173.

11. J. Loach, *Edward VI*, plate 3, and appendix by Penry Williams.

12. J. Scarisbrick, *Henry VIII* (1968), p. 474.

13. Loades, *Mary Tudor; a Life* (1989), pp. 134–70.

14. W. K. Jordan, *The Chronicle and Political Papers of King Edward VI* (1966), p. 55.

15. *Ibid.*, p. 5.

16. G. W. Bernard, 'The downfall of Sir Thomas Seymour', in G. Bernard, ed., *The Tudor Nobility* (1992).

17. W. K. Jordan, *Chronicle*, p. 7.

18. *Ibid.*, p. 8. The Chantries Act is 1 Edward VI, c.14 and may be found in *Statutes of the Realm*, IV, pp. 24–33.

19. In Hayward's Life and Reign of King Edward VI, where his lamentation is recalled from an unknown source. A MS copy exists in BL Harleian MS 2194; Skidmore, *Edward VI*, p. 224.

20. W. K. Jordan, *Chronicle*, p. 75.

21. Loach, *Edward VI*, pp. 151–2. *The Book of Common Prayer Annotated* is RSTC 16441.

22. *Certain Psalmes* (RSTC 2419) sig, A 4.

23. *Historical Manuscripts Commission*, Salisbury MSS, I, p. 129.

24. Memoires de Francois de Scepeaux, p. 341, ii, chs 2–4 in C-B. Petitot, ed., *Collection complete de memoires relatif a l'histoire de France* (1822).

25. Jordan, *Chronicle*, p. 57.

26. *Ibid.*, pp. 57, 77.

27. *Ibid.*, Introduction, pp. xxv–xxvi.

28. *Ibid.*, p. 80.

29. Loades, *John Dudley, Duke of Northumberland* (1996), pp. 147–8.

30. Jordan, *Chronicle*, pp. 181–84.

31. The nearest thing to a male kinsman that the king had was Reginald Pole, the son of Margaret, Countess of Salisbury, the daughter of

George, Duke of Clarence, Edward IV's brother. However Pole was an attainted traitor and exile at this time.

32. The text of the 'Device' survives as Inner Temple, London, Petyt MS, vol. 47, f. 317.
33. Loach, *Edward VI*, pp. 160–62.
34. *Calendar of State Papers, Spanish*, XI, p. 40.
35. S. T. Bindoff, 'A Kingdom at Stake, 1553', *History Today*, iii, 1953, pp. 642–8.
36. *HMC*, Report on the MSS of Lord Montague of Beaulieu (1900), p. 4; D. MacCulloch, ed., *The Vita Mariae Angliae Reginae of Robert Wingfield of Brantham* (Camden Society, 1984), pp. 248–9.
37. There is no trace of it in the Calendar of the Patent Rolls.
38. *Cal. Span.*, XI, pp. 117–9.
39. Loades, *Mary Tudor*, p. 175.
40. *Cal. Span.*, XI, p. 134.
41. TNA, LC2/41. *Archaeologia*, xii, p. 339.
42. A. de Guaras, *The Accession of Queen Mary*, ed. R. Garnett (1892), p. 101.
43. Loach, *Edward VI*, p. 169.

10 The Second Edward Seymour and His Grandson, William

1. *ODNB*.
2. Loades, *Jane Seymour*, p. 28.
3. As William Paget pointed out to Van der Delft, the Imperial ambassador in August 1549. *Cal. Span.*, IX, p. 429.
4. W. K. Jordan, *The Chronicle and Political Papers of King Edward VI* (1966), p. 22.
5. *Ibid.*, p. 33.
6. Eric Ives, *Lady Jane Grey* (2009), p. 184.
7. *ODNB*.
8. *Cal. Pat., 1558–1560*, p. 100.
9. Mortimer Levine, *The Early Elizabethan Succession Question* (1966), p. 16.
10. William Cecil to Nicholas Throgmorton, 8 May 1561. TNA SP70/26.
11. Loades, *The Cecils* (2007), p. 200.
12. Levine, *The Early Elizabethan Succession Question*, pp. 15–30.
13. S. Adams, *Leicester and the Court* (2002), pp. 31–2.

14. *Cal. State Papers, Domestic, 1547–1580*, p. 305.
15. *Cal. Pat., 1558–1560*, p. 58.
16. *Ibid., 1580–1582*, no. 1760.
17. House of Lords Record Office, Original Act, 32 Henry VIII, cap. 74.
18. *Cal. Dom., 1594–1597.* The Queen to the Lord Keeper, 3 January 1596, p. 159. For the Treatise see *ibid.*, p. 339.
19. *Cal. Dom., 1598–1601*, p. 423. 22 April 1600.
20. *Ibid., 1601–1603*, p. 180.
21. *ODNB.*
22. *Ibid.*
23. *Cal. Dom., 1603–1610*, p. 410. 28 February 1608. The edict took the form of an agreement between the Earl of Hertford, Lord Beauchamp and Honora his wife.
24. *Ibid.*, p. 489.
25. *Ibid., 1611–1618*, p. 48. Edward, Earl of Hertford, to the Earl of Salisbury, 26 June 1611.
26. *Ibid.*, 15 July 1611, p. 59.
27. *Ibid.*, p. 48.
28. *ODNB.*
29. *Calendar of State Papers Domestic*, various.
30. *Cal. Dom. 1639*, p. 83. The Council to William, Earl of Hertford, 26 April 1639.
31. G. E. Cokayne, *The Complete Peerage of England*, ed. V. Gibbs (1910–59).
32. *ODNB.*
33. *Cal. Dom., 1644–1645*, p. 464.
34. G. E. Aylmer, *Rebellion or Revolution, England from the Civil War to the Restoration* (1987).
35. M. Kishlansky, *The Rise of the New Model Army* (1980).
36. C. V. Wedgewood, *The Trial of Charles I* (1964); Pauline Gregg, *King Charles I* (1984).
37. *ODNB.*
38. Cokayne, *Complete Peerage*. E. B. Fryde *et al.*, eds, *Handbook of British Chronology* (1986).

Epilogue: Subsequent Generations

1. Cokayne, *Complete Peerage*.
2. *Ibid.*

3. On his estrangement from his wife, see *Cal. Dom., 1672–1673*, p. 143.

4. *ODNB.*

5. Esther Mijers, *News from the Republick of Letters* (Brill, 2012), pp. 25–44.

6. *ODNB.*

7. *Ibid.*

8. E. N. Williams, *The Eighteenth Century Constitution* (1960) pp. 1–7.

9. *Journals of the House of Lords* (1846).

10. *Cal. Dom., 1702–1703*, p. 488.

11. Williams, *The Eighteenth Century Constitution*, pp. 113–15.

12. *ODNB.*

13. *Ibid.*

14. Cokayne, *Complete Peerage.*

15. *ODNB.*

16. J. Swift, *Journal to Stella*, ed. H. Williams (1948), p. 433.

17. *ODNB.*

18. *Ibid.*

19. *Revised Short Title Catalogue.*

20. Cokayne, *Complete Peerage.*

21. Gilbert Burnet, *History of the Reformation in England*, VI, p. 15n; *The Private Diary of William, First Earl Cowper* (1833), p. 50.

22. G. L. Craik, *Romance of the Peerage* (1849), IV, p. 351.

23. *ODNB.*

24. *Ibid.*

25. Cokayne, *Complete Peerage.*

26. *ODNB.*

27. Cokayne, *Complete Peerage.*

28. Horace Walpole, *Correspondence*, XVIII, p. 522.

BIBLIOGRAPHY

Manuscript sources

The National Archive
LC2, 5
SP1, 6, 10, 50, 70

The British Library
Add. MSS 6113, 48126
Cotton MSS Titus B ii, Vespasian D xviii, Vitellius C x
Harleian 249, 2194, 6989

Bodleian Library
Ashmole MS 861

College of Arms
MS 6

House of Lords Record Office
Original Act 32

Inner Temple
Petyt MS vol.47

Printed Primary Sources and Calendars

Acts of the Privy Council, ed. J. Dasent (1890–1907)
Bale, John, *Select Works* (Parker Society, 1849)

Byrne, M. St Clare, *The Lisle Letters* (1981)

Calendar of the Close Rolls, 1259–1261,1425–1435, 1461–1468, 1483–1494, 1494–1509

Calendar of the Fine Rolls, 1430–1437

Calendar of the Patent Rolls, 1452–1461, 1476–1485, 1485–1494, 1558–1560

Calendar of State Papers, Domestic, Edward VI, ed. C. S. Knighton (1992), 1547–1580, 1590–1597, 1598–1601, 1601–1603, 1603–1610, 1639, 1644–1645, 1672–1673, 1702–1703

Calendar of State Papers, Spanish, 1531–1533, 1534–1535

Certain Psalmes (RSTC 2149)

Cokayne, G. E., *The Complete Peerage*, ed. V. Gibbs (1910–1959)

Cox, J. E., ed., *The Miscellaneous Writings and Letters of Thomas Cranmer* (Parker Society, 1846)

De Carles, L., 'De la royne d'Angleterre' in G. Ascoli, *La Grande Bretagne. devant l'opinion Francais* (1927)

Elton, G. R., *The Tudor Constitution* (1982)

Fourth Report of the Deputy Keeper of the Public Records (1843)

Foxe, John, *The Acts and Monuments of the English Martyrs* (1583)

Fryde, E. B. *et al.*, eds, *The Handbook of British Chronology* (1986)

Gorrie, G. E., *The Sermons of Hugh Latimer* (Parker Society, 1844)

Guaras, A. de, *The Accession of Queen Mary*, ed. R. Garnett (1892)

Hall, Edward, *Chronicle* (ed. 1806)

Harrison, James, *An Exhortation to the Skottes* (1547)

Historical Manuscripts Commission, The Salisbury Papers, various reports

Holinshed, Raphael, *The Chronicles of England, Scotland and Ireland* (ed. 1808)

Hughes, P. L. and J. F. Larkin, *Tudor Royal Proclamations* (1964)

Jacobs, A., *The Complete Peerage* (1766)

Jordan, W. K., *The Chronicle and Political Papers of King Edward VI* (1966)

Journals of the House of Lords (1846)

Kaulek, J., *Correspondence Politique de MM de Castillon et de Marillac* (1885)

Knighton, C. S. and D. Loades, 'Lord Lisle and the Invasion of Scotland, 1544', in S. Rose, ed., *The Naval Miscellany*, Vol. VII (2008)

Letters and Papers, foreign and domestic, of the Reign of Henry VIII, ed. J. S. Brewer *et al.* (1862–1910)

Muller, J. A., *The Letters of Stephen Gardiner* (1933)

Nichols, J. G., ed., *The Diary of Henry Machyn* (Camden Society, 1848)

Nichols, J. G., ed., *The Literary Remains of King Edward VI* (1857)

Oxford Dictionary of National Biography

Pollard, A. F., ed., *Tudor Tracts* (1903)

Spont, A., *Letters Relating to the War with France, 1512–1513* (NRS, 1897)

State Papers of King Henry VIII (1830–1852)

State Papers relating to Scotland (1898–1952)

Statutes of the Realm, ed. A Luders *et al.* (1810–1828)

Stow, John, *The Annals of England* (1582)

Tanner, J. R., *Tudor Constitutional Documents* (1930)

The Book of Common Prayer Annotated (RSTC 16441)

Victoria County History of Wiltshire

Wriothesley, C., *A Chronicle of England*, ed. W. D. Hamilton (1875)

Secondary Works

Adams, S., *Leicester and the Court* (2002)

Anglo, S., 'The Foundation of the Tudor Dynasty', *Guildhall Miscellany*, 2, 1960

Anglo, S., *Spectacle, Pageantry and Early Tudor Policy* (2nd ed., 1997)

Aylmer, G. E., *Rebellion or Revolution: England from the Civil War to the Restoration* (1987)

Bernard, G. W., 'The Downfall of Sir Thomas Seymour', in Bernard, ed., *The Tudor Nobility* (1992)

Bindoff, S. T., *Kett's Rebellion, 1549* (1949)

Bindoff, S. T., 'A Kingdom at stake, 1553', *History Today*, iii, 1953

Blomefield, J., *An Essay toward the Topographical History of the County of Norfolk* (1745)

Burnet, Gilbert, *The History of the Reformation of the Church of England*, ed. N. Pocock (1865)

Bush, M. L., *The Government Policy of Protector Somerset* (1975)

Bush, M. L., 'The Lisle/Seymour Land Disputes; a study of Power and Influence in the 1530s', *Historical Journal*, 9, 1966

Cannon, G. and R. S. Sylvester, *The Life and Death of Cardinal Wolsey* (1962)

Chrimes, S. B., *Henry VII* (1972)

Cherry, C. and C. Ridgeway, *George Boleyn* (2014)

Clayton, Joseph, *Robert Kett and the Norfolk Rising* (1912)

Clifford, Henry, *The Life of Jane Dormer, Duchess of Feria*, ed. J. Stevenson (1887)

Craik, G. L., *Romance of the Peerage* (1849)

Cruickshank, Charles, *Henry VIII and the Invasion of France, 1513* (1990)

Daiches, D. and A. Thorlby, *The Medieval World* (1973)

Dent, Emma, *The Annals of Winchcombe and Sudeley* (1873)

Dodds, M. H. and Ruth, *The Pilgrimage of Grace and the Exeter Conspiracy* (1915)

Edwards, John, *Archbishop Pole* (2014)

Elton, G. R., 'Reform and the Commonwealth men of Edward VI's reign', in *The English Commonwealth, 1547–1640*, ed. A. G. R. Smith and N. Tyacke (1979)

Gregg, Pauline, *King Charles I* (1984)

Gunn, S. J., 'The Duke of Suffolk's March on Paris, 1523', *English Historical Review*, 101, 1986

Gwyn, Peter, *The King's Cardinal* (1990)

Hoak, Dale, *The King's Council in the Reign of Edward VI* (1976)

Hoyle, R. W., *The Pilgrimage of Grace and the Politics of the 1530s* (2001)

Ives, E. W., 'Henry VIII's will: a forensic conundrum', *Historical Journal*, 35, 1992

Ives, E. W., *The Life and Death of Anne Boleyn* (2004)

Ives, E. W., *Lady Jane Grey; a Tudor Mystery* (2009)

James, Susan, *Catherine Parr; Henry VIII's Last Love* (2008)

Jordan, W. K., *Edward VI: the Young King* (1968)

Jordan, W. K., *Edward VI: the Threshold of Power* (1970)

Kishlansky, M., *The Rise of the New Model Army* (1980)

Legg, Wickham, *English Coronation Records* (1901)

Levine, Carole, *The Heart and Stomach of a King; Elizabeth I and the Politics of Sex and Power* (1994)

Levine, Mortimer, *The Early Elizabethan Succession Question* (1966)

Loach, J., *Edward VI* (1999)

Loach, J., *Protector Somerset* (2001)

Loades, D., *The Tudor Court* (1986)

Loades, D., *Mary Tudor: a Life* (1989)

Loades, D., *John Dudley, Duke of Northumberland* (1996)

Loades, D., *The Six Wives of Henry VIII* (2005)

Loades, D., *Essays on the Reign of Edward VI* (2004)

Loades, D., 'The Mary Rose and the Fighting Ships', in Marsden, P., ed.,
   Mary Rose, Your Noblest Shippe (2009)

Loades, D., *The Boleyns* (2011)

Loades, D., *Henry VIII* (2011)

Loades, D., *Catherine Howard* (2012)

Loades, D., *Thomas Cromwell* (2013)

Loades, D., *Jane Seymour* (2013)

MacCulloch, D., *Thomas Cranmer* (1996)

Maclean, John, *The Life of Sir Thomas Seymour, Knight* (1869)

Mattingly, Garrett, *Catherine of Aragon* (1942, 1963)

Mijers, Esther, *'News from the Republick of Letters'* (2012)

Morgan, O. and J. Wakeman, *Notes on Parham Castle* (1867)

Muller, J. A., *Stephen Gardiner and the Tudor Reaction* (1970)

Murphy, B. A., *Bastard Prince* (2001)

Nichols, J. G., 'The Second Patent appointing Edward, Duke of Somerset,
   Lord Protector', *Archaelogia*, 30, 1844

Pierce, Hazel, *Margaret Pole, Countess of Salisbury, 1473–1541* (2001)

Pollard, A. F., *England under Protector Somerset* (1900)

Richards, Judith, 'Love and a female monarch; the case of Elizabeth
   Tudor', *Journal of British Studies*, 28, 1999

Richardson, Glenn, *The Field of Cloth of Gold* (2013)

Rose-Troup, Frances, *The Western Rebellion of 1549* (1913)

Rowley Wlliams, J., *The Ladies of the Tudor Court* (2015)

Rule, Margaret, *The Mary Rose* (1982)

St Maur, H., *The Annals of the Seymour Family* (1902)

Scarisbrick, J. J., *Henry VIII* (1968, 1997)

Singer, S. W., *The Life of Cardinal Wolsey by George Cavendish* (1827)

Skidmore, C., *Edward VI; the Lost King of England* (2007)

Starkey, D., ed., *The English Court from the Wars of the Roses to the
   Civil War* (1987)

Strype, J., *Ecclesiastical Memorials* (ed. 1822)

Swift, J., *Journal to Stella*, ed. N. Williams (1948)

Walker, Greg, 'The Expulsion of the minions in 1519 reconsidered',
   Historical Journal, 32, 1989

Wall, Sarah E., 'Editing Anne Askew's examination; John Bale, John Foxe
   and Early Modern Textual Practices', in *John Foxe and His World*, ed.
   J. N. King and Christopher Highley (2002)

Warnicke, Retha, 'The Fall of Anne Boleyn; a reconsideration', *History*,
   70, 1985

Warnicke, Retha, *The Rise and Fall of Anne Boleyn* (1989)

Warnicke, Retha, *The Marrying of Anne of Cleves* (2000)
Watson, J. Foster, *Vives and the Renascence Education of Women* (1912)
Wedgewood, C. V., *The Trial of Charles I* (1964)
Williams, E. N., *The Eighteenth Century Constitution* (1960)

LIST OF ILLUSTRATIONS

14. Henry VIII's will, dated 30 December 1546. (Courtesy of Jonathan Reeve JRCD2b20p961 15501600)
15. Lucas de Heere's *Allegory of the Tudor Succession*, from around 1572, painted as a gift to Queen Elizabeth. (Courtesy of Yale Center for British Art)
16. The coronation procession for Jane's son Edward VI in February 1547, passing Cheapside Cross on its way to Westminster Abbey. (Courtesy of Stephen Porter)
17. Edward VI's 'device' for the succession, naming Lady Jane Grey as his heir. (Courtesy of Jonathan Reeve JRCD2b20p987 15001550)
18. The unfortunate Lady Jane Grey. (Courtesy of Elizabeth Norton)
19. John Norden's 1593 plan of Westminster. (Courtesy of Stephen Porter)
20. The White Tower of the Tower of London, from a mid-fifteenth-century illumination. (Courtesy of Jonathan Reeve JR992b4p640 14501500)

Tudor History from Amberley Publishing

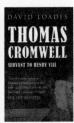
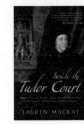
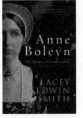
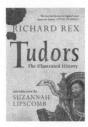

THOMAS CROMWELL
David Loades

'Fresh, fair, lucid and a pleasure to read'
HILARY MANTEL

£9.99   978-1-4456-4001-3   368 pages PB   27 col illus

INSIDE THE TUDOR COURT
Lauren Mackay

'A superb, sound, engagingly written & much needed study...
highly recommended '
ALISON WEIR

£20.00   978-1-4456-0957-7   272 pages HB   40 col illus

ANNE BOLEYN
Lacey Baldwin Smith

'The perfect introduction'
SUZANNAH LIPSCOMB, BBC HISTORY MAGAZINE

£20.00   978-1-4456-1023-8   240 pages HB   60 illus, 40 col

TUDORS: THE ILLUSTRATED HISTORY
Richard Rex

'The best introduction to England's most important dynasty'
DAVID STARKEY

£25.00   978-1-4456-4371-7   256 pages HB   200 col illus

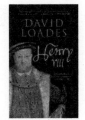

KATHARINE OF ARAGON
Patrick Williams

'Forty years' familiarity with the Spanish archive gives Williams the
courage to march in where most biographers have feared to tread
– notably in the bedroom'
SARAH GRISTWOOD, BBC HISTORY MAGAZINE

£9.99   978-1-4456-3592-7   512 pages PB   40 col illus

CATHERINE PARR
Elizabeth Norton

'Norton cuts an admirably clear path through tangled Tudor intrigues'
JENNY UGLOW

£9.99   978-1-4456-0383-4   312 pages PB   49 illus, 30 col

IN BED WITH THE TUDORS
Amy Licence

'Explores what really went on in Henry VIII's bedroom... a fascinating
book'
THE DAILY EXPRESS

£9.99   978-1-4456-1475-5   272 pages PB   30 illus, 20 col

HENRY VIII
David Loades

'David Loades Tudor biographies are both highly enjoyable and
instructive, the perfect combination'
ANTONIA FRASER

£12.99   978-1-4456-0704-7   512 pages PB   113 illus, 49 col

JASPER TUDOR
Terry Breverton

£20.00   978-1-4456-3391-6

336 pages HB   36 col illus

THE SIX WIVES AND MANY MISTRESSES OF HENRY VIII
Amy Licence

£20.00   978-1-4456-3367-1

448 pages HB   70 illus, 45 col

THE BOLEYNS
David Loades

£10.99   978-1-4456-0958-4

312 pages PB   34 illus, 33 col

MARGARET BEAUFORT
Elizabeth Norton

£9.99   978-1-4456-0578-4

256 pages PB   70 illus, 40 col

Also available as ebooks
Available from all good bookshops or to order direct
Please call **01453-847-800 www.amberley-books.com**

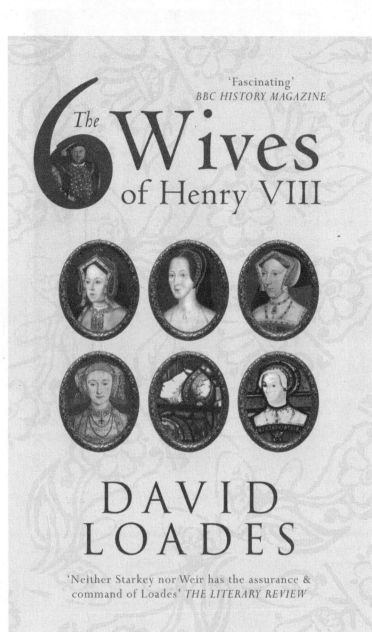

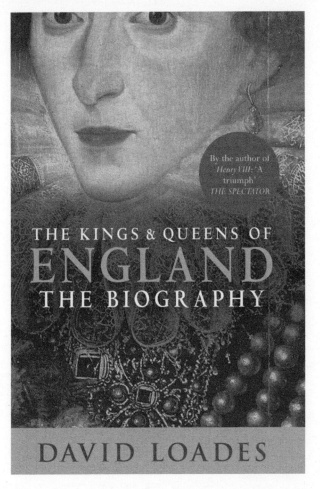